READING
PAUL MULDOON

Clair Wills

BLOODAXE BOOKS

ISBN: 1 85224 347 3 hardback edition
      1 85224 348 1 paperback edition

First published 1998 by
Bloodaxe Books Ltd,
P.O. Box 1SN,
Newcastle upon Tyne NE99 1SN.

PR
6063
.U367
29
1998

Bloodaxe Books Ltd acknowledges
the financial assistance of Northern Arts.

Cover printing by J. Thomson Colour Printers Ltd, Glasgow.

Printed in Great Britain by
Cromwell Press Ltd, Trowbridge, Wiltshire.

40423631

In memory of Thaddeus

ACKNOWLEDGEMENTS

Acknowledgements are due to the editors of *Essays and Studies* and *Princeton University Library Chronicle* in which earlier versions of chapters from this book first appeared.

Extracts from Paul Muldoon's work are reprinted by kind permission of the following publishers: *New Weather* (1973), *Mules* (1977), *Why Brownlee Left* (1980), *Quoof* (1983), *Meeting the British* (1987), *Madoc – A Mystery* (1990), *The Annals of Chile* (1994), *Hay* (1998): Faber and Faber Ltd; *The Wishbone* (1984), *The Prince of the Quotidian* (1994): The Gallery Press.

I am also most grateful to Paul Muldoon himself for providing me with a copy of the manuscript of *Hay* in advance of publication, and for allowing me to refer to informal conversations I had with him in Princeton on 12 October 1996, 20 November 1996 and 9 January 1998. All unreferenced quotations which appear in the text are taken from those conversations.

CONTENTS

Introduction

What makes a poem by Paul Muldoon a Muldoon poem? Muldoon is at once the most characterful of contemporary poets, and the most elusive. There's a distinctive Muldoonian (or should it be Muldoonesque?) ring to his work which may be easy to spot, and even to imitate, but is perhaps less easy to define. Take the following poem, 'Twice', which appeared in Muldoon's seventh poetry collection, *The Annals of Chile*, published in 1994:

> It was so cold last night the water in the barrel grew a sod
> of water: I asked Taggart and McAnespie to come over
> and we sawed and sawed
> for half an hour until, using a crowbar as a lever
>
> in the way Archimedes always said
> would shift the balance, we were somehow able to manoeuvre
> out and, finally, stand on its side
> in the snow that fifteen- or eighteen-inch thick manhole cover:
>
> that 'manhole cover' was surely no more ice
> than are McAnespie and Taggart still of this earth;
> when I squinnied through it I saw 'Lefty' Clery, '*An Ciotach*',
>
> grinning from both ends of the school photograph,
> having jooked behind the three-deep rest of us to meet the Kodak's
> leisurely pan; 'Two places at once, was it, or one place twice?'

Searching here for the fugitive Muldoon trademark we might note, first of all, the poem's characteristic whimsical, almost throwaway tone; for all the learned presence of Archimedes there's a chatty familiarity about these lines (those off-beat verbs, 'squinnied' and 'jooked') which sits lightly with the traditional sonnet form. The relaxed conversational measure cuts across the rhyme scheme to such an extent that we hardly notice the strict formal patterning, but it also complements it. You have to admire the poet's technical aplomb – the rhyming of 'manoeuvre' with 'manhole cover', or the Irish word '*ciotach*' (meaning left-handed) with 'Kodak'. These bold, inventive rhymes are a definite mark of the Muldoon style. The finnicky precision with which he describes the 'fifteen- or eighteen-inch thick' lump of ice is also typical. Muldoon writes as though he has all the time in the world to get his description exactly right, but at the same time bends to the extreme concision of the sonnet's laconic form. Then there's the weird, rather disconcerting image of ice forming as though growing 'a sod of water'. But the real flourish is the final image – so concise and so revealing – but perhaps above all, so impudent. Muldoon takes a childish Peter Pan-like pleasure in the self-replicating grinning schoolboy – how delicately he implies that the poet's gift too lies in his refusal to grow up, to act according to propriety. This cheeky tone befits a poem about doubleness, about having it both ways, about messing about with the laws of space, time and perspective. Clery is a trickster figure, a kind of magician who is able to divide himself in two, to clone himself, by running from one end of the photograph to the other. He is able to disrupt the normal laws of space and time, and this is an art he shares with the poet. The poet too is adept at self-creation by sleight-of-hand.

The notion of self-creation here might be opposed to ideas of lyrical self-expression – Muldoon's poems often seem like marvellous edifices which have been spun out of themselves. (His fellow Northern Irish poet Seamus Heaney once described Muldoon's technique as 'walking on air'). The upshot of this is that although the poem projects a very definite voice, we get precious little idea of the person behind that voice. 'Twice' masquerades as an anecdote – a personal recollection. But the memory of the frozen barrel of water is so unlikely that we know we are on surreal terrain even before Muldoon admits his fiction (the ' "manhole cover" was surely no more ice / than are McAnespie and Taggart still of this earth'). This isn't a personal memory after all. Then there's the difficulty of relating the two halves of the poem. The grammar of the poem (it's all one sentence) insists on connection through the use of colon and semi-colon. Yet we puzzle over the link between the image of Muldoon and a couple of friends levering a lump of ice out of a barrel, and the schoolboy prankster. At one level these elements are yoked together by the round piece of ice, which – when the poet 'squinnies' through it – acts as the lens of a camera. The 'manhole cover' becomes a kind of lens which offers a vision onto another, parallel realm. The image recalls the passage in Frost's poem 'After Apple Picking' where the poet skims a pane of ice from a drinking trough and holds it up to the world 'of hoary grass' ('I cannot rub the strangeness from my sight.'). In 'Twice' the circle of ice is much harder to access (it's so thick it has to be sawed out); it becomes a device for viewing the past in a particular way. It offers a slant on reality – or perhaps, given the image of the camera, a take. And if we follow the logic further we might notice that the two moments are related on another level, through the figure of Archimedes. As the poet tells us, the Archimedean point is the point at which a lever is balanced, but Archimedes also invented the first lens (he used polished mirrors arranged in an arc to focus light in such a way that the Romans' ships caught fire). So far from a reflection on remembered experience the poem is an intellectual conceit. Though the comparison is perhaps not as violent as many in Muldoon's work it is certainly ingenious; it works by means of the juxtaposition of heterogeneous ideas – reminding us that Donne, and metaphysical poetry as a whole, is a key influence on Muldoon.

There's a further twist in the poem found in the hints of the underworld, of something corrupt. The names Taggart and McAnespie signal "Irishness", but (again, typically) they are also emblematic, even allegorical. Etymologically the name Taggart derives from the Irish for 'son of the priest' (*sagart*), and similarly McAnespie means 'son of the bishop'. (The poem was published soon after the scandal surrounding the discovery that the Catholic Bishop of Galway, Eamonn Casey, had fathered a son in the 1970s – a fact which may, or may not, be relevant!) When we realise that Clery too is a "cleric", and a left-handed one at that, it's clear that something "sinister" is going on. We might read Clery as an ill-omened figure, on the side of the devil and the underworld, able to harness divine power through illegitimate filial sucession. But rather than an occasion for moralism on Muldoon's part the poem revels in this perverse lineage, in Clery's brazen ability to play with the rules. Despite the suggestions of godlike power, this is a conjuring trick not a miracle. Clery's trick upsets the laws of perspective – it introduces the element of time so that the still school photograph becomes a moving picture. The Archimedean lever, the lens – these work according to laws or principles, like the principle of perspective, but the poem suggests that once you have mastered the rules you don't have to be bound by them. Like Clery the poem doesn't recognise a terminus, a boundary between here and there – it says you can be in different places at once – you can do it twice, and from opposite ends of the spectrum.

Muldoon has used the word 'whimful' to describe his own poetry. It's a word which conjures all things not grave or earnest, yet at the same time suggests a level of seriousness. Rather than whimsy, this is poetry taking whim seriously, and subverting or diverting the straight lines of authority in the process. This wily, irreverent, even unprincipled side of his work is one of its most attractive aspects – there's something cool, almost glamorous about Muldoon's verbal agility, his mocking legerdemain – but it is also one of the most exasperating, since it offers us no clues to where he stands. Muldoon refuses to position himself, to say where he's coming from. Of course at one level the poetry is very firmly rooted in a sense of

place, in contemporary Northern Ireland: in Belfast where Muldoon
lived for sixteen years, but more often in the rural environment of
his childhood home town, the Moy in County Armagh. In fact,
Muldoon's childhood is represented in the most extreme detail;
the poetry is full of references to his parents, his schooling, his
friends, and above all his books. (Reviewing *The Annals of Chile*,
Helen Vendler complained in exasperation, 'Muldoon would like
us to have read the books important to him, especially the ones he
knew well as a boy.')[1] There's a surfeit of allusions ranging from
the most arcane to the most intimate (even obscene). But paradoxically the wealth of cultural and autobiographical reference doesn't
help to ground the poetry. It's almost as though there are too many
pointers, and no real way of knowing how to read them. The poems
affect a kind of take it or leave it attitude, what one unsympathetic
critic has called a 'cliquish nonchalance'[2] – a cocky assurance that
we'll follow Muldoon down whatever densely private avenues he
chooses to lead us. There's an almost maddening equanimity about
a poem like 'Twice', for example. It remains absolutely balanced
between two separate visions, teasing us with our inability to choose
between the real and the copy. More than just a playful image, this
doubleness is integral to Muldoon's work. It ensures that we can
never be quite sure how to take him; above all this is a poetry which
preserves doubt.

    If we cannot be sure of our ground reading the condensed lyric
poems, we are even more at sea in the long narrative poems for
which Muldoon is renowned – poems such as 'Immram', 'The
More a Man Has the More a Man Wants', 'Madoc – A Mystery'
and 'Yarrow'. Such poems are a maze of semantic levels, with
constant restless metamorphosis of identities, locations and events.
Learned references to literature and history are juxtaposed with
childhood memories, contemporary events in Northern Ireland with
the plight of the American Indians, bizarre and phantasmagoric
visions with the trivia of his day-to-day life. Muldoon draws parallels between different cultures, times and identities, but they are
far too multifarious, kaleidoscopic and chaotic for us to pin any
one of them down. If, as one critic put it, each successive book is
'more like a new religion than a book of poems',[3] how do we find
a way in? Here again doubleness, doing things twice (or three or
four times), is a characteristic poetic device. Muldoon uses repetition as one way of holding the mass of material together. Words,
images and phrases occur in different contexts throughout the
poems, and one of the ways we can begin to make sense of the
narratives is by puzzling over these connections. We can interpret

one occurrence of, say, nutmeg (in 'Yarrow') in terms of another thirty pages later. In 'Madoc' Muldoon parodies the detective story element in his work by announcing the 'mystery' element but offering the reader too many connections ('no body, no motive, but stacks of clues').[4] Muldoon's long poems are large canvases full of relationships which work by addition, by the piling up of elements and the repetition of figures; they lack – or seem to lack – the central focus which would give it all meaning. The last thing we are likely to find in a Muldoon poem is a unifying perspective, a standpoint from which all the multifarious elements can be set in relation to each other. Instead we find distorted perspectives, such as the warping lens in Twice', or perspective split in two, as in the recent poem 'Between Takes': 'I was standing in for myself, my own stunt double.'

So how are we to understand this technique? Mark Ford has described Muldoon's long poems as 'sealed off within the self-reflexive confines of their own ludic patterning, a maze of mirrors one enters arbitrarily and inexplicably'.[5] But can a poem be justified purely in terms of the intricacy of its internal patterning? In response one might point out that Muldoon is not just creating formal patterns, but opening a space in which apparently chance connections and fortuitous verbal echoes can turn into new discoveries. Rather than a subjective journey of discovery, or a drama of consciousness, the poems offer an arena in which layers of meaning, image, story jostle one another, and slip into one another, mutating and transforming in the process. At first sight, this lack of an organising subjectivity in Muldoon's poetry might suggest that his work should be viewed in terms of postmodern practices of random accumulation, as an experiment in serendipity. But at the same time it is impossible to miss the poetry's strong sense of purpose and direction – impossible partly because Muldoon keeps emphasising his authorial control over the proceedings (as in the recent riddling poem 'Rune', which concludes with a message to the reader: 'Go figure'). As opposed to those forms of postmodern poetry in which it is up to the reader to produce connections, Muldoon keeps dropping hints that there is indeed a purpose and a pattern which we should try to understand. Despite the often apparently chaotic surface of his verse, and the lack of a single coherent perspective, there is a sense in which every element has been ordered, and nothing is random. Yet at the same time the poetry's purposefulness sits oddly with its cryptic, arcane and allusive qualities. Take the Irish etymology of the names in 'Twice', for example. We might think that, once decoded, these names would offer a crucial clue to the meaning of the poem. But do they? – or are the names merely another of the false trails which Muldoon likes to lay – and, ultimately, how are we to tell a false trail from a true one? From this point of view, the 'whimful' character of Muldoon's work, far from suggesting arbitrariness, indicates a high degree of authorial control. But this artful engineering of unpredictability is of course something rather different from the way in which a more traditional kind of poem might be said to be unified by the author's subjectivity.

Something akin to this apparent conflict – between a poetry in which the contingent echoes and interconnections of language create meaning for the reader and one where everything is subservient to the author's control – has been acknowledged by Muldoon in a recent lecture. In 'Getting Round: Notes Towards an *Ars Poetica*' he argues on the one hand for a kind of Keatsian negative capability on the part of the poet; it's not the poet's ingenuity which 'sees' a connection between words and images, rather 'a connection sees me'.[6] On the other hand he offers a dizzying reading of Robert Frost's poem 'The Silken Tent' which uncovers (or perhaps forces) mind-boggling levels of literary and autobiographical allusion. So far from 'unknowing', Frost's poem, in Muldoon's reading, exemplifies an intense knowingness. Using a phrase perhaps more fitting for himself Muldoon calls it 'calculated capriciousness'. Muldoon insists that 'it's the poet's job to take into account, as best he or she is able, all possible readings of the poem', a description of his poetic technique which puts it at the furthest remove from serendipity and felicitous accident. What's disorientating about Muldoon's work is that he represents the extremes of both positions. In claiming that the poet is 'the first person to read or, more importantly, to be read by the poem', he stresses the spontaneous and unpredictable creativity of language, in opposition to notions of authorial intention and initiative. Yet he also underlines the primacy of the poet ('the first person to read...'), and so rejects contemporary theories which would put the poet in the same position as any other recipient of the work, or even at a disadvantage. For Muldoon, the massively complex and allusive network of readings, meanings, influences, allusions which is compressed in a poem is both a labyrinth in which even the poet is lost *and* a supreme example of craftsmanship and control – a matter of design.

Certainly there are risks in this kind of poetic technique. Muldoon's poems have been portrayed by the less sympathetic as hermetic, even wilfully inacessible, more dependent on a virtuoso play with language and literary tradition than on considered thought and feel-

ing. Muldoon's sometimes exaggeratedly detached stance, his pref-
erence for complicated and "artificial" verse forms, his fondness
for obscure literary and historical allusions, and the technical brilliance of his work have led to suggestions that the stylistic surface
of his poetry, while dazzling, hides a philosophical and moral
emptiness, that his verbal ingenuity outstrips his capacity for genuine empathy and insight. So Helen Vendler can write, 'When I
first read Muldoon, I thought – to put it bluntly – that his lyrics
were impressively constructed but too often had a hole in the middle
where the feeling should be.' [7]

Vendler's comment is a telling one, indicative of the kinds of
doubt and insecurity that haunt us as we read Muldoon. An ironic
stance often suggests superior knowledge, authority and control. If
we took his irony in this way, then Muldoon's poetry might indeed
appear committed to a process of rarefying the real world, transforming it into an aesthetic object which follows the whim of the
writer. But paradoxically Muldoon's characteristic ironic tone may
also be a sign not of cynicism, but of engagement. For irony can
also articulate the consciousness of failure, and of lack of authority.
True to the legacy of romanticism, Muldoon's poetry continually
struggles with the desire to transform experience into an aesthetic
artefact, while recognising the impossibility of fully grasping it. Lack
of knowledge, failure, the elusiveness of understanding – these are
not phrases readily associated with Muldoon's work, and certainly
the knowing tone of many of the poems seems to belie such a stance.
But the tension between these dimensions of irony, between control
and lack of control, is central to an understanding of Muldoon's
poetry as a whole.

The difficulty of locating the 'feeling' in Muldoon's poetry, of
figuring out where he is coming from, is part of the experience of
reading his work, and it would be foolish to deny it. On the contrary it seems fitting that we should have difficulty in situating a
poetry which so consistently refuses to situate itself, and it may be
that such scepticism about Muldoon's achievement is a paradoxi-
cal sign of its importance. Though thoroughly immersed in poetic
tradition, Muldoon's poetry could be characterised as avant-garde
in so far as the terms on which it might be accepted are not quite
settled – we have a choice about whether we follow him or not,
and in what way. On the one hand it isn't enough to interpret the
work as a virtuoso performance of a new critical extended aesthetic
pattern. But Muldoon doesn't sit easily in an experimental or postmodern framework either (an experimentalism which is at any rate
in danger of becoming codified into an established and all too

recognisable set of techniques). Muldoon's poetry forces us to take a risk, to gamble on its significance. In a sense this is true of all good poetry, of course – innovative work will always need to create the conditions in which it can be read. But Muldoon's work raises risk and doubt to a new level – it refuses to resolve uncertainties in the consolations of groundedness and authenticity; it remains radically undecided on questions of poetic efficacy and poetic significance.

In fact, what seems most compelling about Muldoon's work is precisely that his adroitness and ingenuity in the use of language are not deployed at the cost of feeling. So far from banishing nostalgia, or as a recent poem puts it, feelings of 'longing and loss', the poetry maintains an exquisite tension between sentiment and cynicism, yearning and a self-conscious suspicion of yearning. Muldoon's sense of cultural and geographical displacement, as a pervasive feature of contemporary experience, is interwoven with the nostalgic pull of his rural childhood in Armagh, most obviously in poems about his family, and his father in particular. His poetry keeps returning to a historical and biographical ground which, in one sense, is astonishingly, almost obsessively specific. But at the same time it voices the deep modern suspicion that such returns can never give us the security we seek, are never quite to be trusted. It is this very tension which gives his work its particular poignancy. In one sense, then, it would be gauche to appeal to the "facts" of Muldoon's life for some purchase on his poetry, for there the borderline between fact and fantasy, reality and imagination, the apparent fixity of the past and the flux of the present is a blurred and shifting one. But at the same time, to deny the relevance of such details entirely would be to go against Muldoon's own sense of those indelible traces which survive through all the dislocations of the contemporary world.

Paul Muldoon was born in 1951, eldest child of Patrick Muldoon, later a mushroom farmer and vegetable gardener, and Brigid Regan, a schoolteacher. After a few years living in the village of Eglish in County Tyrone, the family settled on a farm in the townland of Collegelands, near the small town of the Moy in Armagh. It is this childhood landscape which, through all his many later migrations, has remained the constant in Muldoon's work. Indeed it might almost seem that his increasing temporal and geographical distance from the life of the Moy has caused an ever more urgent encounter with that inheritance in his poetry. For Muldoon has moved many times. In 1969 he left home to study for a degree in English at Queen's University Belfast, and it was here that he established a close relationship with the poet Seamus Heaney, who was teaching at that time at Queen's. This was an immensely important encounter for Muldoon. Heaney encouraged the younger author's writing, and introduced him to other figures of the Belfast 'Group', including the poets Michael Longley and Derek Mahon. But as important as the support of older writers were his relationships with the other young aspiring poets among his fellow students, such as Ciaran Carson, Frank Ormsby and Medbh McGuckian. It was at university, too, that he met his first wife, Anne-Marie Conway. The vibrant poetry scene in Belfast at this time, its sense of new energies, undoubtedly helped to accelerate his poetic apprenticeship. Seamus Heaney brought Muldoon's work to the attention of Faber and Faber, and at the age of 21, Muldoon published his first collection, *New Weather*, to considerable critical acclaim.

After leaving university in 1973, Muldoon stayed on in Belfast, working as a producer of an arts programme at BBC Radio Northern Ireland for the next thirteen years. These years were turbulent ones for Muldoon personally. His marriage ended in divorce, and his subsequent relationship with the artist Mary Farl Powers also broke up painfully. They were also years of terrible political violence in Northern Ireland – with frequent terrorist bombings, riots, sectarian warfare and the repeated failure of political settlements. The many traumatic events of the period included the hunger strikes at the Maze prison, which provoked extreme levels of violence outside the prisons and claimed the lives of ten Republican prisoners. The experience of living in a society literally being torn apart by conflict is explored, often in oblique and phantasmagoric ways, in *Mules*, in *Why Brownlee Left*, and above all in *Quoof*, which was written at the time of the hunger strikes and is perhaps his most disturbing volume.

In 1986, after the death of his father, Muldoon left Northern Ireland. He spent short periods living in Dingle in the Irish Republic (on a writer's grant) and in England on academic fellowships at Caius College, Cambridge and the University of East Anglia in Norwich. In 1987 he settled permanently in the United States with his new wife Jean Hanff Korelitz. Since his emigration Muldoon has published several books, including the major collections *Madoc – A Mystery*, *The Annals of Chile*, and – most recently – *Hay*. And at the same time he has ventured into new forms of writing – for television, for theatre, and for the opera. He now lives in Princeton, New Jersey, where he is Professor of Creative Writing.

Muldoon's poetry is intimately bound up with his own personal history, with the local histories and people of his home town of the

Moy, with his experiences of living in Belfast during the 1970s and early 80s, with emigration, with childhood, marriage and family. His preoccupations with the power of the past, with the nature of violence, as well as the resources which might combat it, are always focused though the lens of his own family and locality, filtered through an understanding of his personal inheritance. Yet despite this autobiographical aspect Muldoon's poetry could never be described as confessional, anecdotal or conventionally self-expressive in the manner of much contemporary lyric poetry. One of the most striking aspects of his work is his habit of mythologising elements of his biography – so for example in his second volume of poetry the relationship between his mother and father becomes emblematic of larger dualities and conflicts. He represents himself as a 'mule' or go-between in a mixed marriage between his school-teacher mother and farming father, between the "English" and "Irish" elements of Northern Irish identity, between the longing for poetic transcendence and a stubborn sense of materiality. In later work, figures such as Brownlee and the mercenary Gallogly become emblematic versions of aspects of his own experience, ways of thinking about the nature of destiny, our capacity for violence, and the work of poetry itself.

For obvious reasons Muldoon is often compared with his fellow Northern Irish poet Seamus Heaney, with whom he shares a rural, farming background. Both grew up as members of the Catholic minority in the North, in a society laden with religious and political tensions. Heaney was certainly an important model for Muldoon. Not only was he producing work in Belfast, but more importantly he showed how poetry could be made from the inconspicuous everyday details of a rural farming life. Beyond Heaney, this sense of a world of possibilities concealed in seemingly inauspicious situations can be traced back to Patrick Kavanagh. All three poets have their roots in the border country, though in Kavanagh's case his birthplace was County Monaghan in the Irish Republic. A sense of the epic potential latent in the apparently trivial incidents and conflicts of rural life is something all three poets have in common. Indeed in 'Epic' Kavanagh's mock concern about writing about a local village feud in the year of 'the Munich bother', is allayed by the ghost of Homer: 'He said: I made the Iliad from such / A local row. Gods make their own importance'.

But at the same time the emphasis in Muldoon's work on reinvention as much as expression of the self suggests other points of comparison, notably another Northern Irish poet, Louis MacNeice. MacNeice's interest in parable, allegory and the creation of mythopoeic worlds is an important influence on Muldoon's early poetry, and on *Why Brownlee Left* in particular. Indeed, it is telling that the *Faber Book of Contemporary Irish Poetry*, which Muldoon published in 1986, begins with selections from Kavanagh and MacNeice, almost as though he were nominating them as the poetic godfathers of current Irish poetry. Of course current Irish poetry includes his own, but Muldoon performs a typical disappearing act in this book, offering neither an editorial introduction nor any selection of his own work. Yet somehow the fact that he's nowhere in the book implies that he's everywhere. Muldoon takes his poetry out of an Irish context, and suddenly it all looks like a context for his work. The only trace of him to be found is in a poem by Seamus Heaney dedicated to Muldoon, 'The Widgeon', a poem which is itself an eloquent comment on Muldoon's felicitous yet suspect habit of ventriloquising others and thus turning everything into himself. Finding the voice-box of a bird which he has shot, he 'blew upon it / unexpectedly / his own small widgeon cries'.

Muldoon's airy metamorphoses and his distrust of "the authentic" should perhaps warn us not to appeal too readily to the facts of a life history, or the pressures of a particular social and cultural climate, in seeking to understand his work. These circumstances have been reconfigured and transformed by the imagination from the very moment they begin to take effect. Nevertheless, as Muldoon himself has stressed, the poet 'is necessarily a product of his or her time', and may even be the person 'through whom the time may best be told', though he insists that for that very reason he should remain free of politics. The very fact that Muldoon finds it necessary to comment on the poet's political role is some measure of the importance of his Northern Irish background. In contrast to Britain or North America, poets in Ireland, throughout the twentieth century, have found themselves confronted with the inescapable question of the poet's responsibility, the balancing of political loyalties and engagements against the duty to the imagination, the relation of poetry to the realm of public affairs. Again, Heaney is an important figure here, who has conducted a serious debate on these questions in his poetry over many years. In several hugely influential discussions Heaney has written lyrically of the need to stay true to the imaginative power of poetry, its metaphysical force, in order to be faithful both to external reality and to the inner laws of the poet's being. For Heaney the efficacy of poetry is unequivocally aesthetic. In his collection of essays, *The Redress of Poetry*, Heaney discusses the particular ways poetry makes imaginative redress, and considers how this differs from political redress. He describes the redress of poetry in metaphysical terms, stressing its liberating effect on the spirit. Poetry presents

> a reality which may be only imagined but which nevertheless has weight because it is imagined within the gravitational pull of the actual and can therefore hold its own and balance out against the historical situation. This redressing effect of poetry comes from its being a glimpsed alternative, a revelation of potential that is denied or constantly threatened by circumstances.[8]

It is no qualification of Heaney's judgement to acknowledge that the specific social and historical pressures in Ireland, and Heaney's need to bear witness to them, have a bearing on his concept of redress. But it does confirm a sense that it is almost impossible to think of poetry in Ireland outside a broad rhetoric of response, responsibility and redress. Indeed Heaney himself has acknowledged that his idea of 'poetry as an answer, and answering poetry as responsible poetry', derives from his biography. And it is perhaps inevitable in any country with a wounded history that the relation of poetry to society, lyric to history becomes central.

We tend to think of lyric as the representation of an inner life through personal address, or solitary meditation and reflection. Certainly the concept of an inner life is not an easy one, particularly in the current philosophical climate, and arguably it has never really been possible to abstract it from social and historical forces. Indeed one way of understanding the concept of an inner life is as something social – peopled by the past (through mourning) and the future. It may be, however, that Irish poetry is particularly well placed to represent this, for lyric in Ireland has always been thought through history. I mean by this that the close relationship between poetry and politics or history in the Irish literary tradition, which at various moments has been a cause for concern or a matter for censure, may instead be the source of the vibrancy of contemporary lyric. Yeats's early invocation of the nineteenth-century poets Davis, Mangan and Ferguson, for example, was an attempt to forge an alliance with highly politicised verse; his own poetry, though often in the service of self-definition, always attempted to define that self in relation to social parameters, in the context of national and nationalist upheaval. More recently, Heaney's early insistence that he wanted to open the English 'well-made lyric' out to the pressures of Irish history also registers a sense of the limitations of anti-modernist lyric verse. It is here that we see a traditional rural inheritance being used to radical poetic effect, perhaps precisely because it is a dislocated inheritance. In volumes such as Heaney's *Wintering Out* and *North* and John Montague's

The Rough Field, a new and challenging relation between language, landscape and history is forged, one which demands that the traditional lyric make room for mythic, epic and historical dimensions.

The burden of much recent Irish poetry has been to take account of the ghosts of the Irish past, without being trapped by them into inherited forms. There has been an intense and widespread re-thinking of the relation between lyric and history – and this context is fundamental for an understanding of Muldoon. But though the question of what poetry 'makes happen' is central to Muldoon's work, his response is subtly different from that of Heaney. For Heaney's discussion is couched in terms of balance and resolution; he presents poetry as offering a vision of 'illuminated rightness', a 'glimpsed alternative' to the confusions of society. Alluding to Robert Frost, he argues that the poems of the Ulster poet John Hewitt are best read as 'personal solutions to a shared crisis, momentary stays against confusion'. Referring to the situation in Northern Ireland, he suggests that poetry represents 'a principle of integration within such a context of division and contradiction'. While this account is of great importance for Muldoon (who, like Heaney, is greatly indebted to Robert Frost), he is resistant to any claims for poetry's moral or social force. Muldoon has described his stance as a consequence of his religious background: 'This may be largely an emotional response to the baggage of my religious upbringing – all these ideas of "solace" and "succour", never mind "restitution" and "redemption", which are perfectly appropriate to religious, but not, I think, literary discussion.'[9] Yet there may also be a generational effect here – unlike Heaney and other slightly older writers who took part in the early civil rights movement in Northern Ireland, Muldoon's adolescence was overshadowed by the beginning of the Troubles, perhaps fostering a feeling of political impotence rather than ethical responsibility. Either way Muldoon doesn't seek to bring the issue of redress to imaginative resolution in the manner Heaney suggests. Rather, his is a poetry of disturbance, of lack of fit, a poetry whose elements are always somehow awry. Muldoon's poetry poses redress as a problem – it registers the need to balance real life with an imagined counterpart, but worries about whether this is possible. In other words it is not that the poems achieve balance (with its connotations of equilibrium and even stillness), but that they keep struggling with the problem.

"Struggle" may a misleading word in this context however. For, despite the seriousness of the issues with which Muldoon's poetry is concerned, he deals with them with sharp-sighted wit and humour. This humour is integral to Muldoon's belief in what poetry can do.

A harmonious imaginative redress may lie beyond the grasp of even poetic language, which – like all language – cannot escape the contingency and instability of meaning. But in its ability to offer insight into what seems like a blind play of forces, to distance us from ourselves through humour, perhaps even to offer us glimpses of the transcendent, poetry can give us 'relief' – as Muldoon suggests in his long poem 'Yarrow' – a temporary cure or respite from our pervasive ills.

   At the risk of oversimplification I want to suggest that it is this hesitancy about the idea of poetic significance or utility which is distinctive to Muldoon, and sets him (along with certain of his contemporaries) apart from the older generation of contemporary Irish poets. As I have said, the desire for redress, for cure, even for liberation is fundamental to Muldoon's work. But the longing for poetic redress is pitched against a consciousness of poetry's failure to balance out against the historical situation which we most commonly call irony. In one sense the distinction I am drawing is between a poetry attuned to the traditional reflexes of romanticism and one imbued with a postmodern suspicion of poetic efficacy, but Muldoon's, of course, is both. He is a poet who doesn't offer us, as readers, the security of either political solutions or aesthetic resolutions. Muldoon's genius lies in his ability to transgress established borders and boundaries, between England and Ireland, and Ireland and America, but also between forms and styles of poetry.

This book is primarily a study of a poetic sensibility, and my critical judgements have been directed towards this end. In the pages that follow I have tried as far as possible to enter into the movement of Muldoon's poetry. Although I have elucidated references and allusions where necessary, I have always stayed close to the texture of the poems. This texture is in turn part of a broader interweaving of echoes, through which Muldoon builds the coherence of each collection. The individual poem invariably resonates, through a pattern of chimes and allusions, with the distinctive voice of the volume in which it appears. Muldoon has said that 'I look upon each poem as being a little world in itself',[10] and we enter each book too as though it were a self-contained world. Accordingly I have devoted a chapter to each of the major collections, exploring the development of Muldoon's concerns, and of his conception of the poet's task, from volume to volume. Muldoon's is a broad and varied body of work, but for reasons of space I have regretfully left aside a critical consideration of his opera libretto, his plays, his children's books and translations.

The Argentinian author Jorge Luis Borges once remarked that a good reader is harder to find than a good writer. Since he was quite clearly a very good writer he may well have felt he could afford to be generous about readerly virtues. But even if we need to reckon with an element of flattery in Borges' remark, he was still making a serious point. It is not just that reading properly is a skill, but also that it is extremely demanding. It requires of us, amongst other things, an effort of the imagination, the kind of openness which allows unexpected connections to come into view, and a readiness to live with indeterminacy. But perhaps most of all reading presupposes a willingness to follow the writer on unknown paths – a readiness to learn from him how to read him, and so be led in directions which open up new ways of thinking. Reading Muldoon involves a curious doubleness on the part of the reader. One the one hand, we need to be alert to the many levels of artifice and allusion which have gone into the making of the poem. On the other, we have to relax our reassuring hold on any unifying perspective, travelling across the canvas of the poem, rather than trying to stand back from it and survey it. We have to be open to contingent, unpredictable encounters, taking pleasure in the accidental, serendipitous interconnections of language. Only such a double stance will enable us to acquire the right style of attentiveness, to be traversed by the language of the poem – or to be 'read by it', as Muldoon puts it in his discussion of Frost. This book is the record of my experiments in being 'read by' Muldoon – and so learning to read him.

CHAPTER ONE

New Weather

Paul Muldoon started out early on his poetic career, publishing his first book at the age of twenty-one. *New Weather*, which appeared in 1973, made an unusually strong impression on reviewers and readers alike, who recognised the force of something new and important within the poetry. An unpublished autobiographical essay helps to explain what made this striking debut possible.[1] Muldoon recalls his early intellectual development at school, which took place under the tutelage of several inspiring teachers who encouraged his writing. In April 1968 one of his English teachers at St Patrick's College, Armagh, introduced him to Seamus Heaney after a poetry reading in Armagh Museum:

> I had already written dozens of poems by this stage, including one or two – 'Thrush', 'Behold the Lamb' – that I now sent to Heaney for his opinion. Heaney approved, published these in an issue of *Threshold* he was guest-editing, and steered my work toward Karl Miller, literary editor of *The Listener*, as well as to Charles Monteith, poetry editor at Faber and Faber. By the time I went to Queen's University, Belfast, in 1969, I had already published poems in *The Honest Ulsterman*: by the time I left, in 1973, I had published a pamphlet with Ulsterman Publications, a selection in Faber's *Poetry Introduction 2*, and at the age of twenty-one, my first Faber collection, *New Weather*, for which I had also received an Eric Gregory Award.

Several of the poems in *New Weather*, then, were written while Muldoon was still at school, and the majority while he was at University, where he studied English Literature, with subsidiaries in Celtic and Scholastic Philosophy. Certainly not all the poems in this early volume work, but many are interesting, both in themselves and for what they augur of Muldoon's later work. The volume contains poems of rural boyhood, as well as poems concerned with personal and sexual relationships, but also poems which respond, in an oblique way, to events in Northern Ireland in the early seventies. The Troubles erupted again in the North while Muldoon was at university, and it would have been strange indeed had they not made some mark on his work. No doubt the fact that Northern Ireland was again the focus of civil strife and guerilla warfare helps in part to explain the degree of notice which was given to the book, as does the fact that Muldoon could be read as coming from the same stable as Seamus Heaney, who was then achieving a considerable degree of success as a poet. Both were Northern Irish Catholics,

both came from a rural, farming background, both now lived in
Belfast – and Muldoon had been taught by Heaney.

In retrospect it is clear that the editors at Faber were keen to
establish a link between the two poets; Muldoon had wanted to
title his first volume *The Electric Orchard*, after the first poem in
the book. However, the editors suggested *New Weather*, a significant
title for the book to follow Heaney's *Wintering Out* which had been
published earlier that year. The bizarre and unlikely "accident" of
the volume being printed throughout in italics also helped to signal
the book as something new, something to take notice of. However,
the general enthusiasm of the book's reception can't be put down
entirely to fortuitous circumstances. Paradoxically it may have been
precisely the poetry's superficial resemblance to Heaney's early work
(which made readers think they knew where they were going) which
emphasised Muldoon's originality (as they ended up somewhere
very different). It is in the gap between what the poems promise,
and what they deliver, that their real force resides.

Muldoon was brought up on a farm near the small town of the
Moy in Armagh, and from his earliest work he has taken this local
ground as his poetic terrain. In this he was clearly influenced not
only by the young Seamus Heaney, whose poetry was unapologeti-
cally bound up with local people and local places, but – like Heaney
– by Patrick Kavanagh. Kavanagh, perhaps the leading poet of the
Irish Republic after Yeats, was from Monaghan (across the border
from Armagh), and a champion of the artistic value of the parochial:
'The parochial mentality... is never in any doubt about the social
and artistic validity of his parish. All great civilisations are based
on parochialism.'[2] Muldoon's early work is a moving testimony to
this belief. But unlike the tangible locality presented in much of
Kavanagh's and Heaney's work, Muldoon's home is not a place of
security and groundedness, but a shifting and unstable terrain. It is
a site of trauma and violence as much as of childhood safety, and
this is connected with Muldoon's sense of the disturbing, even
shocking histories which lie concealed just below the surface of
everyday life.

Thus the poem 'Dancers at the Moy', which Muldoon chose to
head his 1996 volume of selected poems, tells the story of a bizarre
historical tragedy. During 'one or other Greek War' the people of
Armagh, and further afield, heard that any horse brought to the
Annual Horse Fair at the Moy would be bought up for the military
campaign. The 'one or other' is important here, as the phrase encompasses suggestions of Homeric fratricide as well as more modern battles. In his opera libretto, *Shining Brow*, Muldoon makes

reference to the year 1912 as one moment when both Greece and
Ireland were involved in war and civil disturbance:

> Nineteen twelve. The Greeks and Turks
> fight a familiar duel.
> The Piltdown Men of Planter stock
> scuttle Irish Home Rule.

If this is also the reference in 'Dancers at the Moy', the irony is
that the Irish traders were hoping to benefit from a war which was
to cause similar suffering to that which they experienced at home.
Hundreds of horses were brought to the fair, without the necessary
food to sustain them, since they were to be sold immediately. But,
unknown to the hopeful traders, the war had ended a week before
market day:

> No band of Athenians
> Arrived at the Moy fair
> To buy for their campaign,
>
> Peace having been declared
> And a treaty signed.
> The black and gold river
> Ended as a trickle of brown
> Where those horses tore
> At briars and whins,
>
> Ate the flesh of each other
> Like people in famine.
> The flat Blackwater
> Hobbled on its stones
> With a wild stagger
> And sag in its backbone,
>
> The local people gathered
> Up the white skeletons.
> Horses buried for years
> Under the foundations
> Give their earthen floors
> The ease of trampolines.

The broken rhythm and repetition of words and phrases such as
'the flat Blackwater' give this poem the feel, not only of a rhythmic
dance, but an incantation – a macabre dance for the dead. The
starving horses, 'like hammocks of skin', point to the poverty and
starvation suffered by the local Irish population. But the poem goes
on to make the analogy explicit, by comparing the horses to 'people
in famine', as though the latter were the more unremarkable in
Ireland. The reference here is not only to the Great Famine of
the 1840s, but to the recurrent famines in Ireland until the late
nineteenth century. At the same time, in mentioning the treaty

following the war, the poem obliquely refers to the Treaty following the Irish war of independence – which partitioned Ireland into North and South, and gave rise to the Civil War, and eventually to contemporary warfare in the North. Ironically Muldoon's poem suggests that this history of starvation and violence has led to the freedom of the dancers, in the macabre foundations of their houses. The point is not, of course, that such tragic histories can be overcome or forgotten, but rather that they cannot. The rhythms of poetry, like that of the dancers, are underpinned by this history. The ironic turn which the poem takes at the end, so far from being cynical, suggests that *all* activity, not only grieving, takes place in the shadow of the dead generations. This is a question not of sentiment or pathos, but of responsibility.

That responsibility towards the dead involves a continuing enquiry into how their deaths should and do affect the living is a central preoccupation of Muldoon's work, a preoccupation which is explored both in terms of peoples and races, and in his elegies for particular individuals. This poem does not succumb to elegiac pathos or sentimentality however – we are left with the unsettling image not of human but of *horses'* bones, prompting us to wonder whether we are supposed to be moved by this history, but also raising more pressing questions, questions which will be central to Muldoon's later work: how can we give due recognition to the dead? In what sense can history help us to place ourselves and understand who we are? As I've suggested there is also an adumbration here of Muldoon's later political sophistication. He hints that the greed of Irish *horse-traders* is in part responsible for the tragedy (they hope to profit from someone else's aggression). In other words the Irish are not simply a victim people, but also capable, in their turn, of causing suffering, or of furthering it elsewhere.

'Dancers at the Moy' is a poem about the discord which underlies harmony, which is constitutive of the rhythms of harmony. The poem creates a rhythmic dance even as it reveals the impossibility of ever fully assimilating the traumatic history which underlies it: it creates itself out of (literally on top of) suffering, but at the same time lays bare the foundations of the aesthetic artefact. This exploration of the relation between experience (and perhaps in particular the experience of suffering) and the work of art is central to *New Weather*. The idea of writing as a compensation for and a defence against suffering and loss is of course familiar from much Romantic poetry (and is a feature of the elegy in particular). More generally the classic Freudian psycho-analytic model of creativity depends on similar notions of compensation and sublimation. Indeed the very familiarity of this idea may have been one of the ingredients of *New Weather*'s success. But what is remarkable for so young a poet is that Muldoon is by no means happy with a straightforword notion of poetic consolation through transfiguration. On the contrary, the poems struggle with the central paradox that to transform something into poetry is to hide it as much as to reveal it. From the very beginning, Muldoon's work is involved in a questioning of the value and costs of the poetic enterprise.

'Dancers at the Moy' is concerned with the question of communal history, but many of the poems in *New Weather* sound discordant notes on other, more intimate levels. Set for the most part within the boundaries of the local parish, the abiding tone of the volume is personal, a wry questioning of the boundaries of self and others. This tone is set by the poem 'Wind and Tree' which, while announcing a new talent for readers to reckon with, also sets out Muldoon's dilemma – a struggle between the wish to remain isolate and inviolate, and the knowledge that only through relations with others can change, progress, feeling (and, implicitly, writing) occur. The poem is also a gritty rewriting of the Romantic trope of the inspirational wind stirring the strings of the harp. As he watches the branches of trees crashing against each other in the wind:

> Often I think I should be like
> The single tree, going nowhere,
>
> Since my own arm could not and would not
> Break the other. Yet by my broken bones
>
> I tell new weather.

Change is registered in the damage inflicted by contact with others, and it is these marks, the stories of his 'broken bones' which he will 'tell' in the broken lines of his poems. The stories he tells are very far from the personal, confessional lyrics we might be led to expect, however. The poems tell of private desires and wishes, while at the same time preserving an air of secrecy, as though Muldoon is unsure how much trust he can place in the reader. Again and again he seems to draw the veil of secrecy aside, while never quite owning up to the meaning of what is found there.

The suggestion of hidden troubles, unsettling the polished surfaces and neat, balanced conclusions of Muldoon's poems derives in part from the influence of Robert Frost. Muldoon's interest in Frost while at university and afterwards has been well-documented, and 'Wind and Tree' owes something to both 'The Most of It' and 'The Tree at My Window'. But perhaps as telling is the background presence here, which Muldoon has mentioned, of D.H. Lawrence's early poem 'Discord in Childhood'. Lawrence's poem compares the 'terrible whips' of the tree outside shrieking in the wind, to the noise of parents fighting inside the house:

> Within the house two voices arose, a slender lash
> Whistling she-delirious rage, and the dreadful sound
> Of a male thong booming and bruising, until it had drowned
> The other voice in a silence of blood, 'neath the noise of the ash.

Muldoon's reliance on the stark distinctions between father and mother derived from Lawrence's *Sons and Lovers* is clear in later poems such as 'The Mixed Marriage' in *Mules*. Here the Lawrentian undertones suggest a hidden narrative of parental strife and paternal violence in Muldoon's poem, yet significantly this traumatic narrative remains secret, present only in an oblique allusion, and this is typical of Muldoon's strategy in the volume. The lyrical voice of the poems remains oblique and allusive, refusing to reveal directly the fund of experience on which it draws. Thus the important point is not whether Lawrence's poem lies in the background for purely contingent reasons (because it is about wind in a tree), or because Muldoon was drawn to it as a way of addressing his own childhood experience. In other words it doesn't matter whether the relationship between Muldoon's parents was similar to that presented by Lawrence or not. Either way, like 'Dancers at the Moy', the poem is built upon the aestheticisation, or transformation, of suffering. But 'Wind and Tree' tries to bury the genesis of the poem, to hide rather than lay bare its foundations, even as it insists on the necessity of the suffering. After all, bones are only broken for a while; they then knit back together. Is it only while still broken that the prophecy can occur?

This reading of 'Wind and Tree' is interesting for the insights it gives into Muldoon's use of buried allusions. Some of Muldoon's own comments about his work, for example that he is drawn to poems with seemingly simple surfaces, 'underneath which all kinds of complex things are happening' have encouraged the assumption that the meaning of his work lies hidden within a poetic kernel. Such comments seem to equate secrecy, or hidden narratives, with poetic depth and seriousness, and this attitude has led to an approach to Muldoon's poetry which seeks to uncover hidden meanings, laying bare references and submerged connections between images. Undoubtedly this approach has been of tremendous value, illuminating aspects of meaning which would otherwise remain obscure. But the danger here lies in the assumption that the poems wrap everything up, or create a balanced whole, which may be coded but can be unravelled with enough time and ingenuity. What this approach

misses is the poetry's concern with the failure to articulate, with
something fallen away, with things that don't add up.

The opacity of hidden meanings might suggest that it is only
through very indirect, circuitous, metaphorical language that emotions, motives and actions can be brought to light at all. Or it could
suggest that language can cover up these motives as much as reveal
them. The poem can, in part, act as a defence against 'telling', an
idea which is explored in 'Thrush'. The subject of the poem is
reading a letter, which perhaps ends a relationship, or at any rate
signifies a withdrawal:

> I guessed the letter
>   Must be yours. I recognised
> The cuttle ink,
>   The serif on
> The P. I read the postmark and the date,
>   Impatience held
> By a paperweight.
>   I took your letter at eleven
> To the garden
>   With my tea.

The physical marks of writing are both expressive of the individual
('I guessed the letter must be yours'), and a defensive gesture –
the cuttlefish expels ink when in danger, but cuttle ink is also a
very rare 'artsy' material, suggesting that this is stylised writing.
But if the letter-writer is protecting herself, her missive is also
experienced as something to be worried about, certainly not to be
treated lightly. The antiphonal lines and measured rhythm reinforce the tone of apprehension mixed with impatience as he sets
about reading the letter. Instead of the contents of the letter we are
given the image of a snail retreating inside its shell, which tells of
her 'withdrawal' from him.

> And suddenly the yellow gum secreted
>   Halfwayup
> The damson bush
>   Had grown a shell.
> I let those scentless pages fall
>   And took it
> In my feckless hand. I turned it over
>   On its back
> To watch your mouth
>   Withdraw. Making a lean, white fist
> Out of my freckled hand.

Clearly this letter makes an impression. The white fist suggests
anger and power, and the title implies an analogy between the
freckled hand and the speckled thrush in crushing the shell. The

speaker is compared to a thrush (a thrush, particularly aptly, being
a song-bird or poet) as, in the girl's absence, he punishes the snail
for her refusal. But in the rhythm's emphasis also on 'bush' and
'hand' we can hear echoes of the adage that 'A bird in the hand is
worth two in the bush'. If the poet loses the girl, then, at least he
retrieves something from the situation – the 'bird' he ends up with
is the poem. Language is both a defence and a retreat from emotion,
precisely because it has the power to transform it into something
else. There is a complex process going on in the poem, as emotion
is turned into language (in the letter), and then that language is
transformed into other signs – the shell, and the poem as shell or
container, which in turn work their own transformations. We can
only learn metaphorically, through the use of poetic tropes and
analogies, what is too painful to be expressed directly, prosaically.

Of course, this returns us to the question we have already
encountered in 'Wind and Tree', and at a different, less personal
level, in 'Dancers at the Moy': what is the relation between the
formalised patterns of poetic language, its rhythmic dance, and the
histories which are its origin? Does poetic language open the individual up to experience and emotion, or work as a defence against
it? Does it maintain the individual in splendid isolation, or – like
the tree in the wind – does it bring him into (possibly damaging)
contact with others – among whom the readers of poetry surely
figure highly?

The power of language as defence and compensation for loss and
withdrawal is also evident in those poems in *New Weather* which
create alternative or parallel lives. Like his later explorations of this
theme in *Why Brownlee Left* these other lives are projected into
both past and future, and thus in part act as a defence against the
present. An early example of this is 'The Waking Father' which
begins with an account of the 'benevolence' and righteousness of
Muldoon and his father out fishing, and throwing the little fish
they have caught back into the river. Muldoon then imagines an
alternative scenario:

> When my father stood out in the shallows
> It occurred to me that
> The spricklies might have been piranhas,
> The river a red carpet
> Rolling out from where he had just stood...

The poem beautifully articulates the precariousness of Muldoon's
world: all could be so easily destroyed, even by thinking differently.
Having fantasised his father's death, Muldoon goes on to describe
the care he would take of his grave:

I would turn the river out of its course,
Lay him in its bed, bring it round again.

No one would question
That he had treasures or his being a king,
Telling now of the real fish farther down.

There is a great deal going on in these few short lines. It is, firstly,
tempting to read this poem as a straightforward celebration of the
father's world, and a tribute to his great worth, along the lines of
Patrick Kavanagh's 'Inniskeen Road, July Evening' ('I am king /
Of bank and stones, and every blooming thing'). But it is surely
as double-edged as Kavanagh's poem, for the poet can afford this
benevolence to the father having orchestrated his violent death, if
only in his imagination. In a conventional elegy the poet's memorial duty is balanced by the meditative freedom which the death
allows him. By creating substitutes for what death has taken away
the elegist attempts to compensate for loss. Like Yeats's premature
elegy for Maud Gonne, 'An Epitaph' ('She was more beautiful
than thy first love / But now lies under boards'), Muldoon's poem
exposes the hidden logic, and ambivalence of the genre – the idealisation of the beloved depends on his or her prior death and burial.
Since Muldoon's father is not yet dead, he will have to be done
away with, so that his absence from the scene can allow the son's
righteousness. The visions of violent death and the riches of an
otherwordly kingdom are thus both images of wish-fulfilment. The
brilliance of this poem lies in the fact that each image is double-
edged: he offers him the red carpet even as he reduces him to a
river of blood. This is the mark of Muldoon's best poetry – a simple
linguistic knot, which captures the complexity of relationships and
emotions.

At the same time the poem returns to the issue of the monumentalising and aestheticising role of the poet. The glorious picture of the father depends on his death, suggesting the difficulty
of articulating the meaning or significance of his life while alive
and subject to change. Yet here again the poem revolves around a
contradiction, as it stills the picture of the father fishing. The
poem suggests that death will monumentalise the father, put him
among the 'real fish', even as it convinces us of the reality and
significance of the everyday father. The lines imply that poetry
can't grasp the nub of experience, while at the same time showing
that perhaps it can.

'The Waking Father' contains many of the ingredients of Muldoon's later, mature work. Here, as elsewhere, the wonder at and
celebration of the transformative power of language underlies and

cuts across Muldoon's characteristic understated tone. The demotic, throwaway, conversational mode of much of Muldoon's work side-steps the outspoken rhetorical traditions developed from Yeats (and also Heaney). Yet there is clearly also a fascination with the power of the poetic word, with the magical and with revelation, which will surface later in his interest in other worlds, in the shaman figure, in surrealism. Muldoon's interest in the incantatory power of poetry is revealed partly in his use of pattern and repetition. Even this early volume plays with the repetition of images, ideas and sounds across poems (fists, shells, corn, edge and centre), and also within poems. So the poems play, for example, on the movement from feckless to freckled, nippling to nibbling, whinged to winch, or father to farther. They revel in the ability of language to transform one thing into another, to create its own reality.

Alternative worlds are present too within the texture of words themselves. Several of the poems in the volume trace the hidden stories lying behind Irish place-names. (Here Muldoon is experimenting within a well-known tradition in old Irish poetry – the 'Dinnseanchas' tradition, or lore of the place-name – which has drawn several contemporary Irish poets such as John Montague and Seamus Heaney.) In 'Macha' Muldoon uncovers part of the history of the goddess who is said to have built Ard Macha (Armagh), bringing together physical geography with the later history of conquest and civil war. In 'Clonfeacle' he turns to a later, Christian age, as he plays with the power of language to convert. The place-name means, literally, 'meadow of the tooth':

> I translate the placename
>
> As we walk along
> The river where he washed,
> That translates stone to silt.
> The river would preach
>
> As well as Patrick did.
> A tongue of water passing
> Between teeth of stones.

Just as Patrick and the river convert one thing into another, so the lover in this poem is able to translate the speaker's meaning from one register into another, a sexual one:

> You turn towards me,
> Coming round to my way
>
> Of thinking, holding
> Your tongue between your teeth.

As in 'Thrush' there is a double or triple movement here as event

(and body – tongue and tooth) is translated into language, language
into speech, and speech back again into body. This transformation
parallels the movement from pagan to Christian, and from Christian
to sexual and secular. But the poem also implies that both preach-
ing and poeticising are morally dubious, breaking down ancient
things – stones into silt and virginity into availability.

Muldoon is often read as the most secular of poets, and certainly
he is keen to distance himself from the narrow-minded repressions
associated with organised Catholicism. Yet his concern with poetic
transformation is echoed by his interest in the ambiguities of that
other crucial form of transfiguration, the religious. What is striking
in 'Clonfeacle' is the relation he draws between pagan, Christian
and poetic forms of revelation (he will go on to explore the connection between these ways of understanding the world in *Mules*).
He finds a deeper, perhaps even a sacred meaning in the colloquial and quotidian, at the same time as he takes an ironic distance
from such belief. In a similar vein, another poem in *New Weather*,
'The Cure for Warts', maintains a wonderful tension between faith
and lack of it, as it explores the world of magic and folklore:

> Had I been the seventh son of a seventh son
> Living at the dead centre of a wood
> Or at the dead end of a lane,
> I might have cured by my touch alone
> That pair of warts nippling your throat,
>
> Who had no faith in a snail rubbed on your skin
> And spiked on a thorn like a king's head,
> In my spittle on shrunken stone,
> In bathing yourself at the break of dawn
> In dew or the black cock's or the bull's blood,
>
> In other such secrets told by way of a sign
> Of the existence of one or other god,
> So I doubt if any woman's son
> Could have cured by his touch alone
> That pair of warts nibbling your throat.

The whole poem is one sentence, whose subordinate clauses make it
difficult to determine the designation of the pronouns (as does the
suggestion of vampirism). Who is it who lacked faith? Importantly it
is precisely the lack of faith rather than the invalidity of folk medicine
which causes the cure to fail. The poem's loving catalogue of folk
remedies suggests not only that there are indeed other forces at work,
but also that the power of the imagination and incantatory poetic
language is a related form of shamanism. (In *Mules* the requirement
of poetry becomes stronger – not simply protection from personal
hurt, as in 'Thrush', but a defence against and remedy for evil.)

The power of the unknowable lies also behind 'Good Friday, 1971. Driving Westward'. This poem is very obviously based on John Donne's 'Good Friday, 1613. Riding Westward', a poem in which Donne plays on the fact that he is riding away from Jerusalem in the East (and from the Sun's – God's – course), on this the day of Christ's Crucifixion, in order, paradoxically, better to know God. Muldoon's poem is a conceit built upon a conceit, and some of the rather forced metaphors seem to acknowledge this wryly (so a newspaper is 'the first edition of the truth'). The poem begins with the narrator 'going along with the sun' on a drive out west, accompanied on the road by families beginning their Easter break. As Donne says in mitigation of his own dereliction of duty on Good Friday morning, 'Pleasure or businesse, so, our Soules admit / For their first mover, and are whirled by it'. Pleasure gets the better of the Muldoon figure even more decisively as he gives a lift to a girl 'out of love', just before crossing the border with the Republic. (Importantly, the journey from east to west is, in the case of Northern Ireland, also a journey from North to South, as the Irish place-name, Gaoth Dobhair, reminds us.) The road and mountain are figured as the couple in the car:

> Where the road had put its thin brown arm round
> A hill and held on tight out of pure fear.
> Errigal stepped out suddenly in our
>
> Path and the thin arm tightened round the waist
> Of the mountain and for a time I lost
> Control and she thought we hit something big
> But I had seen nothing, perhaps a stick
> Lying across the road. I glanced back once
> And there was nothing but a heap of stones.
> We had just dropped in from nowhere for lunch
>
> In Gaoth Dobhair, I happy and she convinced
> Of the death of more than lamb or herring.
> She stood up there and then, face full of drink,
> And announced that she and I were to blame
> For something killed along the way we came.
> Children were warned that it was rude to stare,
> Left with their parents for a breath of air.

Despite the obvious model of Donne, this poem owes something to Frost's dramatic poems, seemingly inconsequential narratives which peter out, merely hinting at some underlying significance. Superficially this is a poem about the foolishness of religious guilt, as the girl embarrasses everyone with her unwanted confession (with the very obvious Christian symbolism of 'lamb or herring'). Yet the narrator's supreme confidence in his own view is surely to be distrusted, with the implication that he is unable to see anything but a heap of stones simply because of his blinkered vision. The narrator is unaware of the significance of his own words, which betray his culpability. Like many of Muldoon's later poems this is set on the border – between this world and the next, between Northern and Southern Ireland. Of course, given the context of illicit border-crossings and military manoeuvres there is a very real sense in which secret deaths may happen on this road. But the poem also suggests shadowy connections between Christianity, politics and violence. The 'event' in the poem remains undecided, not least because a death on Good Friday is not really a death, an ending, but a prelude to resurrection. Unlike the confident narrator, the reader is left with a nagging question, as the poem explores a sense of the unknowable, of that which leaves a hole in our customary ways of explaining the world.

Another characteristic theme which 'Good Friday' broaches, one which will play an increasing role in his work, is the association of young love and nascent sexuality with violence. As the poem 'Wind and Tree' suggests, growing up means taking pain on oneself – through relationships with others – which is something to be feared and desired at the same time. In general, the move into adulthood is a move from listening or observing discord from the outside, to experiencing the violence at its heart. In 'Skeffington's Daughter', 'The Upriver Incident' and 'Cuckoo Corn' the violence is paternal, and bound up with Catholic and familial values. Other poems such as 'February', 'Good Friday', 'Party Piece' and 'The Year of the Sloes, for Ishi' suggest that what the young must learn as they move into adulthood is that relationships are haunted by violence on every side. All forms of authority, whether familial, religious or political threaten youth and hope with destruction.

'Skeffington's Daughter' tells of an enforced backstreet abortion – the title of the poem, which refers to an instrument of torture, reinforces the intimations of hypocrisy and cruelty on the part of the father:

> Being his daughter,
> She would have
> Another chance.
> No one would suffer,
>
> It would be nothing
> Like a death
> In the family.

A companion poem, 'Cuckoo Corn', shows the daughter choosing death as the preferred alternative to telling the father. The poem

begins with a piece of folk wisdom – that seed planted late in the
year, after the first cuckoo, grows 'short and light / As the beard of
a boy'. It goes on to 'explain' the death of a girl:

> They claimed that she had no errand
> Near the thresher,
> This girl whose hair floated as if underwater
> In a wind that would have cleaned corn,
>
> Who was strangled by the flapping belt.
> But she had reason,
> I being her lover, she being that man's daughter,
> Knowing of cuckoo corn, of seed and season.

The fact of the girl's pregnancy is alluded to only in the implicit
links between images. Gaps are left in the tale, leaving the reader to
construct a telling narrative by reading the hinted-at connections
between seed and season. Similarly the fact that these are secret
lovers is not stated but left to be deduced. The balance between
telling and not telling, knowing and not knowing, which was the
subject of 'Wind and Tree' is maintained here by the narrator, whose
position outside the main events structures the reader's access to
information. This narrative pattern is repeated throughout the book
as the speaker looks on while events unfold around him, or attempts
to reconstruct events from signs and clues (taking up a position
similar to that of a reader of the poems). While in 'Cuckoo Corn'
the girl's lover obliquely tells her tale, there is no one to tell the
story of the secret lovers, one with a belly 'hard and round', who
are washed up downstream in 'The Upriver Incident' – their narrative must be deduced from the presence of their bodies, and their
suicides traced all the way back upstream, over the hills to their
homes. Even those poems which do place the poet centre-stage
maintain a wistful yearning for fulfilment or consummation, coupled
with fear of its consequences. Several poems express envy of those
at the centre of tragedy, recapitulating the wish in 'Wind and Tree'
to be broken, not simply to hear or observe violence. The Indian
in 'The Year of the Sloes, for Ishi' knows 'it harder / To live at the
edge of the earth / Than its centre'. The narrator of 'Party Piece'
envies the lovers their violent consummation:

> Their heads,
> Lifted clean off by the blast,
> Lying here in the back seat
> Like something dirty, hold our
> Sadness in their eyes, who wished
> For the explosion's heart, not
> Pain's edge where we take shelter.

The distanced position of the narrator points again to the issue of
secrecy, and the protective mechanism of a poetry which does not
openly tell. This is different from claiming that the poetic narratives
are encoded however, for the point is not that there is a particular
message to be dug up. Instead the poems seem to be ruminating
on the implicit logic of poetry, whereby language protects us from
or cures us of emotion by transforming or burying it within another
creation. However, in the context of the political violence in Northern
Ireland, the passivity of the narrator threatens to become a moral
issue – for at what point does passivity become indifference?

The violence of sexuality, and the violence of authority, clearly
play an important role in Muldoon's early work. But of course, for
a young poet working in Northern Ireland in the 1970s, a more
pressing form of violence sprang from the political conflict around
him. Perhaps not surprisingly, it is precisely with reference to contemporary politics that Muldoon's indirect metaphorical transformations come closest to being coded. Muldoon has admitted that
some of his references are encrypted:

> Though my student days coincided with a period of extreme political
> unrest in Northern Ireland, I myself never took any direct part in pol-
> itical activity. My family would have had Nationalist or Republican
> leanings, of course, but were firmly opposed to political violence. I've
> often considered how easily, though, I might have been caught up in the
> kinds of activity in which a number of my neighbours found themselves
> involved. As it was, I preferred to try to come to terms with the polit-
> ical instability in Northern Ireland through poetry, often in an oblique,
> encoded way: in *New Weather*, for example, a poem like 'The Year of
> the Sloes, for Ishi' was written as a direct response to Bloody Sunday,
> 1972, a fact that may not be immediately apparent to many readers.[3]

'The Year of the Sloes' is the final poem in *New Weather*; its twelve
stanzas (one for each month of the year) relate in repetitive and
incantatory language a ritualised tale of racial murder. Ishi was the
last surviving member of a Californian tribe, the Yahi. Following
the massacres of nearly all the members of the tribe, a few survivors
hid in the canyons east of the Sacramento river where they remained
concealed for nearly fifty years. In 1911, several years after the
deaths of his last companions, Ishi made his way into white civilisation expecting to be killed. He died in 1916 of tuberculosis. Like
'The Indians on Alcatraz', 'The Year of the Sloes' takes the Native
American experience as emblematic of the destruction of a race
through conquest and colonialism. The poem is as much indebted to
Bury My Heart at Wounded Knee, an account of white American
westward expansion from a Native American perspective, as it is to
Ishi's story. This book charts the progressive destruction of Native

American tribes, focusing in particular on nineteenth-century westward expansion, the wars for the Black Hills and the Great Plains between the Indians and white settlers, and the effect of the American civil war on Native American lives and livelihoods. Muldoon has said that he read this book at about the same time as Bloody Sunday occurred, when thirteen civilians were shot dead by British soldiers during a Civil Rights demonstration in Derry on 30 January 1972.

Both Ishi's story and the narrative of *Bury My Heart at Wounded Knee* are woven into Muldoon's poem. The poem charts a creation, and nascent love between two young people within the context of the wars for the Black Hills and the Great Plains, and the Indians' struggle for survival. Muldoon makes use of tropes and a linguistic style derived from *Bury My Heart at Wounded Knee*, borrowing Native American epithets, and employing a remarkably stilled measure and incantatory rhythm:

> In the Moon
> Of the Red Cherries,
> She pledged that she would stay
> So long as there would be
> The Two Legged
> And the Four Legged Ones,
> Long as grass would grow and water
> Flow, and the wind blow.
> None of these things had forgotten.
>
> In the Moon
> Of the Black Cherries,
> While he was looking for a place
> To winter,
> He discovered two wagons
> Lying side by side
> That tried to be a ring.
> There were others in blue shirts
> Felling trees for a square.

The man and woman in the poem are alone in the American landscape, seemingly the last survivors of their tribe. Their threatened existence is interrupted firstly by wagon trains, and then by the murder of the woman by six blue-shirted Union troopers. The defeated man turns to suicide for, as the sole survivor, 'Any day now would be good to die'. This story of genocide is told as a tale of the destruction of young lovers (like 'Cuckoo Corn' and 'The Upriver Incident'). In terms of Muldoon's professed analogy with Bloody Sunday the blue-shirted troopers represent the soldiers who fired on the peaceful crowd of protestors in Derry. By drawing a parallel such as this, between the contemporary conflict in Northern

Ireland and frontier struggles over land and colonisation of the American West, Muldoon is saying more than that Ireland too suffered under colonialism, and at the same time reminding us of the genocide of the American Indians. He is also implicitly suggesting that the Troubles in Northern Ireland have as much to do with struggles over land and land-ownership as with sectarian divisions and religious fundamentalism. It is surely this basic insight, along with his own rural background, which lies behind the agrarian concerns of his next book, *Mules,* and the emphasis on the *geography* of violence in his work as a whole. Yet as important here is the emphasis on tribalism, and the difficulties involved in writing about a lost tribe. Ishi represents the last, poignantly suicidal impulse of a dying tribe; we could think of this as an alternative to the presentation of a lost tribe in Seamus Heaney's *Wintering Out.*

While many of the poems in *New Weather* play with the distance between the narrator and the events he relates, the final two stanzas of 'The Year of the Sloes, for Ishi' effect a sudden turn, as the narrator reflects on his own involvement in the story he tells. The narrative switches into the first person:

> In the Moon
> Of the Leaves Falling,
> I had just taken a bite out of the
> Moon and pushed the plate
> Of the world away.
> Someone was asking for six troopers
> Who had lain down
> One after another
> To drink a shrieking river.
>
> In the Moon
> Of the Trees Popping, two snails
> Glittered over a dead Indian.
> I realised that if his brothers
> Could be persuaded to lie still,
> One beside the other
> Right across the Great Plains,
> Then perhaps something of this original
> Beauty would be retained.

Here, by a terrible irony, the poet is as blameworthy as the troopers. Like the elegist, the poet here weighs the aesthetic profit to be gained from loss: as in 'The Waking Father', aesthetic beauty requires the stillness of death. The poem addresses the culpability of poetic language as it buries events and emotions in order to transform them into art. Poetic language, while it may offer more intense insight into the world around us, carries us at the same time into a realm of fantasy and even moral irresponsibility where violence and suffering are transformed into objects of disinterested contemplation.

For the work of a young author, *New Weather* already displays a remarkable sense of the complexities of poetic transfiguration. As I've suggested, Muldoon is much concerned with the ways in which experience maintains its ghostly presence behind the work of art. The lyrical impulse, and the sense of personal testimony which goes with it, are strongly present in the poetry. But this emotional core is often oblique and concealed, refracted by an intense awareness of the poem's artifice. Muldoon acknowledges that poetic contrivance is necessary – it is the only way in which experience can be rendered with the kind of precision which brings insight. But at the same time, such contrivance can act as a form of protection and containment, as the means of securing a questionable detachment.

But even this is only half the story. For Muldoon also suggests that what remains oblique or concealed at the level of the poem's content remains essential to the formal dynamism of the poem. The very energy of poetry, we might say, is in some sense the energy of evasion, as Muldoon's fondness for fanstasy excursions and parallel realities suggests. As 'Dancers at the Moy' implies, it is concealment and forgetting, the literal 'burying' of the past, which makes possible the exuberance of the dance. And yet, in a way which is not easy to decipher, the dance itself is a displaced acknowledgment of 'forgotten' suffering. A sense of the moral and aesthetic difficulties of this process will remain a central feature of Muldoon's work. In his next book, *Mules*, he will approach this issue from another angle, exploring the tension between the poet's political responsibilities, his obligation to tell the straight 'truth' on the one hand, and his duty to the imagination on the other.

Mules

If *New Weather* exhibits a sense of the power of poetic language to create and destroy, that power is put into question in Paul Muldoon's startlingly accomplished second volume, *Mules*. In part, the reasons for this may be biographical. The volume was published in 1977, and – among other events – responds to the death of Muldoon's mother from cancer in 1974, and the intensifying conflict in Northern Ireland. Muldoon wonders what poetry can offer in the face of bereavement and loss, appalling violence and social breakdown. In what sense, if any, can poetry bring light into these dark places? What meaning can it point towards in a world apparently governed by senseless and brutal contingencies? One might hope that poetry could help us to make sense of our lives, by coming to terms with our own origins and finding a pattern in our life history. But perhaps the poetic enterprise is too immersed in the contingencies it explores to have any genuine enlightening impact upon the world. How are we to define the awkward status of poetry, torn as it is between the confusion of the here-and-now and an elusive 'beyond', or between the desire to take a political stand, and the demands of aesthetic detachment?

This basic ambivalence is built into the image which gives the volume its title. A mule is the sterile offspring of a horse and a donkey, and – throughout the book – Muldoon is concerned with all kinds of bizarre and unlikely liaisons, and the ambiguous entities to which they give rise. At the most general, metaphysical level, Muldoon is concerned with the relation between transcendence and immanence, sky and earth, and the uneasy position of poetry suspended midway between the two. Mules variously represent the hybrid heirs to a mixed marriage between Christian and pagan traditions; masculine and feminine qualities; literary and farming worlds; good and evil. But the image also suggests the sterility born of such cross-breeding since mules do not reproduce. On a more mundane level, the image suggests stubbornness and the impossibility of reconciliation: the cover of the Faber edition shows two mules, superimposed on one another, and facing in opposite directions. And the image conjures not only Muldoon's farming childhood but also evokes, implicitly, the American West and the struggles between Mexicans, Native Americans and white settlers over land and livestock. But 'mule' is also, of course, a self-description, a

curtailment of his own name. The relationship between his mother
and father, with its tensions and inversions, which will become an
abiding preoccupation of his work, is already a central issue here.
Again, the reasons for this focus on marriage and parenthood may
be biographical. Muldoon's marriage to Anne-Marie Conway took
place in May 1974, the year in which his mother later died.

The note of irony and scepticism which will come to the fore
in *Quoof* is well in place in *Mules*, yet at the same time many of
these poems are lyrical and elegiac, seeking a way of understanding and writing about love and death. The volume encompasses a
wide variety of forms and modes, as the poems vary between short,
wry autobiographical pieces, dramatic monologues, and sonnets
alternately meditative and celebratory. All, though, are bent towards
story-telling. Muldoon explores both childhood memories and
tales or fables of a more allegorical nature, peopled with emblematic characters such as Mercy, Will, Faith and Grace, a merman
and a bearded woman. It is not easy to separate the autobiographical from the allegorical poems, however, as Muldoon plays with
the boundary between the reality of personal and material existence and larger, more transcendental or metaphysical structures.
One of the ways in which this is achieved is through the power of
the imagination, able to raise the mundane to higher levels (the
stars and the heavens) and also to bring things down to earth, as
in the powerful opening image from 'The Centaurs':

> I can think of William of Orange,
> Prince of gasworks-wall and gable-end.
> A plodding, snow-white charger
> On the green, grassy slopes of the Boyne,
> The milk-cart swimming against the current
>
> Of our own backstreet.

The child deflates the proud conqueror by transforming him in his
imagination into an everyday occurrence, though the milk-cart also
achieves a certain grandeur by the comparison. The imagination's
capacity for transformation is celebrated throughout this book, as the
poems enjoy their own creativity. This is particularly true of the
series of exuberant poems in praise of love and sex, such as 'Largesse':

> It fits like a dream!
> What's the fish-pond to the fish,
> Avocado and avocado-dish,
> But things shaped by their names?

As with the almost magical verbal transformations of his first volume, the poems in *Mules* applaud the power of the language to

transform, to create, and to play, but in a darker mood they also
meditate on their own failure to heal. While poetry may be able to
celebrate and to praise, and perhaps also offer solace, it cannot
ultimately find a remedy for trauma and loss.

The mention of William of Orange recalls another of the dicho-
tomies which Muldoon is intent on exploring in this book. He
makes the issue of the poet's responsibility to address the situation
in Northern Ireland, and the possible conflict between this duty
and the poet's unique task a central concern. *Mules* appeared two
years after the publication of Heaney's *North*, which had caused
controversy over the writer's supposed involvement in speaking
for the Catholic community in Northern Ireland. Heaney had
figured the poet's dilemma as one of 'tribal' affiliation and responsibility balanced against the desire to be freed into the realm of
the imagination, tied to no creed. *Mules* deals with similar concerns, albeit in an oblique and ironic mode. Muldoon's opening
poem, 'Lunch with Pancho Villa', describes a fictive meeting with
the 'celebrated pamphleteer', living on 'a quiet suburban street',
who upbraids the Muldoon figure for his self-indulgence in writing about rural themes and images irrelevant to the current 'revolution'. (The irony here is that the Mexican revolution, which was
led by Pancho Villa, was a predominantly rural one):

> 'Look, son. Just look around you.
> People are getting themselves killed
> Left, right and centre
> While you do what? Write rondeaux?
> There's more to living in this country
> Than stars and horses, pigs and trees,
> Not that you'd guess it from your poems.
> Do you never listen to the news?
> You want to get down to something true,
> Something a little nearer home.'

The second part of the poem exposes Muldoon's 'invention' of the
pamphleteer, 'All made up as I went along', and asks rhetorically:

> 'When are you going to tell the truth?'
> For there's no such book, so far as I know,
> As *How it Happened Here*,
> Though there may be. There may.
> What should I say to this callow youth
> Who learned to write last winter –
> One of those correspondence courses –
> And who's coming to lunch today?
> He'll be rambling on, no doubt,
> About pigs and trees, stars and horses.

Muldoon is of course both the pamphleteer (he lived at the time on a suburban street in Belfast, while working for BBC Radio Northern Ireland), and the callow youth, a young man from the country. So 'home' is both Belfast and the farm in Armagh where he grew up. While the poem seems to ridicule the idea of poetry's political and social "truthfulness", in the figure of the blinkered Pancho Villa, at the same time it raises the question in such a way that it cannot be entirely dismissed, for Muldoon himself is on both sides at once. So that while the reader might have been inclined to take the poems about 'stars and horses, pigs and trees' at face value, we are encouraged instead to read them as versions of 'how it happened here'. The poems in the book do try to tell something of the truth both of the streets of Belfast and the border country, articulating something between the truth of the pamphleteer and the truth of the romantic, pastoral youth. For if Muldoon inhabits a position somewhere in the middle between these two poles, this suggests not simply that he rejects both sides, but also that he is persuaded by both.

Nonetheless most of the poems in *Mules* do take the reader back to Muldoon's childhood and adolescence in Armagh, or (like the final sonnet sequence 'Armageddon, Armageddon') revisit it. This emphasis on the border country is not only of autobiographical significance; it also signals the importance of struggles over land and land ownership to Northern Ireland's conflict. In effect Muldoon is insisting that the urban 'revolution' stressed by Pancho Villa cannot be understood in isolation from the roots of the troubles in sectarian struggles over land between Protestant settlers and dispossessed Catholics. To write this, however, may be erroneously to suggest that *Mules* is a volume with an explicit argument, and to deny the tone and wry ambiguities of the poetry. If there is argument here it is Muldoon's debate with himself as he explores his own background and the kinds of explanation – for the Troubles, violence, death and love – which are open to him. So far from offering explanations, the poetry puts explanation itself into question.

Traditionally, one of the main ways in which sense has been made of such fundamental facts of human life has been religion. Religious faith offers an explanation for the meaning of death, through the concepts of the well-lived life and the after-life (and, in a more pragmatic vein, religion or sectarianism provides an 'explanation' of the conflict in Northern Ireland). Yet religion enters the book in the form of ambiguous and irresolvable images, rather than as a source of orientation. The languages of Christianity (particularly in apocalyptic mode), popular faith and fate are central to this book, as Muldoon explores the concept of a life lived 'between' heaven and earth, between fate and history, and also (perhaps less obviously) between romanticism and realism (or youth and pamphleteer). He attempts to carve out a space in between these poles, to write a poetry which is connected to 'home' and at the same time transformative, even transcendental. This attempt to bring together everyday life and the transcendental is, of course, a familiar preoccupation in both Romantic and Modernist poetry, one which Heaney had explored in *North* in his poems about Hercules and Antaeus. (Hercules lifts the earthbound Antaeus to the sky, an image which Heaney used to figure his own attempt to find a middle way between committed, 'grounded' poetry, and a freer poetry of the imagination.) Muldoon is clearly following on from these concerns as he explores the "ideal" realm of poetic insight as both product of and mirror back on to his life in Northern Ireland. But while for other poets the need to stay grounded in the particularities of history is an issue of personal responsibility, Muldoon portrays his search for a middle ground very differently. His use of the image of the mule, a genetic cross-breed, allows him to think about the work of poetry not in terms of the poet's duty or obligation to the world around him, but as something fated, a condition of writing.

The complexities of this image are explored in the title-poem, which also reveals a connection between stars and horses:

> Should they not have the best of both worlds?
>
> Her feet of clay gave the lie
> To the star burned in our mare's brow.
> Would Parsons' jackass not rest more assured
> That cross wrenched from his shoulders?

Surprisingly perhaps, it is not the mule, but the mare and the donkey who should have 'the best of both worlds', since they are caught between lives themselves. The mare is associated with the earth, despite the heavenly star on her brow; the donkey with Christianity, although the cross sits uneasily on his back. Yet the union between mare and jackass is not only a union between pagan and Christian, but also between Catholic and Protestant (the neighbour is a 'Parson'), and between two men:

> It was as though they had shuddered
> To think, of their gaunt, sexless foal
> Dropped tonight in the cowshed.
>
> We might yet claim that it sprang from earth
> Were it not for the afterbirth
> Trailed like some fine, silk parachute,
> That we would know from what heights it fell.

The grammar of these final lines is baffling; to explicate 'that we would know' as 'by which we could tell' negates the ambiguity of 'that' as well as the biblical resonance of the phrase, and the sense that such knowledge is also to come in the future. The afterbirth 'gives the lie' to the mule's earthly origins, its own feet of clay, revealing that it has dropped from the sky. Muldoon has said that the germ of this poem came to him after watching some footage of the Korean War (a civil war between North and South, with one side supported by an imperial power and one by a dictatorship – with obvious analogies with Irish history) in which mules carrying supplies were dropped by parachute over an airfield. The otherworldly image here is one intimately bound up with earthly violence, a kind of perverse incarnation. The poem adumbrates a central Muldoon concern, that parents may not be the "real" ancestors. Despite the mild and friendly tone of this poem, we should remember that falling stars are associated with the devil, and augur the apocalypse which Muldoon himself heralds in the concluding sequence of the book, 'Armageddon, Armageddon'.

As I have suggested, Muldoon uses the image of the mule in many ways, but partly as a way of exploring alternatives to the opposition between poetry as pamphleteering on the one hand, and romance on the other. But if the mule, or cross-breed, in some sense symbolises the art of poetry it is not simply because of its association in Muldoon's work with transcendence, but rather precisely because of its mediation between earth and sky. For the mule is also a farm animal, as far as possible from anything transcendent, with a reputation for obstinacy and recalcitrance – it cannot be persuaded to go where it doesn't want to. And even in its earthbound guise the mule has a lot to offer; it is a very useful animal primarily because it is able to carry a great deal of weight. Through 'cross-breeding' Muldoon emphasises both the functionality of poetry – the fact that it is able to work hard, to carry meanings and tell the truth – and its possibilities for imaginative liberation.

The hybrid coupling of mare and donkey in 'Mules' is echoed in the other unusual liaisons which characterise this book. Perhaps the clearest example is 'The Bearded Woman, by Ribera'. The picture draws the poet's eye beyond the 'so unlikely Madonna' whose beard is 'so luxuriantly black', and her unchildlike child, to her husband in the background:

> the figure in the shadows,
> Willowy, and clean-shaven,
> As if he has simply wandered in
> Between mending that fuse
> And washing the breakfast dishes.

Part of the point here must surely be the very normality of this
seemingly abnormal couple, whose domestic life continues in
much the same way as others despite the genetic confusions. The
'willowy' husband is feminised just as his wife is masculinised.
The 'masculation' of women is a theme also in 'The Girls in the
Poolroom' (though this time the reference is surely to non-repro-
ductive sexual activity as much as biology or social role): 'The
girls in the poolroom / Were out on their own limbs // How could
I help / But make men of them?'

   Unsurprisingly perhaps, given the dynamics of the sexual relationships represented in the volume, 'the merman' – another hybrid
creature – in the poem of that name chooses to avoid getting mixed
up in family at all. He shuns 'friendship, love', in order to plough
his 'single furrow'. The land farmer warns him that nothing will
come of it – his choice is infertile, yet like 'Wind and Tree' the
poem hints at the discord which haunts relationships:

> He remembered these same fields of corn or hay
> When swathes ran high along the ground,
> Hearing the cries of one in difficulties.

The cries are associated with life on land, suggesting that the farmer
is drowning in his harvest, and giving an ominous inflection to the
biblical saying that you reap what you sow. Bearing in mind that
mules, and those others who live 'in-between' in the world of this
book, have no reproductive life, it is clear that the merman's choice
is rational. Being of mixed breed he is infertile, and the implication is that he is therefore possessed of special insight, enabled to
see the world in a new (and clearer) light. These poems offer a
different angle on the abortive pregnancies of *New Weather*, suggesting that while the sterile offspring may be a harbinger of disaster (a fallen angel), it may also partake of special poetic insight.
The association of sterility and insight is even clearer in 'Ned
Skinner', who explains to the young Muldoon the results of the
castration of a litter of pigs:

> 'It doesn't hurt, not so's you'd notice,
> And God never slams one door
> But another's lying open.
> Them same pigs can see the wind.'

There are of course biographical reasons why Muldoon might have
been interested in the structure of familial and marital relationships at this time, for not only was his own family disintegrating
with the death of his mother, but he was also creating another
union in his recent marriage. However Muldoon is also playing

here with the traditional association between poetic production and biological reproduction. Male poets such as Rilke, who famously wrote of 'the serious motherhood of men', have often used the analogy of reproduction in order to sanctify their writing practice. We might recall too Yeats's ironic apology for childlessness in 'Pardon Old Fathers' when he laments, 'I have no child, nothing but a book to prove your blood and mine'. Over and above the traditional association of creativity and procreativity Yeats here implies a connection between ancestry and poetic insight.

Muldoon takes this idea even further when, in an audaciously arrogant move, he suggests in 'The Mixed Marriage' that the hand of fate has decreed him to be a mule or 'go-between', through the ingredients of his autobiography. He thereby likens himself to a sterile farm animal but also to a fallen angel and a clear-sighted visionary, possessed of special awareness. (This association of sterility and poetic insight continues until the birth of Muldoon's daughter in 1992, which also proves the occasion for him to rethink his family history.)

Muldoon is making an interesting move here, as he removes the link between writing and childlessness from the realm of choice and places it in the realm of biology; he is suggesting neither that he wishes his poem were a child, nor that his poem is better than a child (as Yeats does), but that poetry *entails* childlessness. This is not to be understood as a personal or autobiographical matter (such as it is for some women writers who have felt that the career of writer has necessarily excluded motherhood), but as a generic situation, and a matter of fate. This is an interesting, if highly questionable, proposition because it means that the fact that one is a poet, and what one does as a poet, is predetermined by inheritance, and thus cannot be subject to moral judgement – mulishness is a question not of responsibility but of destiny.

In 'The Mixed Marriage' Muldoon implies that he is himself the product of a union between earth and stars. The poem sets up an exaggerated distinction between the parents (the learned lady and the farmhand) which, as Muldoon has pointed out, is reminiscent of the relationship portrayed in Lawrence's *Sons and Lovers*. As elsewhere, the mother is associated with schooling and books, and the father with farming and land. But the differences are even starker than that for the father is described as a 'servant-boy', and the mother a 'schoolmistress'. Paul acts as go-between in this master-servant relationship:

> I flitted between a hole in the hedge
> And a room in the Latin Quarter.

When she had cleared the supper-table
She opened *The Acts of the Apostles,*
Aesop's Fables, Gulliver's Travels.
Then my mother went on upstairs

And my father further dimmed the light
To get back to hunting with ferrets
Or the factions of the faction-fights,
The Ribbon Boys, the Caravats.

The poem follows a shape repeated in several other poems in the
book – a move from light to darkness. The mother's classical learning ('The world of Castor and Pollux') gives her access to the night
sky and its constellations, and all the fateful auguries which go
with it. The "pagan" concepts of fate and fortune are fused with a
religious moralism, for she is also associated with reading tales of
righteousness, moral education and enlightenment; certainly she is
a school-teacher who takes the idea of "lessons" seriously. In contrast to this drive towards enlightenment through literature and
religion, the father's darkness (dimming the light) is a world of
the land, and of struggles over the land. The Ribbon men and the
Caravats were secret agrarian societies which orchestrated violence
against landlords over high rents, injustices and evictions. Strong
during the early and mid-nineteenth century these secret organisa-
tions were associated with the revolutionary societies of the late
eighteenth century, although they were far more local in their
aims. The father's interest in such events is natural given the
description of him as one who would 'win the ground he would
never own', but he also acts as an earth-bound counterpoint to his
wife's heavenward gaze. There is also a suggestion that his fac-
tionalism and anti-landowner activities are related to the dynamic
of his marriage, too, since he isn't even master of his own house.
As in 'The Bearded Woman' there is a reversal of gender roles
here; not only are learning and intellect the preserve of the female
in this marriage, but the father is associated with gaudy colours
and fabrics, ribbons and ties.

'The Mixed Marriage' is an early example of Muldoon's habit of
offering his readers a framework in which to read the poetry. This
"autobiography" suggests themes and images from Muldoon's
childhood and early education which are important to him, and
sure enough we find these emblems – stars, biblical rhetoric, moral
lessons, eighteenth-century Irish literature, nineteenth-century
Irish agrarian struggles – elsewhere in the volume. But the central
image which 'The Mixed Marriage' develops is that of the opposition and coming together of the earth and cosmology; the Irish

land and its history coupled with the world of faith, fate and literature. Slyly, the poem suggests that the framework for the volume
lies in Muldoon's autobiography, and of course there is some truth
in this. But in fact the representation of the parents' marriage is
crafted so as to illuminate the central themes of the book. While the
religious and moral sentiments associated with the mother ultimately
fail as a route to understanding, biblical rhetoric, *Gulliver's Travels*
and Aesop are incorporated and recreated in the son's fabular tales
of good and evil, where they are fused with an earth-bound, historical and material perspective. Throughout the volume the par-
ticulars of autobiography merge with fable and allegory.

One example of how Muldoon fictionalises his autobiography is
that his parents owned and did not rent their farm, as he suggests
– and here perhaps he could be accused of simplifying Irish history,
erasing the owner-occupying Catholic middle class, in order to make
it fit in with his imaginative schema. This is not the only danger
which arises when organising a volume around recurring images.
While cross-referencing and intercutting poems can enrich the
meaning of each individual poem, the poems suffer if they seem to
be written in order to flesh each other out. The book as a whole is
extraordinarily well crafted so that the connections between poems
illuminate hidden aspects of the poetry as a whole. For example the
twins, Castor and Pollux, reappear in 'Armageddon, Armageddon'
as the sign of the zodiac and also the twins who in Irish legend
were born to Queen Macha after her husband forced her to race
against horses. As Macha died in childbirth she called down a curse
on Ulster, so that the twins augur the evil which is now visited on
Northern Ireland. Occasionally Muldoon seems guilty of confusing layered meanings and dense references with profundity, but
for the most part he avoids the dangers of poems fitting together
too neatly, because the thematic connections themselves remain
resonant and shadowy in meaning. Despite appearances it is in
fact not possible to draw a map of associations between poems,
and parallel meanings, because the poems themselves resist total
explanation. Like the mule, the elements of the poems are always
more than functional, with reference outwards to a realm of metaphysical and transcendental concerns.

Such concerns are inevitably most to the fore in those poems
concerned with experiences of death and bereavement, and with
the question of what sense can be made of such experiences. Perhaps the finest examples are the series of poems commemorating
the death of Muldoon's mother, including the very moving poem
'Ma':

Old photographs would have her bookish, sitting
Under a willow. I take that to be a croquet
Lawn. She reads aloud, no doubt from Rupert Brooke.
The month is always May or June.

Or with the stranger on the motor-bike.
Not my father, no. This one's all crew-cut
And polished brass buttons.
An American soldier, perhaps.
                                        And the full moon
Swaying over Keenaghan, the orchards and the cannery,
Thins to a last yellow-hammer, and goes.
The neighbours gather, all Keenaghan and Collegelands,
There is story-telling. Old miners at Coalisland
Going into the ground. Swinging, for fear of the gas,
The soft flame of a canary.

This poem heralds Muldoon's mastery of the sonnet form, the
possibilities of which he will go on to explore in his next four
books. A certain formal mulishness is invoked here: the octet and
the sestet do not remain separate, as is traditional, but are subtly
blended into one another. The conversational tone of the octect is
accentuated by using seemingly redundant colloquial phrases
which suggest we are being given the poet's thoughts as he thinks
them ('I take that to be', 'no doubt', 'not my father, no', 'perhaps'),
and reinforced by the very marked enjambement. In contrast the
rhythm and tone of the sestet are more reflective, as the pace slows,
the line lengthens, and the measure echoes the syntax of the sentences. The switch from the colloquial to a gentler rhetoric mirrors
the move from the picture of the mother captured in photographs
to the more general picture of the community of her neighbours,
but it also heralds the move from the sunlight of summer to the
darkness of the grave and of the underworld. The old photographs
show the mother in her youth, in summer, when it is warm enough
to sit outside, or with light reflecting off polished buttons. On the
morning of the mother's waking the moon as it disappears into the
daylight is likened to a yellow-hammer, which departs. As daylight
breaks the neighbours gather to mourn the passing of one of their
community through storytelling, and the storytelling supplants the
light of both sun and moon, which cannot reach underground (to
where Brigid Muldoon will be buried). The swaying moon gives
way to the swinging flame of the canary, a warning and protection
against death, and a light in the underworld. (Canaries were used
to warn miners of the presence of gas in the mines before the
invention of the Davy Lamp.) The sadness of this poem lies in
the fact that, just as the yellow-hammer departs, so too the yellow

canary will die. The tenuousness of the mother's hold on life, as well as of the neighbours' attempts to protect themselves is beautifully articulated in the phrase 'soft flame'. The control of the sonnet form is remarkable, as the rhymes fit so well with the flow of the sentences that we hardly notice them, and it is perhaps the contrast between this formal mastery and the profound sense of loss and fragility which makes the poem so moving.

The movement from light to darkness which shaped 'The Mixed Marriage' reappears in 'Ma' and is repeated in many of the poems in the volume, where light is associated with the language of Revelation and the divine protections of the twenty-third Psalm. But 'Ma' remains resolutely secular, no biblical world of light enters to redeem the community, and this is part of the poem's sadness. The failure of redemption through religion casts a shadow not only over the neighbours' hopes and prayers, but over the mother's life, lived in accordance with such prayers. 'Ma' appears in a sequence of poems, including 'Keen' and 'Vaquero' which touch on death and its effects on the living. But it has perhaps more in common with poems such as 'Our Lady of Ardboe' and 'At Master McGrath's Grave' – poems which do not take death as their primary subject-matter but which, like 'Ma', articulate a sense of loss and powerlessness.

'Our Lady of Ardboe' is a poem in three sections. The first six lines recount a moment in the 1950s when a young rural girl saw a vision of the Virgin Mary:

> The girl leaning over the half-door
> Saw the cattle kneel, and herself knelt.

The second section of the poem offers Muldoon's reflections on this incident as he considers the efficacy of such visions: 'I suppose that a farmer's youngest daughter / Might, as well as the next, unravel / The winding road to Christ's navel.' Rather than condemn such faith as naive, Muldoon seems jealous of the girl's innocent ability to merge aspects of Christianity with popular faith in the world of faeries and auguries from nature. Surely this girl too is a type of mule living in between organised religion and popular faith, and this makes her a visionary, seeing something beyond the limitations of ordinary domestic and material life:

> Who's to know what's knowable?
> Milk from the Virgin Mother's breast,
> A feather off the Holy Ghost?
> The fairy thorn? The holy well?
>
> Our simple wish for there being more to life
> Than a job, a car, a house, a wife –

The final six lines of the poem seem to mirror the first in offering up a prayer to the Virgin Mary, 'Mother of our Creator, Mother of our Saviour, / Mother most amiable, Mother most admirable.' However the death of Muldoon's own mother is surely also a subtext here. Muldoon's mother was a 'farmer's youngest daughter', and possessed of strength of faith similar to this visionary. Muldoon uses her own religious discourse in a silent lament for her, which is also a lament for his own inability to gain solace from such faith. The final lines evoke a profound sense of loss, as they parallel the girl kneeling before the Virgin.

> And I walk waist-deep among purples and golds
> With one arm as long as the other.

The purple and gold flowers bring together the colours of the Catholic church with the world of natural beauty, but to have one arm as long as the other means to be carrying nothing, to be empty-handed. Unlike the farm-girl, Muldoon (a sadder sort of mule) can take comfort and meaning from neither tradition, and he is conscious of his own impoverishment. Where will he find solace?

One answer to this question must be that he finds it in art. Poetry can offer a form of transcendence which is neither solely dependent on redemptive faith nor on revelatory history. But what is striking about *Mules* is the way that this enlightenment is always tenuous or provisional. 'At Master McGrath's Grave', for example, offers a vision of a world imbued with otherworldly meaning which cannot quite be grasped. Master McGrath was a greyhound who, in 1869, won the Waterloo Cup, an important race in England. His victory was celebrated in a well-known ballad, as he became symbolic of the possibility of eventual victory of the Irish over the English. In Muldoon's poem the dog is described as 'touched' by the heavens in a similar way to the mule: he is an Irish 'shooting star'; the white marks on his back are like hail which 'had fallen and never melted'. While the meaning of McGrath's life remains obscure for the poet, and therefore for the reader too, this inability to explain the power of such images seems very much to the point in the poem. The final image in the poem echoes 'Our Lady of Ardboe' in suggesting that the poet is at the mercy of a world which is beyond him. The world brings him to his knees, or overwhelms him:

> The overhanging elm-trees
> And the knee-high grass
> Are freshly tinged
> By this last sun-shower.

> I'm not beside myself with grief,
> Not even so taken by McGrath,
>
> It's just the way these elm-trees
> Do more and more impinge,
> The knee-high grass
> Has brought me to my knees.

The poet reaches a moment of transcendence even as he is engulfed by the earth. Strangely, for a poet who seems to reject organised religion, his aesthetic here, though secular, owes a great deal to the concept of incarnation. It is its very earth-boundedness which enables poetry to capture something of those moments when the everyday seems to open onto a transcendent dimension. The mulish nature of poetry, both temporal and sublime, can represent this experience, but cannot entirely control it. It is worth noting here how Muldoon has moved on from *New Weather*'s faith in the ability of the imagination to transform loss and suffering into art. In 'The Waking Father' (which was, of course, not a true elegy) Muldoon displayed his control of representations and 'events' through poetry – he was able to kill and resurrect his father at will. But many of the poems in *Mules* seem to question this sense of the power of poetic language as they show events and their meanings to be beyond the control of the poet. Poetry, we might assume, by offering insight and enlightenment can help us to come to terms with our condition. But, in *Mules* this enlightening conception of poetry is often counteracted by the movement of the poem itself – not from darkness into light, but from light into darkness. At best, it seems, poetry may be able to offer a form of solace and meditation, but it is unclear whether its insight can heal.

Mules is much concerned with the question of what meaning, if any, can be found in one's personal history, and in experiences of death and loss. But at the same time, the conflict-ridden history of Ireland, the wider context of Muldoon's own life, presses with ever more insistence on his attention. Master McGrath's grave lies 'at the edge of Lord Lurgan's demesne', recalling the world of landlords and tenants and religious sectarianism which was touched on in 'The Mixed Marriage'. Yet the lines of demarcation between master and servant are complicated. Lord Lurgan (of the Brownlow family), who owned Master McGrath, was hugely supported by his tenants as his dog became symbolic of Irish nationalism, and at the same time as land-owner Lurgan was the object of anti-landlord sentiment. (Lord Lurgan too can be thought of as a type of mule – divided between English and Irish national attitudes. The name 'Brownlow' is one source of the 'Brownlee' of Muldoon's next book.) Lurgan's ancestor, another Brownlow, was a conservative member of Parliament and instrumental in founding the Orange Order, a pro-Union organisation set up in order to combat the influence of the United Irishmen, in the late eighteenth century. Armagh has in fact been the site of some of the most bitter sectarian conflicts in Irish history, primarily because of the abrupt juxtapositions of Catholic, Presbyterian and Anglican population areas. Muldoon has described the population of his townland in North Armagh in this way:

> The 'college' of Collegelands was Trinity College, Dublin, and many of our neighbours had been tenants of Trinity College for several generations, up until the founding of the Irish Free State. This, then, was a little enclave of Roman Catholics living within the predominantly Protestant Parish of Loughgall, the village where the Orange Order had been founded in 1795. [1]

Following the founding of the Orange Order, increased anti-Catholic terror led to the Armagh expulsions of 1795 and 1796, when hundreds of Catholic families were banished 'to Hell or Connaught' (a western province of Ireland). South Armagh is a far more firmly Catholic area however, and a stronghold of the Defender movement – a south-Ulster based secret society which had evolved in the 1780s, and would later merge with the United Irishmen to champion the ideals of the French Revolution. During the nineteenth century Catholic agrarian secret societies such as the Ribbonmen were strong particularly in South Armagh. In more recent history too this border area has become known as 'bandit country' – the site of many clashes between the IRA and security forces (including the murder of Captain Nairac, a British undercover officer), as well as loyalist sectarian murder. It is this violent history which lies behind the melodramatic events figured in 'Armageddon, Armageddon', the final sonnet sequence in *Mules*. Thus the apocalyptic vision offered in the poem is on one level ironic, but on another it is a reply to Pancho Villa: to write about land is very far from being an avoidance of the Troubles in Northern Ireland.

  The sonnet sequence brings together the local and the cosmic, as the title announces not only 'Armagh', but the battle which heralds the end of the world. Like the revelation to St John, this is a vision of apocalypse. Muldoon was married in 1974, and he has said that the poem describes his honeymoon and return home during the Ulster Worker's Council Strike in May of that year, when his mother was already dying of cancer. The Strike aimed to bring down the Power-Sharing Executive set up in the wake of the Sunningdale Agreement in 1973. The executive, which gave a measure of minority control over affairs in Northern Ireland to moderate nationalists, was seen by many loyalists as an act of betrayal, a shameful sell-out of Protestant rule over a Protestant state. The Strike paralysed not only industrial activity but power supplies, sewerage systems, transport and the whole infrastructure of Northern Ireland. After two weeks, at the end of May, the Power-Sharing executive was abandoned.

The sequence begins in the 'dazzling' light of an enchanted island (actually an island near Corfu where Muldoon and his wife took their honeymoon). The seven sonnets echo the movement from light to darkness which recurs throughout the volume as they chart the process of returning home to Northern Ireland. The couple make their way back to Armagh by plane, train, and eventually on foot. In the second sonnet Muldoon retells the story of Oisin, the legendary figure who spent three hundred years on an enchanted island with his faery lover. Muldoon draws a wry analogy between Oisin's return to Ireland (when in falling from his horse he accidently touches the earth and ages three hundred years in an instant) and his own return from the land of plenty and fulfilment in Corfu: 'And I know something of how he felt.' As they 'land' like Oisin, it is as though the honeymooners have been away for ever. Sonnet III tries to make the best of the situation; with the whole province at a standstill, they will have to find some way to amuse themselves:

> Not to worry. From where I lived
> We might watch Long Bullets being played,
> Follow the course of a pair of whippets,
> Try to keep in time with a Lambeg Drum.
>
> There'd be Derryscollop and Cloveneden,
> The parish where W.R. Rodgers held sway.
> And where the first Orange Lodge was founded,
> An orchard full of No Surrenders.
>
> We could always go closer if you wanted,
> To where Macha had challenged the charioteer
> And Swift the Houyhnhnm,
> The open field where her twins were whelped.
> Then, the scene of the Armagh Rail Disaster.
> Why not brave the Planetarium?

Perhaps more than any other poem in the volume this sonnet highlights the difficulties which court Muldoon's attempts to stay true to 'something a little nearer home'. The history of Armagh is balanced on the land side of the poetry's mulish equation, but this history can read like a list of obscure references to those not already in the know. At first sight this is an eclectic gathering of local historical and legendary events, a tourist's guide to Armagh. But in

58

fact the images increasingly intimate disaster as they move from
loyalist celebrations, via the Protestant poet Rodgers, who was from
Loughgall, to Unionist intransigence symbolised by the Orange
Order. The fated nature of Northern Ireland's troubles is hinted
at in the story of Macha's ancient curse on Ulster, a fate which is
surely written in the stars at the Planetarium. Imminent destruction threatens even more clearly in Sonnet V, with Muldoon and
his wife near enough to his parental home to walk there in the
dark (all transport systems having come to a standstill during the
strike). Muldoon fuses the apocalyptic language of Revelation with
the fate written in the signs of the Zodiac, which prefigures the
chaos he will find at home:

> Why should those women be carrying water
> If all the wells were poisoned, as they said,
> And the fish littering the river?
> Had the sheep been divided from the goats,
> Were Twin and Twin at each other's throats?

This is a fascinating experiment in writing melodrama and apocalyptic narrative (a genre not common in poetry). The poem pushes
our ideas of suitable subjects for lyric poetry to the limit, in order
to give a sense of complete breakdown and trauma. Muldoon has
said that at the back of this poem lies the powerful image in John
Ford's film, *The Searchers*, of returning home in the knowledge
that you will find everyone dead or disappeared, and the lonely
settler house burned out by Indians. The melodramatic events (rape,
murder, madness) described in the sixth sonnet are too sensational
to be taken seriously and yet at the same time given the nature of
the apocalyptic fable the exaggerated traumas do convey a real mood
of fear and hopelessness. But it is the meditative final sonnet which
carries much of the weight of the sequence as a whole:

> A summer night in Keenaghan
> So dark my light had lingered near its lamp
> For fear of it. Nor was I less afraid.
> At the Mustard Seed Mission all was darkness.
>
> I had gone out with the kettle
> To a little stream that lay down in itself
> And breathed through a hollow reed
> When yon black beetle lighted on my thumb
> And tickled along my palm
> Like a blood-blister with a mind of its own.
>
> My hand might well have been some flat stone
> The way it made for the underside.
> I had to turn my wrist against its wont
> To have it walk in the paths of uprightness.

The poem conjures a very simple, but resonant image for the hopes and uncertainties which shape this volume. 'Armageddon, Armageddon' began in the blazing sun of an enchanted island, but by the end not even the light of the stars survives. The pitch darkness resulting from the cutting of all power supplies figures the extinction of hope. Muldoon borrows from Westerns the favourite image of escaping danger by hiding underwater and breathing through a straw, but he intensifies it. Here the water itself tries to preserve itself from the surrounding danger and chaos in this way. Into this benighted world 'lights' a black beetle – a kind of scarab, associated with hope, and the possibility of rebirth. The lyricism of the final lines seems to offer an uplifting and redemptive conclusion to this traumatic narrative. 'Armageddon, Armageddon', and the volume as a whole, yearns for the kind of solace and protection from evil offered in the 'paths of righteousness' of the twenty-third psalm: 'Even though I walk through the valley of the shadow of death / I will fear no evil.' The evil and distress which haunt this volume lie not only in the collapse of civic society in Northern Ireland, but also in the death of the mother. Muldoon is asking not only can poetry shed light on such darkness (a darkness in many ways bound up with religion), but can it offer consolation? The speaker's action in turning his hand over suggests perhaps the ease with which the world can be righted, or the need for the opposing sides in the conflict in Northern Ireland to act 'against their wont' in order to find a solution. But the lines are complex, for the image also suggests the illusory nature of such solutions. The action of turning the hand over reminds us also of how easily it can be turned back (flipping the wrist back and forth is a common gesture of equivocation and uncertainty).

This is surely an image for the equivocal nature of poetry, which inhabits a space in-between the redemptive language of religion and the earth-bound language of history. Muldoon gives us several ways to think about this mixed heritage. Thus, on the one hand poetry seems to offers a way of healing the split between temporal and eternal, a means of orientation to rival the systems of both mother and father. On the other hand, as 'neither one thing nor the other', poetry may partake of the special perversion of the fallen angel. Rather than rejecting pamphleteer and romantic youth, Muldoon is looking for a way to fuse the two – and the resulting genetic mix may be neither good not evil, neither moral or immoral, but beyond the categories of moral judgement. Muldoon is treading a difficult line here, for he seems to suggest that poetry stands outside moral judgement because it doesn't have a purpose, because, like the mule, it doesn't have children. (In Muldoon's eyes it differs from the languages of religion and politics precisely in its refusal to project a definitive aim, to subordinate imagination to the goal of future liberation whether on earth or in heaven.) This is different from claiming that poetry doesn't have effects, however, and Muldoon needs a way of affirming the value of purposelessness without denying the importance of poetry's capacity to shift our perspective. The direction that poetry should take, if it has no end in view, is the burden of Muldoon's next volume *Why Brownlee Left*.

CHAPTER THREE

Why Brownlee Left

One of the most striking aspects of Paul Muldoon's work is his
ability to write autobiography as poetic form. He represents elements
of his own autobiography – childhood, family life, the farm, marriage, Northern Ireland – not simply as thematic preoccupations
but as stylistic principles, pressures on the style, form and genre
of his poetry. This transformation of personal narrative into poetic
form may be one reason why the autobiographical drive behind
Muldoon's work has not been fully recognised, for this is as far as
possible from confessional verse. In *Mules*, as we have seen, Muldoon's
personal life history (partly fictionalised) is channelled into a consideration of the way to write poetry in Northern Ireland, as he
rejects both literal and allegorical, or emblematic, registers (earth
and stars) in favour of a mixed marriage between the two. But if
the poems seem to strive towards a balance between a human
measure, and a sublime or transcendent one, that balance is as
often upset. Rather than resolution, it is the tentativeness of the
poetic vision which is emphasised, the fact that with a flick of the
wrist all can be so easily turned upside-down.

Muldoon seems both drawn to and suspicious of the idea that
poetry may offer a redemptive or consoling vision, a road to peace.
Why Brownlee Left intensifies the quality of disturbance in the poetry;
it is a volume preoccupied with lack of fit, with things falling apart,
with lack of resolution. It is hard not to relate such concerns to
elements of Muldoon's biography, in particular the break-up of his
marriage to Anne-Marie Conway in 1977. The idea of leaving is a
central organising principle of the book, which considers many kinds
of departure: departure from a marriage, from traditional poetic form,
from life's predestined plot, and from the heterosexual norm. Along
with this comes, unmistakably, a bleaker, more pessimistic tone, and
a pared down contemporary diction, moulded by colloquial phrasing
and by cliché. The temptation is to read this harsher style as a
rejection of the romanticism of Muldoon's earlier work born of
personal disillusion and disappointment, and there is surely some
truth in this. Yet it would be a mistake to miss the crafted, literary
nature of the tone of *Why Brownlee Left*. The literary and artistic
influences are many, from the Irish legends of Cuchulain and Mael
Duin which frame the book, to the obvious generic borrowings
from film noir and detective fiction in the long poem 'Immram':

I was fairly and squarely behind the eight
That morning in Foster's pool-hall
When it came to me out of the blue
In the shape of a sixteen-ounce billiard cue
That lent what he said some little weight.
'Your old man was an ass-hole.
That makes an ass-hole out of you.'

This is clearly a borrowed music, a distinctively American idiom which recalls the work of Raymond Chandler (a writer to whom Muldoon is obviously indebted throughout 'Immram'). In general *Why Brownlee Left* is fascinated by the language of American popular culture; Muldoon is drawn not only to the highly crafted diction of Chandler's detective novels, but also to the language of comics, popular fiction and westerns. In part this reflects of the importance of American popular culture, particularly the cinema and the serial comic, to Irish youth in 1950s and 60s. Many of the poems in this book return to childhood moments marked by encounters with these cultural imports, but there is more than reminiscence at work here. One of the aspects of this language which draws Muldoon is clearly the element of plain-speaking, straight from the hip talk – a laconic style which will help him sidestep (another 'departure') the rhetorical traditions of Irish verse. But this is very far from being at the expense of complexity. Throughout this book he experiments with what can be said through simple and direct language. In part, this is a matter of twisting plain speech back on itself, taking its clichés literally, and exposing its darker implications and undercurrents. And in this regard perhaps the most pervasive literary influence in *Why Brownlee Left* is another American, Robert Frost – a poet who made his career out of seeming to speak plainly.

Frost's disarmingly frank, yet complex style was an important model for Muldoon from his earliest work, but *Why Brownlee Left* reveals a deeper engagement. Muldoon admires above all in Frost his ability to represent disorder and disturbance within order. He has described the American poet's gift as 'an apparently simple, almost naive, tone of voice and use of language, underneath which all kinds of complex things are happening'.[1] Certainly this is an idiosyncratic reading of Frost, and it casts as much light on Muldoon's own writing as it does on Frost's poetry. In Muldoon's hands such hidden complexity is often experienced by the reader as an irritant, something bothersome which inhibits poetic resolution. Muldoon offers us an image for this kind of disturbance in the niggling thing which disturbs repose in 'The Princess and the Pea':

> This is the dream of her older sister,
> Who is stretched on the open grave
> Of all the men she has known.
> Far down, something niggles. The stir
> Of someone still alive.
> Then a cry, far down. It is your own.

In most of the poems in the book, however, this niggling element,
so far from being imaged concretely appears as an element of confusion or disturbance in the narrative. It accounts for the whimsical tone of much of the verse, as if the poet himself is suprised by
some of the implications of his words. One might recall here Frost's
comment that 'all the fun is outside, saying things that suggest
formulae but won't formulate – that almost but don't quite formulate'. For example, Muldoon's poem 'Early Warning' initially seems
to offer a relatively straightforward comparison of Muldoon's father,
a Catholic farmer, who carefully heeds the warning of apple-scab
in the air, with his Protestant neighbour's self-confidence about
his own immunity. The poem opens with an image of the hard-
working farmer spraying the 'lone crab-apple tree' in his garden
against disease. The tree is a focus for the children's play, much
of which is bound up with warfare and its politics:

> We would swing there on a fraying rope,
> Lay siege to the tree-house,
> Draw up our treaties
> In its modest lee.
>
> We would depend on more than we could see.
>
> Our Protestant neighbour, Billy Wetherall,
> Though he knew by the wireless
> Of apple-scab in the air,
> Would sling his hammock
> Between two sturdy Grenadiers
> And work through the latest *Marvel* comic.

As several critics have commented this poem works with stereotypes:
Catholics are poor, they have lots of children, and they make a
precarious living; the Protestant farmer, by contrast, can 'weather
all'. He feels protected from harm by a military presence – his trees
are 'Grenadiers'. The poem seems to echo the division which Seamus
Heaney sets up in his poem 'The Other Side' (in *Wintering Out*)
between the poor Catholic farmer's 'scraggy acres', and the 'promised
furrows' belonging to his Protestant neighbour – one of a chosen
people. But despite the apparent simplicity of Muldoon's poem,
there is something about it which doesn't quite add up. It is built
around a contrast between visibility and invisibility – between the
sturdy, all too visible trees which bolster Billy Wetherall's confidence,

and the insubstantial hold the speaker's family have over their fortunes (imaged by the fraying rope). And yet to depend on more
than you can see is to have faith – a faith which is belied by the
father's reliance on the material protections afforded by insecticide.
If there seems to be contradiction here, stereotypes are even more
clearly put into question in the description of Billy Wetherall. Far
from embodying the Protestant work ethic, as we might have
expected, it is in fact Wetherall who seems closest to the divine –
he 'works' through marvels. It is hard not to be reminded here of
Frost's poem 'After Apple Picking', a poem about the way that the
Fall (in the seasonal as well as the religious senses) both requires
and redeems labour, among other things. In fact, so far from re-
stating the terms of Heaney's poem, 'Early Warning' uses Frost's
meditation on grace and labour in order to complicate the sectarian
division between neighbours. As Muldoon says ironically of the
'shower of rain' which creates a border in 'The Boundary Com-
mission': 'He stood there, for ages, / To wonder which side, if any,
he should be on.'

There is a similar element of strangeness in 'Lull', a poem which
was presumably written during the long IRA ceasefire in the late
1970s. Here again the subtleties of the poem are inextricable from
its apparent availability. The poem begins with a description of
calm which borrows from the rhetoric of the Sermon on the Mount,
when Christ exhorted his followers to seek first the kingdom of
God, rather than concerning themselves with the needs of this
world. Rather like the 'fowls of the air' who 'sow not, neither do
they reap, nor gather into barns; yet your heavenly father feedeth
them',[2] the people of Northern Ireland seem to be giving themselves up to providence:

> I've heard it argued in some quarters
> That in Armagh they mow the hay
> With only a week to go to Christmas,
> That no one's in a hurry
>
> To save it, or their own sweet selves.
> Tomorrow is another day,
> As your man said on the Mount of Olives.
> The same is held of County Derry.
>
> Here and there up and down the country
> There are still houses where the fire
> Hasn't gone out in a century.
>
> I know that eternal interim;
> I think I know what they're waiting for
> In Tyrone, Fermanagh, Down and Antrim.

'Lull' seems to overcome the built-in binarism of the sonnet form, which so often splits into question and answer, problem and solution. We are offered firstly an image of timelessness, of lack of concern about time, and the practical requirements of this world. The sestet seems initially to reinforce the sentiments of the octet – the turf fires damped down at night to be rekindled in the morning conjure images of traditional rural life, lack of change, and an acceptance of the boundaries to experience dictated by fate or faith. But this is to miss the poem's oddness. For the fact that the 'fire / hasn't gone out in a century' is if anything the opposite of 'tomorrow is another day'. To keep the fire lit implies a concern for tomorrow, a wish to have all in readiness for the next day. And it is also an image for keeping the passions lit, implying that these country homes are still burning with unfulfilled political ambitions (which might be Unionist as well as Republican). So far from being unconcerned about the future, such ambitions are entirely directed towards a future end; moreover that imagined future is dependent on a particular experience of the past. Thus the poem imperceptibly moves from stating one thing, to stating the opposite. The idea of faith in providence shifts from being something which offers an alternative to the struggles and ambitions of everyday life, to conjuring an image of lack of progress and the impossibility of moving beyond the political impasse in Northern Ireland precisely because of struggle and ambition. The poem suggests that the ceasefire is only a lull (i.e. it is temporary), because the fires are eternal. At the same time by comparing the religious deferral of action in favour of future consolation within the kingdom of God, with the Republican assumption of future national liberation, Muldoon indicts both. For both reasons Ireland is eternally stuck in a warp.

'Lull' reveals a profound and philosophical use of language and form. The tensions between the temporal and the eternal, between progress and timelessness are figured in the poem's syntax; there is no clearly identifiable point at which the poem shifts ground, and one of the consequences of this is that there seems to be no progress in the poem. Indeed the oppressive and threatening atmosphere of the final lines derives in part from the poem's circularity. This conflict between purposeful movement, directed towards an end, and circularity (or being determined by the past) is repeatedly echoed in *Why Brownlee Left*, which is preoccupied with matters of purpose and direction, and thus also with the implications of choice. Muldoon's most obvious specific indebtedness to Frost in this volume is to his poem 'The Road Not Taken'. Famously, when coming upon a fork in the road Frost's speaker decides on the road 'less travelled by', and is haunted ever after by the impossibility of ever knowing what his choice may have meant, since he doesn't know where the other road would have led him. Muldoon seizes on the idea of destiny which lies within destination, and considers the alternative life histories which might have been, and yet might be, opened up by choosing another road.

In a sense the whole book explores the meaning behind the cliché of life as a journey, or (perhaps more aptly) a pilgrimage. Initially this has to do with the idea of making the most of your life, being open to all its possibilities. Suspicion accrues to those who set out on their journey already knowing where they are going to end up. Yet at the same time Muldoon asks whether it is possible to avoid your predetermined destination even if you take another route – fate will always catch up with you. Fate, both arbitrary and determining, is that which moulds as well as that which undermines purpose. Thus the concepts of choice and destiny implicit in the metaphor of life as a journey allow Muldoon to meditate further on the issue of purpose and purposelessness which had preoccupied him in *Mules*. In part, as in 'Lull', Muldoon is addressing those philosophies which are built around the idea of an ideal resolution, or final consolation.

The poetry is at odds with those social forces – not only Christianity but also nationalist politics – which seem based on a clear, predetermined direction, from darkness into light, from bondage into freedom. But this also implies an argument about poetry. For Muldoon, alert to the dangers poetry confronts, is also concerned with those it creates. Throughout this book he asks how poetry may enlighten without underwriting a simplistic idea of progress, without seeming to offer solutions. In 'I Remember Sir Alfred' Muldoon images his poetic method as one of indirection. He rejects the straight lines prized by a bevy of Irish predecessors and possible models, including Charles Stewart Parnell and the IRA, as well as Sir Alfred McAlpine, the construction engineer:

> Watching Irish navvies drinking pints
> This evening in Camden Town
> I remember Sir Alfred McAlpine –
> The shortest distance between two points
> Is a straight line.

Rather like the use of 'Grenadiers' in 'Early Warning', here Muldoon plays on the hidden military metaphor used popularly to describe the army of Irish navvies drafted in to build England's transport system: McAlpine's Fusiliers. (The word 'navvy' here is important too. It derives from 'navigator', reminding us that Irishmen were employed to build first the canals and only later the roads of England. The term thus signals the links between these men and all the Irish navigators of the past and present who people this book, from the most ordinary, such as Muldoon's father – himself once a navvy – to perhaps the most famous, Brendan the Navigator.) While both armies, or labourers and revolutionaries, seem wedded to the idea of the straight line, the shortest distance from here to there, the poem suggests that all straight lines are really bent – purpose is cut across by personal motivations, emotions, addictions, desires and short term goals:

> Charles Stewart Parnell, the I.R.A.,
> Redheaded women, the way back to the digs,
> The Irish squire
> Who trained his spy-glass
> On a distant spire
> And imagined himself to be attending Mass.

> Now Sir Alfred has dislodged a hare
> That goes by leaps and bounds
> Across the grazing,
> Here and there,
> This way and that, by singleminded swervings.

It would not be too fanciful, I think, to discern in these lines an echo of the 'straight crookedness' prized by Robert Frost in his important essay 'The Figure a Poem Makes'. Frost is in part discussing the process of writing, which he argues must follow the dictates of feeling and association: 'The impressions most useful to my purpose seem always those I was unaware of and so made no note of at the time when taken, and the conclusion is come to that like giants we are always hurling experience ahead of us to pave the future with against the day when we may want to strike a line of purpose across it for somewhere.'[3] Frost suggests that the freedom of this method of composition allows the poem to find its own direction – the results are both 'unforeseen' and at the same time 'predestined' from the poem's point of departure:

> The figure a poem makes. It begins in delight and ends in wisdom. The figure is the same as for love. No one can really hold that the ecstasy should be static and stand still in one place. It begins in delight, it inclines to the impulse, it assumes direction with the first line laid down, it runs a course of lucky events, and ends in a clarification of life – not necessarily a great clarification, such as sects and cults are founded on, but in a momentary stay against confusion. It has an outcome that though unforeseen was predestined from the first image of the original mood – and indeed from the very mood. It is but a trick poem and no poem at all if the best of it was thought first and saved for the last. It

finds its own name as it goes and discovers the best waiting for it in
some final phrase at once wise and sad – the happy-sad blend of the
drinking song.

Frost's famous definition of the poem as a momentary stay against
confusion has been of immense importance in contemporary Irish
poetry, not least because of Seamus Heaney's adoption of the phrase.
Heaney interprets Frost as meaning that the poem can act as a
place of potential resolution, 'beyond confusion': 'And just as the
poem, in the process of its own genesis, exemplifies a congruence
between impulse and right action, so in its repose the poem gives
us a premonition of harmonies desired and not inexpensively
achieved. In this way, the order of art becomes an achievement
intimating a possible order beyond itself, although its relation to
that further order remains promissory rather than obligatory'.[4]
Muldoon's interpretation of Frost is very different however; he
emphasises not promised integration, repose or resolution, but
instead the impulsive nature of the path which the poem follows, its
outcome 'unforeseen' and yet 'predestined'. What kind of destination
do you arrive at if you follow the kind of route 'that goes by leaps
and bounds'? For Muldoon it's important not to claim that poetry
leads directly to anything, though it may result in something.

Many of the poems in *Why Brownlee Left* explore the possible
connections between the seeming opposites: randomness or contingency, and fate or predestination. These are merged together as
the arbitrary constraints of what one poem calls 'family plots'. The
volume complicates the idea of a genetic poetic inheritance which
informed *Mules*. In 'The Mixed Marriage' Muldoon was predestined to poetry through his mixed ancestry, which placed him in
between the worlds of heaven and earth. Here destiny, rather than
being something written in the stars, becomes a matter of historical
contingency – in other words fate is equated with the past. It is
reduced to the accidents of sex – such as the sexual encounter in
'Whim' which ordains the man's fate, in a bizarre embodiment of
the Freudian maxim that anatomy is destiny ('Once he got stuck into
her he got stuck / Full stop.'). In 'History' the course of the lovers'
relationship as well as, by implication, history's larger structures,
can be put down to the arbitrary first encounter: 'Where and when
exactly did we first have sex? / Do you remember?' As the events
in the recent history of Northern Ireland become personalised –
channelled into the memory of the different addresses known by the
lovers – Muldoon implies that the difficulty with not being able to
remember the past, or not being sure of it, is that the future too
remains hidden. This is surely also the significance of the 'chance

remark' which may have led to Muldoon's own conception in 'October 1950':

> Whatever it is, it all comes down to this;
> My father's cock
> Between my mother's thighs.
> Might he have forgotten to wind the clock?

The last line here echoes the beginning of Laurence Sterne's novel *Tristram Shandy*, where the narrator searches in vain for the precise moment when he began, only to find his origin slipping further and further back into the history of his family. The arbitrariness of the moment of conception is not merely to do with the timing of sex, therefore, but also the arbitrariness of taking conception as the moment of beginning, as the source of explanation for all the later details of the poet's life.

> Whatever it is, it goes back to this night,
> To a chance remark
> In a room at the top of the stairs;
> To an open field, as like as not,
> Under the little stars.
> Whatever it is, it leaves me in the dark.

This poem surprises with its harsh diction, emphasised particularly by the end-stopped lines in the first stanza. There is nonetheless a suggestion of romance or fantasy in the 'open field' and the little stars of these final lines, but it is allowed little purchase. The stars here resist allegorical or fateful significance, since there is no order to be found. As in the final lines of 'At Master McGrath's Grave' (where the poet, brought to his knees, seems swallowed by the earth) this poem too pulls away from the seductions of the sublime, and towards the contingent and everyday. At the very point when the poem reaches towards a visionary moment, it is put into question, a movement which is emphasised by the clichéd, colloquial phrasing of the last line. To be left in the dark evokes both the dark of the night of conception, as well as the darkness of the future which stems from that conception.

Why Brownlee Left is preoccupied with the ways in which departure or origin predetermines the nature of the journey and the place of arrival. One of the things Muldoon is saying in 'October 1950' is that he doesn't know where he is going, since he doesn't know where he has come from, and yet his destiny may be no less inescapable for being hidden. The poet sees his own fate as largely bound up with the choices his father made: everything from whether or not he wound the clock, to the name which he bestows on his son is part of the destiny the son bears. The volume as a whole is peopled with characters, such as Wetherall, Brownlee, Coulter, Joseph Mary Plunkett Ward, even Mael Duin himself, who fulfil or refuse the destiny which has been laid out for them – indeed, which is signalled by their names. As in *Mules* the characters' names bear an allegorical significance – they are emblematic of the destiny they are to fulfil. For example Mael Duin (Muldoon), which means literally 'bald head', is a euphemism for seer or devotee. Destiny, then, while inescapable, is not presented as transcendental, but as a matter of chance – it depends on matters such as when and where you (or your parents) have sex, or how you were named.

Yet if historical contingency moulds the path of the poet's life, Muldoon is at liberty to consider alternative scenarios. The final long poem of the book, a reworking of the medieval Irish voyage poem 'Immram Curaig Mael Duin' ('The Voyage of Muldoon'), is an extended meditation on the possibility of alternative origins, including possible literary foster fathers: the anonymous scribes of Irish legend, Chandler, MacNeice, Frost, Tennyson. Muldoon has made a habit of recreating or reinventing his father, as is clear in early poems such as 'The Waking Father', but 'Immram' takes the process much further, suggesting that it is lack of imaginative potential in the father that prompts the poet's flights of fancy. Muldoon states the problem boldly: 'This was how it was. My father had been a mule' (although we already know that mules are very complex creatures). Despite such recalcitrant material, the poet transforms the mulish farm labourer into his dangerous, exotic namesake, the drugs smuggler:

> He had flown down to Rio
> Time and time again. But he courted disaster.
> He tried to smuggle a wooden statue
> Through the airport at Lima.
> The Christ of the Andes. The statue was hollow.
> He stumbled. It went and shattered.
> And he had to stand idly by
> As a cool fifty or sixty thousand dollars worth
> Was trampled back into the good earth.
>
> He would flee, to La Paz, then to Buenos Aires,
> From alias to alias.
> I imagined him sitting outside a hacienda
> Somewhere in the Argentine.
> He would peer for hours
> Into the vastness of the pampas.
> Or he might be pointing out the constellations
> Of the Southern hemisphere
> To the open-mouthed child at his elbow.
> He sleeps with a loaded pistol under his pillow.

Such exoticisation of the mundane is a recurrent motif in this book, which dwells on the transformative possibilities of the imagination. In a companion poem, 'Immrama' (Voyages), Muldoon speculates about a similar alternative life history for his father (and therefore also for himself), taking his cue from a real life alternative which in the end his father did not take. In the 1930s his father and a friend decided to emigrate to Australia, and arranged a meeting place at a crossroads in Tyrone, from where they were to make their way to Belfast and beyond. As Muldoon tells the story (which turns out to be apocryphal) his father made it to the meeting place, but returned home again when his friend did not arrive:

> It's an image that's troubled me for ages, since it underlines the arbitrary nature of so many of the decisions we take, the disturbingly random quality of so many of our actions. I would speculate on my father's having led an entirely different life, in which, clearly, I would have played no part. And suddenly my poems were peopled by renegades, some of them bent on their idea of the future, some on their idea of the past. All bent, though. All errantly going about their errands.[5]

'To be bent upon' suggests both singlemindedness, and deviation. (The phrase echoes the 'singleminded swervings' of the hare escaping at the end of 'I Remember Sir Alfred'.) It encompasses both the straight road and the tangent, and fittingly both kinds of journey are contained in the poem.

> I, too, have trailed my father's spirit
> From the mud-walled cabin behind the mountain
> Where he was born and bred,
> TB and scarlatina,
> The farm where he was first hired out,
> To Wigan, to Crewe junction,
> A building-site from which he disappeared
> And took passage, almost, for Argentina.
>
> The mountain is coming down with hazel,
> The building-site a slum,
> While he has gone no further than Brazil.
>
> That's him on the verandah, drinking rum
> With a man who might be a Nazi,
> His children asleep under their mosquito-nets.

Like many of the poems in *Mules* this brings together real and imagined histories. The poem begins in the realm of fact, as a passage from Muldoon's autobiographical essay attests:

> My father's parents were Hugh Muldoon, a thatcher, and Mary Hamill, a housewife, while my mother's were Francis Regan, a tailor, and Mary Donnelly, also a housewife. Both families were poor. After his mother died when he was seven and his father remarried an unsympathetic

woman, my father was forced to hire himself out as a farm labourer at the age of eleven or twelve, and therefore received no secondary education. He could read and write only with difficulty, needing help to manage official documents and forms. He continued to work as a shepherd, navvy, farm-worker, builder's labourer, cauliflower- and mushroom-grower. [6]

The realms of fact and fiction diverge in the poem with the word 'almost'. To 'almost' take passage suggests both that he thought about leaving but decided against it in the end, and that he almost made it as far as Argentina but actually got 'no further than Brazil'. The poem imagines an alternative past for the father, and the consequences of this past in an alternative present. This other life involves family (children if not a wife) as well as suggestions of a political underworld. The poem creates an uncertain balance between past, present and future, which is embodied in the see-sawing rhymes of the final lines. The rhyme-scheme of the poem may not at first seem unusual; the octet's two quatrain's rhyme loosely with each other *abcd/abcd*, although only the four-syllabled rhyme words, scarlatina/Argentina, draw attention to themselves. The sestet seems to rhyme *ababcc*, but if this is the case the final couplet rhymes 'Nazi' with 'nets', although it is as much an assonantal rhyme for 'hazel' and 'Brazil'. Just as the word 'Nazi' seems to look both forwards and backwards in the poem, so the father seems to be pulled both by his 'real' past and his imagined present in the west.

Yet another way to read these final lines (rather like the example of the 'mule' in 'Immram') is as an exotic treatment of the father's real choice, which was to leave the building sites in England and travel westwards home to Ireland. In this reading 'Brazil' is the rural home in Collegelands were Muldoon was brought up, transformed in the poet's imagination. In fact Muldoon has repeatedly used the image of the pampas and the hacienda to describe his childhood home:

> This image of the 'pampas', or as it appears in another poem, 'That hacienda's frump / of pampas-grass' ('The Earthquake') is particularly evocative for me. There was, in our garden, a great 'frump' of pampas-grass that has, for me, come to stand for something along the lines of Eliot's 'rose-garden' from the opening section of 'Burnt Norton':
>> 'What might have been and what has been
>> Point to one end, which is always present.
>> Footfalls echo in the memory
>> Down the passage which we did not take
>> Towards the door we never opened
>> Into the rose-garden.' [7]

It seems that this 'pampas-grass' includes not only an idea of 'what might have been' but some notion of 'what might yet be'.

The image of the hacienda, then, evokes both possible pasts and possible futures, like the rhyme words which face towards the future as well as the past in 'Immrama'. At the same time the other world to which the father flees, Brazil, evokes the other world of Irish legend, Hy-Breasil, an enchanted island situated in legend somewhere off the West coast of Ireland. In addition to an exotic treatment of Muldoon's rural home in Armagh, then, this is also surely a secular vision of heaven, with a geographical rather than transcendental location. Given that this other world contains the father's spirit, should we read this as another poem (like 'The Waking Father') in which the father is killed off to be reimagined?

'Immrama' imagines an alternative life for the father, in which the absence of a wife is telling. But while roads both taken and not taken seem to co-exist here, alternatives can also be experienced as missed chances. In 'Promises, Promises', for example, the promises of the title (marriage vows, promises to return, being promised to someone else, but also perhaps broken promises) seem to have limited the alternatives available to the speaker. Unlike 'Immrama', where the present contains both past and future, 'Promises, Promises' records an overwhelming sense of loss, and the finality of the past. The poem begins with the poet in North Carolina, unable to respond to his surroundings because of his nagging memories of departing from a 'girl in Bayswater' in London – a departure which has left him without hope.

> Yet I am utterly bereft
> Of the low hills, the open-ended sky,
> The wave upon wave of pasture
> Rolling in, and just as surely
> Falling short of my bare feet.
> Whatever is passing is passing me by.

In the central section of the poem Muldoon draws an analogy between his situation and Raleigh's failed attempt to colonise Virginia, the Roanoke settlement of 1585. Although Raleigh keeps his promise to return, the ships he sends back to America arrive too late to save the colonists from extinction.

> I am with Raleigh, near the Atlantic,
> Where we have built a stockade
> Around our little colony.
> Give him his scallop-shell of quiet,
> His staff of faith to walk upon,
> His scrip of joy, immortal diet –
> We are some eighty souls
> On whom Raleigh will hoist his sails.

He will return, years afterwards,
To wonder where and why
We might have altogether disappeared,
Only to glimpse us here and there
As one fair strand in her braid,
The blue in an Indian girl's dead eye.

Ironically the sign of continuity – that extinction is not complete, that we only 'might have' disappeared – can only be found in death, which finalises the extinction. The mark of presence is discovered too late. The third to sixth lines here quote from a poem attributed to Raleigh (thought to have been written while he was awaiting execution for treason) entitled 'The Passionate Man's Pilgrimage'. This title in turn suggests analogies for Muldoon – both passionate and engaged in a kind of pilgrimage – but the poem implies that the object of his quest is unattainable – he writes under sentence of death. The third stanza returns to the image with which the poem began, but substitutes the girl in Bayswater for the Indian girl:

The cardinal sings from a redbud
For the love of one slender and shy,
The flight after flight of stairs
To her room in Bayswater,
The damson freckle on her throat
That I kissed when we kissed Goodbye.

The damson freckle acts like the blue of the eye, or the fair strand of hair: all are glimpses of what you can't reach, tortuous signs of hope, and at the same time the extinction of hope. (One might note here in passing that for Muldoon the plum and the damson seem to be signs emblematic of sexual loss – for example the damson bush in 'Thrush' is associated with rejection; in 'Something of a Departure' the lovers' last time together is symbolised by a 'plum-coloured beauty-spot'; in 'The More a Man Has the More a Man Wants', damsons and plums are again associated with damsels and disappearance.)

It is worth considering for a moment the significance of the westward voyage for Muldoon, since this has been a central pre-occupation for him since his early poem 'Good Friday 1971. Driving Westward'. The west has very rich connotations in Irish history and culture. There is firstly, the importance of the rural west of Ireland as the repository of true Irish identity for Gaelic and Celtic revivalists. Arising out of this comes the description of those who turn to England for their cultural and economic survival as 'West Britons' (hence the nationalist accusation of Gabriel Conroy in Joyce's short story 'The Dead'). But the land to the west of Ireland is America, to which many Irish have accordingly emigrated (and this is what Muldoon puns on in 'Immrama'). Also to 'go west' in popular speech means to die – crossing the border between one world and another. In terms of literary tradition the westward voyage forms an important strand of pre-Christian and Christian legend in Ireland, including the voyages of Oisin, Bran, Mael Duin, and the most famous, Brendan. Muldoon has written poems involving all these figures, and as Edna Longley has pointed out, in this he has surely been influenced by the later 'parable' poetry of his Belfast-born predecessor, Louis MacNeice.[8] One of the models which MacNeice cites as important for his concept of parable is the Irish voyage myth. In *Varieties of Parable* MacNeice loosely defines his topic as occupying an area somewhere between symbolism, allegory, fable, fantasy and myth; he characterised parable as an 'enigmatical saying', a narration in which something is expressed in terms of something else. But most importantly for MacNeice parable is a sort of 'double-writing' or sleight of hand, which plays off both a manifest and a latent content (for him this differentiates it from simple allegory, which is organised in terms of one to one correspondences). One might note here the way that for Muldoon, Brazil can stand both for home (through the image of the pampas grass) and its exotic other. Muldoon has indeed noted the elements of parable in his own versions of these legends:

> One of the ways in which we are most ourselves is that we imagine
> ourselves to be going somewhere else. It's important to most societies
> to have the notion of something out there to which we belong, that
> our home is somewhere else...there's another dimension, something
> around us and beyond us, which is our inheritance. [9]

The concept of 'another dimension' is clearly very important to Muldoon, but he doesn't want to think of this in a narrowly religious way, in terms of a future (life after death), something which orientates the direction of our temporal lives, or lends them purpose. Instead these are parables about a parallel world. In 'Immrama' he suggests that the voyage westwards, towards another life, can take place in the spirit, in parallel to the life lived at home. This movement is even more explicit in 'The Bishop', which meditates more directly on the destiny presupposed by organised religion. Like many of the characters in the book the Bishop arrives at his ordained destination despite having deviated from his route. 'The night before he was to be ordained' as a priest, he changes the course of his life completely:

> He packed a shirt and a safety razor
> And started out for the middle of nowhere,
> Back to the back of beyond.

He returns to his farming background, and builds a life perhaps similar (as we shall see) to the one Brownlee left – a farm, a wife, children, grandchildren. The title of the poem perhaps hints at the name given him by his neighbours (reflecting his book-learning), for whom his alternative life, his road not taken, still lingers. And it is this life which eventually reclaims him:

> His favourite grand-daughter
> Would look out, one morning in January,
> To find him in the chair, in the yard.
>
> It had snowed all night. There was a drift
> As far as his chin, like an alb.
> 'Come in, my child. Come in, and bolt
> The door behind you, for there's an awful draught.'

On one level the poem's subject is the closing down of life's possibilities with age, and the desire to to have been able to follow many different routes. In part the poem suggests that the bishop has lived both lives in parallel, that he hasn't really had to make a choice at all, since he has inhabited the strange state of being in but not of another world.

Like 'Immrama' the poem holds alternatives in tension syntactically as well as thematically. Edna Longley notes the poetry's characteristic 'postponement rather than subversion of the indicative, its distrust of the definitive'.[10] Muldoon's frequent use of 'may' and 'would' (the present habitual, which is a tense in the Irish language), is weighted to suggest an oblique slant on historical time and a temporal place existing between the here and now (indicative) and the may-be (conditional). The present habitual acts as a sort of 'other-wordly' tense which serves to hold alternative lives and places together in one poem. Longley notes how in 'The Bishop' this construction places alternative narratives 'in historical suspension' as it drives ordination in tandem with family and secular life.

Of course another way to read these lines is that the bishop's choice of family over religious life is overridden by fate. The end of the poem suggests at first that the past has reclaimed him, but this is to simplify the poem's dynamic. For the religious dimension which the bishop eschews is also surely an image for his future, the other world to which he hopes he will be admitted. Indeed as the final lines suggest, he has already entered another world, for the present (like life in 'Brazil') contains both past and future possibilities.

The 'bishop' rejects the idea of dedicating his life to a singular journey – towards the life after death. He goes off at a tangent, but in doing so he comes full circle, fulfilling the destiny implied by his name. Of no character in the book is this more true than of

Brownlee himself, the archetypal renegade, who deviates from his predestined script, only to be more than ever twinned with his fate. The jacket note decribes Brownlee as an 'enigmatical figure': 'past shaky, future hazy, present whereabouts uncertain', and this peculiar state of temporal in-betweenness is superbly represented in the poem. 'Why Brownlee Left' is a remarkable poem, technically brilliant, and at the same time richly evocative:

> Why Brownlee left, and where he went,
> Is a mystery even now.
> For if a man should have been content
> It was him; two acres of barley,
> One of potatoes, four bullocks,
> A milker, a slated farmhouse.
> He was last seen going out to plough
> On a March morning, bright and early.
>
> By noon Brownlee was famous;
> They had found all abandoned, with
> The last rig unbroken, his pair of black
> Horses, like man and wife,
> Shifting their weight from foot to
> Foot, and gazing into the future.

Syntactically this poem seems to be telling a straightforward story, with a beginning, middle and (mysterious) end, its straightforwardness reinforced by the absolute plainness of the language. The first stanza (the sonnet's octet) sets up a simple mystery to be solved: why and where did Brownlee go? The simple syntax follows the rhythm and measure of the lines; grammatically, facts follow on from one another in a clear and logical manner. The standard, predictable break between the octect and the sestet suggests that, as is traditional, we will find the answer to the mystery in the poem's final lines. And oddly enough we do, despite the fact that we have been told that the mystery is as yet unsolved. For the strangest thing about this enigma is surely that there is no enigma. The syntactical logic of the poem chimes perfectly with the inevitability of the narrative, for what Brownlee leaves is the image of marriage represented by his horses. The sestet's single sentence pulls inevitably towards the final image, as the poem's measure slows through enjambement to rest on the image of the horses 'like man and wife' suspended in mid-task. This final image is extraordinarily powerful; Brownlee's disappearance leaves the reader contemplating the nearly ploughed field and the horses neither completely still, nor making progress, but shifting 'from foot to foot'.

Here again, it is possible to interpret these lines in different ways. A pessimistic reading of the poem would suggest that Brownlee is indeed swallowed by his fate. He wants to deviate from the marital plot, but in the end he comes full circle: the fated nature of Brownlee's life is signalled in his name – which means, literally, 'brown meadow'. (Muldoon has said that the name, while it recalls the Brownlows of Lurgan, actually came to him because it was the manufacturers' name printed on the toilet doors at the BBC. A name then that he, literally, saw every day.) So Brownlee disappears into his surroundings, fulfils his destiny, even as he seems to depart from the domestic script which has been laid out for him in the first stanza.

And yet the image of the horses is, to say the least, equivocal. On the one hand shifting from foot to foot suggests lack of progress, or near stasis, but it is also an image of perpetual movement. The horses, like Brownlee himself, have come to an end without coming to a stop, and this is an image for the poem too. Like the poem, the ploughed field is constructed of straight lines. The feet of the horses (one would have expected 'hoof to hoof') are the feet of poetic measure, which shifts in the reader's mind, as the poem opens out into a landscape which still harbours possibilities (the last rig is as yet 'unbroken'). We might recall here Muldoon's suspicion of the kind of progress or advancement which is plotted in straight lines. The poem implies that rather than offering a possible solution or clarification, the future can be grasped not by moving forward but by standing (nearly) still. The poem achieves a delicate balance between the two poles of departure and arrival; Brownlee has permanently just departed, the future remains always beyond reach, suggesting a gloss on the line from Robert Frost, 'The only certain freedom's in departure'. (There are in fact several instances of this kind of arrested, perpetual movement in the volume, such as these lines from 'Immram': 'When I nudged the rocker on the porch / It rocked as though it might never rest. / It seemed that I would forever be driving west.')

Muldoon's dissatisfaction with the religious idea of a future (as a future to be *gained*) is rendered more explicit in another poem which has to do with ploughing, 'Come into My Parlour'. The title echoes not only Frost's equivocal invitation in 'Come In', but more obviously the well-known rhyme 'Come into my parlour / Said the spider to the fly', with its connotations of danger and deceit. The parlour in this case is the graveyard at Collegelands which, like the spider's web, offers no way out. Muldoon's bleak vision of the future for his family and neighbours is to be swallowed by the earth (hinted at in the reference to dinner plates):

> 'I've been at the burying
> Of so many of the Souper McAuleys

> I declare they must be stacked
> As high as dinner-plates.
> Mind you, this ground's so wet
> They're away again like snow off a ditch.
> Them, and the best of good timber
> Are come into the kingdom.'
>
> And I saw over his tilting shoulder
> The grave of my mother,
> My father's grave, and his father's;
> The slightly different level
> Of the next field, and the next;
> Each small, one-sided collision
> Where a neighbour had met his future.
> Here an O'Hara, there a Quinn,
> The wreckage of bath-tubs and bedsteads,
> Of couches and mangles,
> That was scattered for miles around.

Coulter, the grave digger (whose name means the shoulder-piece of a plough – that which keeps the plough straight) tries to equate burial with entry into the Kingdom of Heaven, but he cannot see that in fact things are out of 'kilter', they have gone awry. The future the neighbours meet is, like one possible interpretation of Brownlee's fate, one of being submerged, of disappearing into the earth rather than reaching for the sky.

Despite Muldoon's secular impulse, however, the metaphor of the religious journey, and in particular Christian mythology, lies behind many of the poems in this book. It is as if Muldoon were not satisfied with denying the efficacy of the idea of life as a pilgrimage, for he repeatedly uses it as a metaphor for his own life. The dissolution of Muldoon's marriage is imaged in terms of the journey towards Calvary, with poems marking progress along the route entitled 'Palm Sunday' and 'Holy Thursday'. (Although the poem which marks the end of their relationship, 'Making the Move', offers a revision of a different voyage myth, as Muldoon suggests that, were he Ulysses, his would not be a circular journey: 'Were I embarking on that wine-dark sea / I would bring my bow along with me.')

However, the poem which is most clearly based on a religious pilgrimage is 'Immram'. 'Immram' is another of the departures in the book, since Muldoon has not previously attempted such a long narrative poem. Narrative itself is used in the poem as a way of playing around with departures. Muldoon bases his poem on the early Irish 'Voyage of Mael Duin' – the original (as well as the versions by Tennyson and Louis MacNeice to which he alludes) gives him a plot to depart from and return to, to swerve away from, and

circle back to. Like so many of the poems in *Why Brownlee Left*
Muldoon interprets the Mael Duin voyage as a family plot – in his
version it is a narrative about parentage, authority and tradition.
The poem explores a characteristic Muldoon concern (powerfully
imaged in 'Mules') that your mother and father may not be your
"real" parents.

The original legend of Mael Duin has an unmistakable moral
purpose and overtly Christian message. The voyager sails to thirty
islands in search of enlightenment, which is given in the form of a
message of forgiveness from the Hermit of Tory, who tells him to
make peace with his enemies. Muldoon's poem transposes the legend into a contemporary *film noir* setting; the thirty islands visited
by the wanderer become the thirty stanzas of the poem, in which
the Muldoon figure searches for the "truth" of his existence by
trying to find out the truth about his father. The poem offers
many marvels, mostly those associated with drink, drugs and sex,
but little enlightenment. In the end we discover that the keeper of
wisdom is merely a power-crazed Howard Hughes figure:

> He was huddled on an old orthopaedic mattress,
> The makings of a skeleton,
> Naked but for a pair of draw-string shorts.
> His hair was waistlength, as was his beard.
> He was covered in bedsores.
> He raised one talon.
> 'I forgive you,' he croaked. 'And I forget.
> On your way out, you tell that bastard
> To bring me a dish of ice-cream.
> I want Baskin-Robbins banana-nut ice-cream.'

The Muldoon figure in the poem is described as 'like any other
pilgrim', but religion is harshly satirised here. The seekers after
enlightenment are persuaded by many different varieties of transcendence and consolation, all equally delusive – such as the 'angel
dust' cocaine, or the 'wholly new religion' of the surf-board:

> He called it *The Way Of The One Wave.*
> This one wave was sky-high, like a wall of glass,
> And had come to him in a vision.
> You could ride it forever, effortlessly.

If the vicissitudes of 'family plots' place constraints on action in
many of the poems here, this volume also evidences the way that
Muldoon experiments with arbitrary formal constraints. 'Immram'
self-consciously experiments with the possible choices which can
be made within a predetermined script. Not only do the number
of stanzas correspond to the number of islands in the original legend, as though the poem itself were a sea voyage (it begins and

ends in a 'poolroom', and takes in on the way the 'Atlantic Club' and 'Ocean Boulevard'), but specific elements of the original tale are transposed into *film noir* equivalents. So a black cat on one of Mael Duin's islands becomes 'a solitary black cat', 'honking to Blind Lemon's blues guitar'. In addition to the constraints provided by literary models (which have been a feature of his work since 'Good Friday 1971. Driving Westward'), Muldoon is also interested in the limitations and possibilities of writing within traditional literary forms, such as the sonnet, and using traditional poetic devices such as rhyme. To pursue the analogy with an individual's possible departures from life's predestined plot, Muldoon's formal experiments seem designed to explore the relationship between the unforeseen and the predestined through possible departures from literary genres and forms. Just as each departure can be understood only in tension with a standard plot, so formal experiments depend for their effect on the balance achieved between tradition and newness. So the effects of half-rhyme (such as the unusual relation between the rhymes hazel, Brazil and Nazi) depend on our awareness of the structure of traditional rhyme, and our expectations of traditional sonnet form.

As always with Muldoon, however, these formal issues have far-reaching implications. I have suggested that the reflection on journeys in *Why Brownlee Left* is not only a meditation on personal fate, but also (since fate itself is presented in terms of historical contingency), a consideration of the way that the past determines the future. In poems such as 'History' or 'October 1950' Muldoon ironises the idea that the clue to the future lies in the past, yet many of Muldoon's characters seem destined to replay the past. In 'Lull' the inhabitants of the six counties are caught in an endless replaying of the past, entrapped in the circular narrative of Irish history. At the same time, however, Muldoon's formal experiments suggest that it is possible to use the past (poetic tradition) to build a different future – but you must go at a tangent, rather than in a straight line.

Perhaps Muldoon's most equivocal comment on the relationship between past and future occurs in 'Anseo'. This poem repeats the circular structure of 'Promises, Promises'. It is comprised of three sonnet stanzas, with the third returning to the first and repeating it with slight variation. Like the bishop, the central character here goes off at a tangent but in the end comes full circle (in an embodiment of the principle of 'revolution'). Joseph Mary Plunkett Ward is the school rebel, and persistent truant. He is rarely present for the calling of the roll, in which the schoolchildren answer to their

names in Irish: 'Anseo, meaning here, here and now, / All present
and correct.' His punishment is to be beaten by the master, with a
stick he has found for himself in the hedges:

> After a while, nothing was spoken;
> He would arrive as a matter of course
> With an ash-plant, a salley-rod.
> Or, finally, the hazel-wand
> He had whittled down to a whip-lash,
> Its twist of red and yellow lacquers
> Sanded and polished,
> And altogether so delicately wrought
> That he had engraved his initials on it.

Not only does he make his own means of punishment but he also
makes it his own – he engraves his initials on the stick used to beat
him which is then, literally, 'a rod for his own back'. Eventually
Ward takes a place within the hierarchy of the IRA which is equi-
valent to that of the Master of the school:

> And he told me, Joe Ward,
> Of how he had risen through the ranks
> To Quartermaster, Commandant:
> How every morning at parade
> His volunteers would call back *Anseo*
> And raise their hands
> As their names occurred.

A great many things are going on in this poem – there is firstly
the similarity between the disciplinary institutions of school and
revolutionary army, the use of Irish to enforce a sense of belonging,
the linking of the Irish language, nationalism and education. As in
'Lull' Muldoon is not just targeting the the idea of future direction,
but the way that this is dependent on a reading of the past. The
poem sets up a contrast between the writer and the activist revolutionary; the latter is 'making things happen' as opposed to the
passive occupations of reading and writing. But in reality poet and
revolutionary share a great deal, for Ward is also an artist. He creates 'delicately wrought' art out of his method of punishment, but
perhaps more telling is his name. Joseph Mary Plunkett was a poet,
friend of Patrick Pearse, and one of the signatories to the 1916
Declaration of Independence, who was executed after the Easter
Rising. Ward then is named after a poet-revolutionary, but even
his surname reveals his writerly bent. The school-master plays on
the name suggesting he is (or should be) 'a ward-of-court'; but in
fact the name has more in common with Brownlee or Coulter, in
that it hides an etymological meaning – ward means 'son of the
poet' (Mhac an Bháird). So Joseph Mary Plunkett Ward is a

poet/revolutionary twice over, and the contrast between him and the Muldoon figure is in fact a comparison.

Muldoon's wry analogy between poet and revolutionary has several implications; strongest perhaps is the idea that rather than to bring peace or resolution (as Heaney suggests at the end of 'The Harvest Bow' when he writes, echoing Coventry Patmore, 'The end of art is peace'), the poet's task is to disturb and disorder. At the same time, as in 'Anseo', Muldoon allows the possibility that revolution is also creative in its way (the schoolboy makes of his punishment a work of art), although perhaps what Ward needs to learn from the poet's experiments with traditional forms is that it is better not simply to repeat the past (to come full circle) but to learn from the past in order to produce variations on it. Present in the figures of Pancho Villa and Joseph Mary Plunkett Ward, the link between poet and revolutionary becomes even more central to Muldoon's next book through the figure of Gallogly, hero of 'The More a Man Has the More a Man Wants'. In *Quoof* however the focus is on violence, and the destruction which goes hand in hand with creativity. No longer romantic revolutionary, Gallogly is clearly a terrorist and the poet seems to share with him the capacity not merely to represent but to enact violence.

I have focused in this chapter on Muldoon's preoccupation with fate, history and repetition, but the image of the poet-revolutionary highlights another aspect of his concern with destiny and destination – the question of agency or control. Robert Frost is again a background presence here. The title of his poem 'Directive', for example, hints at the fact that to find oneself going in a particular direction is to be under a certain command or order. The debate about how movement or progression occurs in politics or in poetry is figured throughout *Why Brownlee Left* as a tension between accident and design, randomness and purpose. Of course Muldoon is not the first poet to experiment with ways of combining random events or sudden connections with a sense of poetic wholeness or order. We could instance here the poets of the New York School, and those influenced by Abstract Expressionism, and action painting in particular. In Frank O'Hara's work, for example (poems such as 'Personal Poem' or 'The Day Lady Died'), quotidian, seemingly inconsequential or arbitrary details are, almost despite themselves, invested with a sense of purpose. Such poems create an illusion of randomness; indeed paradoxically they use randomness as a way of excluding accident, making everything by definition part of the intent (as Jackson Pollock said of his frantically disordered drip paintings 'There IS no accident'). But although the artists and

writers of the New York School have clearly been important influences
on Muldoon, particularly in *Quoof*, Muldoon dramatises the tension
between control and lack of control rather differently. Rather than
creating an illusion of randomness, Muldoon entices us, draws us
in, by playing on our desire for order and control, our need for
directives. Among contemporary poets he is remarkable for the high
degree of verbal patterning which his work displays. Not only does
Muldoon embrace the discipline of such traditional poetic forms
as the sonnet, but he often imposes even more extreme constraints
of rhyme and verse pattern on himself (such as the complex sestinas
of 'Yarrow'). The poems in *Why Brownlee Left* set up an illusion
of a simple journey from A to B, but as readers our desire for
order and direction is undercut by the actual process in which we
find ourselves involved. Just as Muldoon uses rhyme and traditional forms to undermine our expectations of order (as in the
half-rhymes of the final lines of 'Immrama') so his narrative journeys
are not as straightforward as they seem. Almost imperceptibly they
change direction in the middle. These swervings are not primarily
a result of the actions and events of the narrative – they are not a
response to the unpredictable immediacy of experience (O'Hara's
'you just go on your nerve'). Rather, the poems are pulled off course
by the many different directions implied by the semantic ambiguity
of the words themselves. Muldoon exploits this ambiguity to create
a universe of parallels and alternative possibilities. In poetry, he
seems to be saying, we can escape constraints, disobey orders – we
are not obliged to choose, but can exist on more than one plane,
visit more than one place, live in present and future at once. But
at the same time experience threatens to bring us full circle. In
the midst of our plural imaginative explorations we become aware
of a countervailing movement, or a controlling presence, like the
fate which catches up with the characters in *Why Brownlee Left*.

Muldoon's teasing metaphor of the poem as a journey clearly
has implications for the way we read and understand his poetry –
and for the work of criticism. For throughout *Why Brownlee Left*
Muldoon is not merely arguing that enlightenment and understanding go 'by leaps and bounds', he is demonstrating it. He is
asking us as readers to allow for those oblique and unforeseen tangents of language and thought which may carry us far away from
where we think we are, and leave us somewhere else. In a sense
what he is demanding from us is lack of critical distance; he wants
us to get inside the poems with him, to follow the twists and turns
of their singleminded swervings from within. This is a particular
problem for criticism and explication of course; the critic is being

asked to resist the temptation to abstract or extract the argument or meaning of a poem, since the meaning lies in the journey the poem travels. This is of course true of poetry in general, but in *Why Brownlee Left* it is dramatised in a way which gives it new urgency. Muldoon is suggesting that only by going at a tangent can we be true to poetry's possibilities as a form of knowledge – to its particular ability to bring different imaginative possibilities together, and thereby hold open another dimension, the imaginative space of the future.

CHAPTER FOUR

Quoof

Paul Muldoon's fourth collection, *Quoof*, was published in 1983, during the aftermath of the Republican hunger strikes – a particularly painful time in recent Northern Irish history. It is an unsettling volume, revealing in Muldoon a new darker poetic sensibility. Violence, cruelty and their anarchic ramifications are central to this book which can, at times, be difficult to digest. Readers are treated to a number of disturbing vignettes: a pair of severed hands, a woman 'fist-fucked all night...until the morning that never comes', another tarred and feathered, a local councillor blown to pieces by a car-bomb – the scattered remains of his body impossible to collect. Not only are some of these violent scenarios hard to stomach, but the form in which they are presented can be disorientating, to say the least. The poems cut between the local and the cosmopolitan, as Muldoon weaves together rural childhood reminiscences, drug-induced visions, references to modern art and elements of Native American legend, with phantasmagoric accounts of contemporary events in Northern Ireland.

That Muldoon should have chosen this moment to explore further the relationship between art and violence might have been predicted, but Muldoon himself seemed conscious that he was breaking new ground, with regard to poetry in general, but also with regard to his own work. The book has been hailed by many critics as a tour de force, lauded for its technical brio as well as its hard-edged view of reality ('*Quoof* consistently sets out to assault received notions of decorum and decency with the unpalatable truth: Muldoon employs modern-day realities to crush all forms of sentimentality and idealisation').[1] Highest praise was reserved for the final long poem in the book, 'The More a Man Has the More a Man Wants' – a surreal sonnet sequence following the fortunes of Gallogly, a terrorist mercenary on the run, and his alter-ego and nemesis, Mangas Jones, an American Indian on a revenge visit to Northern Ireland. The poem was celebrated for its wit, energy and iconoclasm, as well as its exploration of 'postmodern' narrative techniques such as a fluid sense of personal identity, narrative instability, and intertextuality. This textual difficulty was also at the root of what some readers criticised as the poetry's wilful obscurity however, as the book was taken to task for an overly cynical and ungenerous tone. In a related vein, other readers disliked the

book for its treatment of women, discerning in the repeated yoking
of sexuality and violence not so much an 'unpalatable truth' as a
self-serving misogyny. Certainly many of the images of women in
the book are both unpleasant and discomforting; women are nearly
always represented as sexualised objects, variously fantasised, discarded, raped, murdered, or violently punished.

It is, I think, a mistake to dismiss criticisms of _Quoof_'s misogyny in the name of Muldoon's iconoclastic, unsentimental realism.
Rather than attempting to match the book's callous tone with a
correspondingly hard readerly attitude, it is important to acknowledge the disturbing aspects of this book. What's distressing about
it is not simply that Muldoon describes unpleasant events, acts,
thoughts and fantasies, but that he acknowledges them as his own.
This book is as personal as his previous work – it's about how violence and brutality coexist with a sentimental vision of the family
and the home, and may, indeed, be nurtured by it. Throughout the
volume Muldoon juxtaposes (and confuses) poems of brutal vision
with highly nostalgic images of his childhood home, and his father
in particular. As always with Muldoon it's difficult to tell exactly
what is meant by this juxtaposition, but one effect is to emphasise
yet again the roots of the poetry within a very specific experience
of rural Northern Irish culture. Inevitably certain questions are
posed: does home confine or liberate vision? Is the powerful paternal presence in the poems benign or corrupting? And perhaps most
pressing, can the poetry which is a product of this background ever
be more than a symptom of the peculiar pressures of Northern
Ireland, or can it also be part of a cure?

Quoof reveals Muldoon to be as suspicious as ever about poetry's
transformative, healing properties, but also more than ever in need
of a cure. The sickness in this volume is in part the violence and
brutality in Northern Ireland, and as the images of violated women
and fragmented body parts suggest, it is represented above all in
physical terms. _Quoof_ places tremendous emphasis on the physical
body and its appetites (nutritional and sexual). The body is of course
the most personal of properties, and therefore perhaps the logical
extension of Muldoon's autobiographical concerns. In part Muldoon
is exploring here the problem of communicating that which is most
personal and corporeal, of how to overcome the individual's con-
finement within the body. But the insistent emphasis on bodies
and body parts in _Quoof_ also has to do with entrapment in very
specific sense – with imprisonment and with the spectacle of the
body then being enacted in Northern Irish prisons.

The Republican prisoners' dirty protests and hunger strikes of the early 1980s are fundamental to an understanding of this volume. In the mid 1970s the British government withdrew special category status from those convicted of terrorist offences. Henceforth they were to be treated as ordinary criminals, and housed in the newly constructed facilities at the Maze prison (formerly Long Kesh). The new buildings came to be known as the H Blocks. The prisoners refused to comply with the new regulations, initially rejecting prison uniform. (Since they were prohibited from wearing their own clothes, they wrapped themselves in their blankets, and the protest came to be known as going 'on the blanket'). This quickly escalated into the no-wash protest, and then the dirty protest, when prisoners refused to use toilet facilities and smeared the walls of their cells with excrement. The protests culminated in the hunger strikes of 1981, ending only after ten prisoners had starved to death. Outside the prisons, assassinations, bombings and sectarian murders continued at a high level; in 1981 alone there were more than one thousand shootings and 530 bombs planted.

It would be difficult, I think, to overestimate the effects of this nightmarish reality on Muldoon. Terrorist bombings, army manoeuvres, shootings, murders and reprisals all feature in this volume as Muldoon focuses on the bodies which suffer this violence. In fact bodies feature in almost every conceivable aspect in this book – there are entrails, human and animal skins, body parts as various as (famously) a blown-off foot 'like a severely pruned back shrub' and a pickled womb, the scattered sexual bodies of women and men. In part this stems from the book's insistent emphasis on sex and sexuality. The personal and autobiographical bent of Muldoon's work is pared down to a meditation on corporeality, so that, for example, in the title-poem the relation between the lovers is, in default of language, a relation (or non-relation) between two bodies. But while the body of the other may be a source of enlightenment it is more often a site of violence, disease and corruption, as the poems focus on the body's vulnerability and injurability. Whether a sprained ankle or a severed hand, it is the body itself which becomes transformed, blown up, twisted by drugs, ecstatic sex and poetic language itself. Indeed, despite my description of the book as 'hard-edged', many of the poems focus on softness – the soft body of a frog which can be squeezed to death, the delicate mound of a trifle, the softness of human bodies which can be so easily damaged and destroyed, and most insistently the softness of the body's products, such as faeces.

Muldoon is clearly responding here to the central images in Northern Irish culture in the early 1980s – the damaged bodies of victims of bombs and shootings, but also the use of the body by Republican prisoners in the dirty protest and the hunger strikes. One thing the Republican prison protests shared was the use of the body to make political statements, the transformation of the body into rhetoric. During the dirty protest the prisoners' bodies, unclothed and unwashed, and their cells, smeared with their own excrement, became the signs of their resistance to the prison guards. But an even more extreme and tragic spectacle was the hunger-strikers' doomed use of their own flesh in the battle with the British government over political status. The special emphasis on the body during this period has to be understood in part as a "negative" response to imprisonment and the increasingly uncompromising stance of the British government over political status. The prisoners began to use the self as a weapon, to sacrifice themselves, because they had no access to other weapons. But at the same time, like the anorexic woman (an analogy used twice in the book), the suicidal behaviour of the hunger-striker is not only a response to entrapment, but a powerful sign of protest. The hunger-strikers drew on a well established tradition in Irish Republican politics of using suffering as a form of attack. Most famously Patrick Pearse, one of the leaders of the 1916 Rising, had claimed, in a warped interpretation of the Catholic emphasis on the body and bodily suffering, that victory comes not to those who are able to inflict the most, but to those who are able to suffer the most.

Yet this preoccupation with imprisonment has implications not only for the content of Muldoon's poetry but for his poetic method. If *Why Brownlee Left* hinted at a comparison between the figures of the poet and the revolutionary, that correspondence becomes central in *Quoof*. In 'Anseo' Muldoon had drawn an analogy between poet and revolutionary based around the issue of 'making things happen'. Here, however, the revolutionary is in jail, and can only make things happen to himself. Muldoon's emphasis on the body in this book may be partly a comment on his own self-consuming poetry, as the autobiographical impulse of his work narrows to focus on the most intimate and private aspects of the self, on what goes into and comes out of the body – food, drugs, semen, urine, faeces. One way of understanding this might be as a critique of any idealistic vision of writing's revolutionary possibilities – here violence becomes violence against the self. At the same time, however, Muldoon is preoccupied with how the body and its products can be creatively transformed – and it is this impulse which lends 'The More a Man Has' its tremendous energy. Gallogly, the "hero" of this surreal and fantastic narrative, is a master of physical transformation,

able to turn himself into many different shapes and sizes in order
to evade capture. His ability to mutate parallels the poem's own
creative impulse – the aesthetic transformations enacted by poetic
language, or the metamorphosis of the traditional meditative sonnet
form into a supple tool of narrative verse. But while such transformations may seem productive, the lesson of the hunger-strikers
(also transforming their bodies for revolutionary ends) suggests
that such activity is as destructive as it is creative. Rather than
fertile imaginative conversions, how far are the physical transformations of poetry merely a doomed response to entrapment?

In addressing this issue in *Quoof* Muldoon repeatedly invokes
the figure of the shaman. The shaman is in one sense a magician,
arousing all kinds of sceptical thoughts about whether his activity
can be more than charlatanry. But at the same time, shamanistic
practices of transformation – in the form of drug-taking, dance,
ritual and magic – centre on the body in a way which picks up the
volume's central concerns. Importantly, these material practices can
give rise to 'visions' comparable to those of the poet. Muldoon seems
fascinated by this connection between the most crudely physical
aspects of our existence and the capacity for vision and illumination. It is the figure of the shaman which first makes a connection
between Muldoon's poetic concerns and the dirty protest: the epigraph to the volume brings together magical physical metamorphosis with sexuality and images of defecation. It tells of a 'great
shaman' in Eskimo legend who turns herself into a man, in order
to marry her adoptive daughter:

> With a willow branch she made herself a penis so that she might be like
> a man, but her own genitals she took out and made magic over them
> and turned them into wood, she made them big and made a sledge of
> them. Then she wanted a dog, and that she made out of a lump of snow
> she had used for wiping her end; it became a white dog with a black
> head; it became white because the snow was white, but it got the black
> head because there was shit on one end of the lump of snow.

Magical transformation is offered here as an figure for the transformations of poetry which throughout the volume circle around
images of defecation, and what can be made of them. But the analogy
carries sinister implications. The shaman uses her body to create a
new sexual identity for herself (she becomes a sham-man), and
throughout *Quoof* Muldoon implies that a similar process of re-
fashioning was at work in the Republican prison protests – but in
this case the process proved deadly.

The hunger-strikers died as their bodies digested themselves,
in a slow and agonising way. Merging dirty protest and hunger

strike, this volume is obsessed with the processes of ingestion, digestion (as well as, inevitably, indigestion) and emission. At one point in 'The More a Man Has the More a Man Wants', Gallogly is described disappearing into himself, as Muldoon implies that it is impossible to separate pain from macabre comedy:

> Disappearing up his own bum.
> Or, running on the spot
> with all the minor aplomb
> of a trick-cyclist.
> So thin, side on, you could spit
> through him.
> His six foot of pump water
> bent double
> in agony or laughter.
> Keeping down-wind of everything.

At this point in the narrative Gallogly has been shot, and he is trying to escape detection in the Armagh countryside. But at the same time he is represented as a clown or jester, performing his death for the public. Like the hunger-strikers, so thin that he practically disappears, he nonetheless enacts for others a grotesque and tragicomic spectacle. (There is too a possible dialogue with Seamus Heaney here. Heaney's *Field Work* (1979) ends with the Ugolino translations, in which people are consuming each other. Human flesh has become food. Muldoon's book takes the notion of devouring hatred further as it contemplates the body consuming itself.)

Food, bodily fluids and the body's waste products circulate throughout this book, each seemingly interchangeable with one another. In the sonnet 'A Trifle' Muldoon is 'working through lunch' in an office block in Belfast – he is engaged in his own small-scale hunger strike. During the subsequent bomb alert he encounters on the stairs an office-worker who treasures the remains of her dessert, holding it 'at arm's length' on a tray. While the sweet 'trifle' may seem tasteless in the context of the deaths of the hunger-strikers, it is saved (and savoured) as a triumph (even though a small one) in the midst of the chaos. Other foods in the book are more unambiguously souring. A woman gulps semen, the poet considers making a meal (quite literally) of his ex-partner's internal organs, or contemplates the 'lemon stain' on his sheets, and Gallogly laps custard from a cow-pat. In 'Trance' Muldoon hints at the circular nature of the relationship between ingestion and emission, as he visualises a shamanistic rite in Siberia:

> Someone mutters a flame from lichen
> and eats the red-and-white Fly Agaric
> while the others hunker in the dark,

taking it in turn
to drink his mind-expanding urine.

Here personal ecstasy, borne of eating an hallucinogenic mushroom, is communicated by drinking the body's products. The Fly
Agaric is poisonous and the shaman risks death, but this self-
sacrificial aspect merely deepens the parallel with the Christian
symbolism of eating the body and blood of Christ – a symbolism
employed to effect by the hunger-strikers.

This image of feeding off one another and consuming the body's
waste products, must in part be read as an indictment of the
Republican movement, for the way in which it fed off and gained
strength from the consumption of the bodies of some of its imprisoned members. But as I have suggested, it is also an image for
the poetry itself. Not only is there wry acknowledgement of the
fact that Muldoon's poetry perhaps feeds too exclusively off his
own past, returning to particular images and obsessions springing
from his childhood – that he is, in other words, 'disappearing up
his own bum'. (In *The Annals of Chile* Muldoon will joke about
this poetic habit, referring to it as his food 'repeating' on him –
inevitably indigestion follows from the endless regurgitation of the
same.) But the image also implies that the poet may be guilty, or
at the very least responsible, for the way his poetry feeds off the
images thrown up by the Troubles.

At issue throughout this book are questions of taste, responsibility and morality, as Muldoon continues his debate with himself about the morality of poetry, its purpose and its effects. 'The
Frog', for example, ironises the attempt, on the part of both poet
and reader, to draw moral and political conclusions. In the poem
frogs become analogous to the new order in Ireland following the
union with Britain in 1801. Yet, the poem asks, what can be made
of this image? And it suggests that in order to make something of
it you have to murder the frog:

> The entire population of Ireland
> springs from a pair left to stand
> overnight in a pond
> in the gardens of Trinity College,
> two bottles of wine left there to chill
> after the Act of Union.
>
> There is, surely, in this story
> a moral. A moral for our times.
> What if I put him to my head
> and squeezed it out of him,
> like the juice of freshly squeezed limes,
> or a lemon sorbet?

Those wishing to draw a moral from the history of Ireland's association with England may find it within the bodies of its inhabitants, but the moral can't be reached except through death. In
part this is a wry accusation of the reader who may be tempted to
kill the poetry by exerting too much pressure on it for a particular
political or social message. But it is also a self-accusation. The
second line hints at the presence of something 'amoral' within 'a
moral'; Muldoon suggests that the poet who uses the body in this
way (not only the body of the frog but other bodies too) lies on
the far side of morality. Indeed the poem goes further than this
for the imagined moral, once extracted, is not simply there to be
contemplated – it is something to be eaten. The dead body provides food for others, but the references to lemon and lime admit
to the sourness of this process. It is not a coincidence either that
certain frogs emit a poisonous liquid, suggesting that if there is a
lesson to be learnt here, it is a dangerous one.

In deliberately raising questions of taste alongside those of
morality, Muldoon may be suggesting that the two have too often
been confused. How far is what is distasteful also amoral, or even
immoral? This is far from an academic issue for Muldoon. He
suggests that the language of good taste may simply be a cover for
mere politeness. But as I've suggested many readers felt that the
boundaries of taste had been overstepped not only in relation to the
descriptions of murdered and mutilated bodies in the book, but
perhaps more insistently in relation to the portrayal of women.

Muldoon seems to revel in the representation of callousness and
disillusionment, particularly in relation to women, and he has, accordingly, been accused of an egotistical misogyny. The stanza break in
these lines from 'The Destroying Angel' seems especially malicious:

> At last, one cockatoo flaps away
> into the snow-dark sky
> and one stays behind to smooch
> in your left ear.
> Another gin and Angostura bitters
> and you are part of her dream
>
> kitchen's ceramic hob,
> the bathtub's
> ever-deepening shades of avocado,
> the various whatnots,
> the row upon row of whodunnits...

In fact the lines are so full of spite that the accusation of misogyny
seems to be deliberately courted. The poet attempts to reserve
decorum for himself (as well as taste, with the implication that
you wouldn't catch him being impressed by an avocado-coloured

bathroom suite), but he knows too that the viciousness of his description will reflect back on him. The lines serve as a satire on his own taste for the exquisite, gestured towards throughout the book in over-refined and discriminating references to colour as taste – lemon, cinnamon, aubergine.

This barbed description of feminine ambition is, however, mild compared to Muldoon's representations of female sexuality. In 'Blewits' he addresses a woman lying 'on the bed / of your own entrails'; in 'Aisling' the traditionally chaste and virginal figure of Ireland as a woman is represented as an anorexic who carries venereal disease. But perhaps the clearest connection between violence and sexuality is drawn in these bitterly ironic lines from 'The More a Man Has' about the fate of a (possible) adultress:

> Someone on their way to early Mass
> will find her hog-tied
> to the chapel-gates –
> O Child of Prague –
> big-eyed, anorexic.
> The lesson for today
> is pinned to her bomber jacket.
> It seems to read *Keep off the Grass.*
> Her lovely head has been chopped
> and changed.
> For Beatrice, whose fathers
> knew Louis Quinze,
> to have come to this, her perruque
> of tar and feathers.

In punishment for sexual transgression against the Republican cause, a woman is tarred and feathered and chained to railings. The religious setting is not coincidental. In essence this is a hard-hitting critique of the link between authoritarian religion and civic intolerance (the 'lesson for today' is transferred from inside to outside the chapel). The poem has a disturbingly 'amoralistic' tone, however, offering neither condemnation nor understanding. Indeed, Muldoon even seems to indulge the violence: as several critics have noted, the line break after 'chopped' is 'no less callously placed for the skill with which it recuperates a cliché'.[2]

The insistent, almost parodic, coupling of sex and violence throughout this book is surely meant to disturb the reader, and could be taken as proof of Muldoon's belief (explored in *Why Brownlee Left*) in poetry as harbinger not of peace but of discord, of the jarring note. But while his descriptions of meaningless sex (and meaningless death) may seem unpalatable, perhaps most shocking is his insistence on the poet's personal engagement with violence. I do not mean that Muldoon dwells on the poet's 'tribal' allegiances,

as, for example, Seamus Heaney does in *North*. In fact the above
lines rewrite the final lines of Heaney's poem 'Punishment' (in
North). Both poems describe the treatment meted out to women
deemed to have betrayed the Republican cause through sex, but
while Heaney confesses his understanding of the 'exact and tribal,
intimate revenge', Muldoon seems, perversely, to be purely interested in effects: the distorted effects of paramilitary justice, which
far outweigh their cause, and his own, poetic, effects.

It would of course be more than stretching a point to suggest
that he takes on the role of perpetrator of violence in *Quoof*. Yet it
is possible, I think, to see in this book a development and consolid-
ation of Muldoon's habitual concern with the relationship between
violence and personal experience. All three of his previous books
trace some kind of connection between violence (or discord) and the
childhood home: parental strife and parental cruelty in poems such
as 'Wind and Tree' and 'Skeffington's Daughter' in *New Weather*;
the discovery of the roots of violence in the Armagh countryside
('something a little nearer home') in *Mules*; the hinted-at link between
writer and revolutionary in *Why Brownlee Left*. *Quoof* makes this
analogy explicit as Muldoon reworks the romantic image of the
poet as both seer and revolutionary. Here however, the seer has
become drug-crazed, and the revolutionary both psychotic murderer
and self-sacrifical prisoner, as well as "creative writer".

One very potent example of the intimate relationship between
violence and writing at this time was the figure of Bobby Sands.
Sands was the leader of the 1981 hunger strikes, and the first of
the ten men to die, and at the same time he was a prolific writer of
propagandistic stories and poetry. (He thus embodies the marriage
of artist and revolutionary in a way similar to the 1916 poet Joseph
Mary Plunkett – alluded to in 'Anseo' – but with contemporary
relevance.) Throughout *Quoof* Muldoon seems to be wrestling
with the symbiotic relationship between art, suffering and violence.
At one point in 'The More a Man Has', Gallogly, the now-imprisoned
revolutionary, escapes from his cell and watches 'a girl at stool'
through the peep-hole of her cell:

> At last. A tiny goat's pill.
> A stub of crayon
> with which she has squiggled
> a shamrock, yes,
> but a shamrock after the school
> of Pollock, Jackson Pollock.

In this witty but rather gruesome vignette, the faeces smeared on
the walls of prison cells during the dirty protest become a national

(and nationalist) symbol. The mention of Jackson Pollock here is interesting. It is only one of several references to modern and modernist art – the poems refer to the Museum of Modern Art in New York, to Picasso, to Gertrude Stein and to other modernists. In part this relates to abstraction, and perhaps more specifically (given the references to Stein and Picasso in particular) to the cubist aesthetic of fragmentation. In paintings such as Picasso's 'Guernica' (referred to in 'The More a Man Has') the violence of war is portrayed through the disruption and fragmentation of the represented body. Stein's experiments with linguistic forms were in part an attempt to apply cubist principles to the written word, and the several references to her in 'The More a Man Has' surely point to the intended cubist effect of that poem, its questioning of representational forms. The question of whether art can be representational, or should be, is clearly very important in this book, and modernist painting is so central here because it is most clearly the art that has evolved pure abstraction in the twentieth century. But there is also a more specific analogy going on in the reference to Jackson Pollock. For Pollock is supposed to have created his method of laying on paint by watching someone (in fact his father) urinate on a rock. What's more, Pollock was also very influenced by Navaho sand-paintings, suggesting another link with the American Indian material in *Quoof* – both sources of Pollock's work were explored by Robert Hughes in *The Shock of the New*, a popular television series on modern and postmodern art which was broadcast on British television in 1980.

In addition to the formal question of abstraction or representation, therefore, at issue here are the sources of art and creativity. Not only are these located in the self (faeces, urine), but in waste products. Human and bodily waste is central to the book: Muldoon contemplates a calf skittering dung, a pony fouling the snow, a cow-pat, and even a clean ass-hole. In 'Gathering Mushrooms' the mushrooms are grown in manure; in 'Trance' insight comes as a result of drinking urine; in 'The Frog' the moral can be extracted from the juice of a frog – and this image highlights an important aspect of the preoccupation with dung. Just as the juice of the frog is poisonous so all animal waste is toxic – it is what the body must rid itself of in order to function.

Muldoon's interest in toxicity in this book is in part a reflection on how to write about contemporary events in Northern Ireland. In the *Poetry Book Society Bulletin* published alongside *Quoof* in 1983, Muldoon commented that one of the impulses behind the book lay in a desire 'to purge myself of the very public vocabulary it employs, the kennings of the hourly news bulletin'. (Remember that since 1974 he had worked for the BBC in Northern Ireland, editing a radio arts programme, and he would therefore have been surrounded by the kind of media language he decries.) One way of understanding this is as championing the vitality of poetic language against the official, public language normally used to describe the violence and the tragic events inside the prisons in Northern Ireland. The implication is that poetry may be able to offer a more "truthful" representation of such horror. Muldoon's often vicious and disturbing lyrics would then be a form of poetic realism, but a realism adequate to the arbitrary and cruel quality of the life he describes.

Yet this interpretation doesn't do justice to the texture of the work itself. To purge is to cleanse, suggesting Muldoon's wish to purify himself of public language, but it is also to vomit up toxic matter (another link between the poet and the hunger-strikers as well as the book's anorexic women). So the purge here is less a purifying ritual, with its connotations of order and ceremony, and more an effort to get out and onto the page the worst aspects inside himself. So far from maintaining a position outside the collective sickness in Northern Ireland, his poems are part of that sickness – they vomit up their poison from within. Rather than an attempt to find a more truthful way of representing violence in Northern Ireland, the volume can perhaps best be understood as Muldoon's own "dirty protest". Bitterness, violence, cruelty, cynicism – all are displayed as the body is turned inside out. And it is surely in this context that the sexually "dirty" poetry in the volume can best be understood. The destructiveness and the misogyny in these poems isn't so much relished as revealed and made public.

Quoof, then, can be seen as Muldoon's protest against imprisonment, making its point by exposing the inner violence fostered by a certain history, with all its constraints and confinements. Thus, as always in Muldoon, the feeling of entrapment is entwined with an awareness of the past, as well as of the body. Muldoon returns again to his origins, interweaving memories of his parental home with contemporary urban scenes of fantasy and violence. The possibility that this volume is Muldoon's own "dirty protest" is introduced in the first poem, 'Gathering Mushrooms', a poem which in a sense encapsulates Muldoon's uncertainties about the confining or liberating aspects of home. This surreal poem offers a wild, almost parodic, fusion of national and familial (or personal) registers, at the same time introducing a number of elements central to the volume as a whole – the relationship between childhood experience and adult perception, the surreal fusion of drug-induced and revolutionary-inspired visions, and the events and rhetoric of the prison protests. Mushrooms are a perfect image for this kaleidoscopic vision: they are both a food and a drug, the body's metabolism is both nurtured and destroyed by the chemicals it takes into itself. (In general the volume is stuffed full of chemicals. Everything from aspirin to cocaine to semtex conspires to change the body, destroying the borders between inside and outside through explosives or mind-expansion – a form of fragmentation which again relates to the book's "cubist" method.)

'Gathering Mushrooms' begins with Muldoon's recollections of his childhood home: his mother's washing, rain-drenched on the line; a delivery of manure, which his father would use to propagate mushrooms:

> The rain comes flapping through the yard
> like a tablecloth that she hand-embroidered.
> My mother has left it on the line.
> It is sodden with rain.
> The mushroom shed is windowless, wide,
> its high-stacked wooden trays
> hosed down with formaldehyde.
> And my father has opened the Gates of Troy
> to that first load of horse manure.
> Barley straw. Gypsum. Dried blood. Ammonia.
> Wagon after wagon
> blusters in, a self-renewing gold-black dragon
> we push to the back of the mind.
> We have taken our pitchforks to the wind.

This poem, like many of the shorter lyrics in *Quoof*, proceeds by cutting back and forth between past and present, between a childhood presided over by an unchanging paternal figure, and a metropolitan "maturity". 'Fifteen years on' from the manure-shovelling incident Muldoon finds himself with a companion in Belfast, ingesting "magic mushrooms" or psilocybin; the hallucinations born of ingesting the mushrooms precipitate a drugged nightmare in which the constituents of his childhood memory become realigned as elements in a Republican song of struggle and sacrifice. If circular journeys formed the basis of Muldoon's meditation on revolution in *Why Brownlee Left*, here they have been replaced by trips:

> We followed the overgrown tow-path by the Lagan.
> The sunset would deepen through cinnamon
> to aubergine,
> the wood-pigeon's concerto for oboe and strings,
> allegro, blowing your mind.
> And you were suddenly out of my ken, hurtling
> towards the ever-receding ground,
> into the maw

of a shimmering green-gold dragon.
You discovered yourself in some outbuilding
with your long-lost companion, me,
though my head had grown into the head of a horse
that shook its dirty-fair mane
and spoke this verse:

Come back to us. However cold and raw, your feet
were always meant
to negotiate terms with bare cement.
Beyond this concrete wall is a wall of concrete
and barbed wire. Your only hope
is to come back. If sing you must, let your song
tell of treading your own dung,
let straw and dung give a spring to your step.
If we never live to see the day we leap
into our true domain,
lie down with us now and wrap
yourself in the soiled grey blanket of Irish rain
that will, one day, bleach itself white.
Lie down with us and wait.

Like the mushrooms themselves, this is not an easy poem to absorb. Several of the references here are obscure, to say the least. As Muldoon points out (on the Faber Poetry Cassette published alongside *Quoof*), 'allegro' refers not only to musical pace but to the writer John Allegro, whose 1970s cult book, *The Sacred Mushroom and the Cross*, claimed that the roots of Christianity lay in an hallucinogenic mushroom cult. The idea that ingesting certain mushrooms brings divine knowledge brings us back to the shaman, whose access to divine wisdom may be mediated by – among other things – the hallucinatory trance. Here shamanistic knowledge comes 'straight from the horse's mouth', and turns out to be a rhetorical plea for conformity with the Republican ideals of suffering and sacrifice. "Divine wisdom" here is fanatical, deluded, masochistic. The context of the prison dirty protests is clear in the references to concrete and barbed wire, to negotiating terms, to blankets and dung. And, as in 'Trance', the link with Christian rhetoric is not hard to see either, as the talking horse calls for sacrifice on earth in return for future liberation. Muldoon targets the same fusion of religion and politics that he had satirised in *Why Brownlee Left*; it is the coercive idea that the endurance of suffering may bring future benefit which he abhors.

However, it is also important to note Muldoon's use of home and a personal past here. The 'gold-black dragon' of farm manure takes on the colours of the Irish Republic as it transmutes into the 'green-gold dragon' of political nightmare; the wagonload of horse

dung turns into the human faeces on the walls of the H Blocks; his
mother's tablecloth becomes a grey blanket, symbol of the prisoners'
resistance to government demands. 'Gathering Mushrooms' transforms the Muldoon figure into an equine mouthpiece for a Republican credo, and readers might well wonder what is going on here.
He gives us an insight into his concerns when he says in his essay
'Chez Moy' that, like many from his home-place, he too might have
been drawn into Republican activity: 'My family would have had
Nationalist or Republican leanings, of course, but we were firmly
opposed to political violence. I've often considered how easily,
though, I might have been caught up in the kinds of activities in
which a number of my neighbours found themselves involved.'
The passive constructions here are interesting; Muldoon is implying that for many Republican activists there is little choice in the
matter – involvement is more a matter of fate than of design. But
the comparison between poet and revolutionary has other levels
too. In 'Gathering Mushrooms', for example, Muldoon suggests
that the basic constituents of Northern Irish rural life can as easily
(if not more easily) be turned to Republican as artistic vision.

All this suggests a new gloss on the idea of fate which was central to *Why Brownlee Left*; rather than future destiny the emphasis
here is on entrapment, and the way we are bounded by conditions.
Entrapment occurs not only in the prisons, but in life in Northern
Ireland as a whole. Many of the poems in the book explore the
difficulty of escaping from cultural forms which have determined
personal life for Catholics in Northern Ireland (as well as Protestants). A crucial question for Muldoon is whether the poet is trapped
in the same way, or is he able, by breaking down and breaking
through forms, to find another way of thinking? (The play with and
against the contraints of the sonnet form is central to this theme.)
Entrapment is often figured in terms of a battle between individual and the state, frequently framed in terms of state violence. The
man in 'The Hands' (based on a poem by Erich Arendt) has his
hands severed by the Guardia Civil (the notorious police force
which backed Franco):

> He lay dead in the field. But his far-fetched hands
> would stir at night, and the villagers heard
> the fists come blattering on their windows, looking for home.

In 'The Sightseers' it is a Northern, Protestant (and volunteer)
police-force which abuses its power. The Muldoon family set out
for a Sunday afternoon ride to see the 'brand-new roundabout at
Ballygawley, / the first in mid-Ulster':

Uncle Pat was telling us how the B-Specials
had stopped him one night somewhere near Ballygawley
and smashed his bicycle

and made him sing the Sash and curse the Pope of Rome.
They held a pistol so hard against his forehead
there was still the mark of an O when he got home.

The roundabout is an almost perfect emblem for the family's
entrapment within the situation. They aren't visiting the roundabout in order to get somewhere – instead the roundabout is an
end in itself. When we speak of things coming 'roundabout', we
often mean that priorities are turned round and hierarchies over-
turned, but to go roundabout is also to go in a circle, to repeat. In
this poem Uncle Pat seems to have moved on, graduating from
bicycle to beaten up Ford, but he (and his relatives) are still dominated by the circle. His circular route is mapped out for him,
with the implication that there is no way out. Yet this is a problem for the poet, for if entrapment is so powerful, from where
does the power to break out, to rework or subvert old forms,
come? Importantly, despite the force of the mark, the O has now
faded. The poem suggests that the family may be too passively
trapped by other kinds of circularity, but that it might be possible
to escape from the situation if you don't just 'lie down and wait'.

'The Hands' and 'The Sightseers' appear on facing pages in
Quoof, a fact which makes it easier to notice that both poems end
with the word 'home'. Other poems in the volume, such as 'Trance'
and 'Cherish the Ladies' repeat the return to and departure from
home, in a development of the cyclical structure used in 'Promises,
Promises' and 'Anseo' in *Why Brownlee Left*. Both 'Trance' and
'Cherish the Ladies' begin and end with glimpses of Muldoon's
parents – his mother emptying the dregs of tea onto Christmas
snow, his father watering the cattle – but the central section of
each poem offers a wayward departure from these everyday scenes,
as Muldoon (and his reader) are transported by visionary fantasy.
This process of encasing poetic vision within the confines of home
and childhood is, of course, double-edged. It suggests that while
poetic creativity (and hallucinogenic visions) may use the materials
of home, they are also contained by it (in another version of the
traffic circle). This benign form of imprisonment (or house arrest)
is the subject of the delicately balanced sonnet 'The Right Arm':

I was three-ish
when I plunged my arm into the sweet-jar
for the last bit of clove-rock.

We kept a shop in Eglish
that sold bread, milk, butter, cheese,
bacon and eggs,
Andrews Liver Salts,
and, until now, clove-rock.

I would give my right arm to have known then
how Eglish was itself wedged between
ecclesia and *église*.

The Eglish sky was its own stained-glass vault
and my right arm was sleeved in glass
that has yet to shatter.

This is a poem about the way that adults remain both trapped and protected by their early experiences, about how memory determines outlook. The child of three is located in a very specific environment, inside the family shop which sells a comfortingly limited supply of goods: basic foodstuffs and the necessary indigestion cure, but also one luxury – clove-rock. Predictably this luxury is also limited – it runs out, and the child himself is the last to savour it. (Here is another instance of the volume's self-consumption – he's eating them out of their own shop!) The clove-rock is sweet, which perhaps makes it easier to digest the religious message it conveys. It carries echoes of the hymn, 'Rock of Ages, cleft for me / Let me hide myself in thee', where the rock represents the Church (through Christ's body, riven on the cross). The rock is a source of comfort and protection therefore, but it also has connotations of the devilish 'cloven hoof'. To cleave is to divide, hinting at the way the community is divided by religion, but the three-year-old child in his innocence is unconscious of this. The village place-name evokes the word 'English', but in fact its roots lie in Latin and French (hence the village is also Roman, and continental). Whatever its roots, for the moment the child's experience is of being inside, rather than outside the church. Indeed the last lines suggest that the child lives inside the church, within the vault and therefore in a treasured and treasuring environment, but also a tyrannical one. He is completely surrounded by religion, which both enhances and limits his vision: the stained glass may be beautiful but it prevents you from seeing outside. At the same time his right arm (perhaps also his writing arm, and therefore the source of his power) is further encased in glass, which is both fragile and enduring, both protective and crippling.

Not only is this protection an illusion of course (you can't hide behind glass), but the image also suggests that the poet is trapped by his past. He is dependent on these childhood moments, still replaying reaching for the last bit of clove-rock all these years later. There is a Proustian element to this self-identity, which holds on to the urban and familial, rather than the natural. At the same time the desire to move beyond the search for childhood sweetness is also endlessly replayed, as the poem looks forward to the moment which has 'yet to' come. Like some of the poems in *Why Brownlee Left* which faced in two directions at once, this poem looks backwards while articulating a sense of tremendous promise, the promise of breaking out of protective yet disabling forms, the promise that things are about to shatter.

The shocking and disturbing character of the language of *Quoof* is clearly in part an exploration of the limits of the poetic, and indeed the limits of language in general. For one of the central preoccupations of *Quoof* is the problem of communicating what is most intimate, even repulsive. Muldoon wonders how one can transform the private, personal world (at the extreme, the body) into something with public meaning. Language is normally taken to be the way in which the raw contingency of our existence (of which the body and its processes are perhaps the most extreme examples) is transmuted into something with publicly acknowledged significance. But the paradox is that the closer language gets to the intimate core of the self, the less it is able to communicate at all. Thus language becomes both the means of escape and a form of containment. The title-poem, another sonnet, and perhaps the most enigmatic poem in the book is also built around ideas of containment and escape. It questions whether it is ever possible to communicate the familial and personal. Here not just an arm but the whole person is encased, in a private language.

> How often have I carried our family word
> for the hot water bottle
> to a strange bed,
> as my father would juggle a red-hot half-brick
> in an old sock
> to his childhood settle.
> I have taken it into so many lovely heads
> or laid it between us like a sword.

'Quoof' sets up a comparison between the father's rural childhood and the adult son's modern, cosmopolitan experience, as the child-hood settle is weighed in the balance against a variety of adult and sexual beds. There is an ominous echo here of the lovely head which is 'chopped and changed' in 'The More a Man Has', but 'Quoof' offers a far less brutal vision. Like 'The Right Arm' this is about partly about comfort, as the sexual body is substituted for the hot water bottle (earlier substituted for the hot brick in a sock) as a human rather than inanimate source of warmth. The word acquires a kind of materiality. It is as warming to the son as the brick was to the father – in other words, it suggests rupture as well as links between them (as in Heaney's 'Digging'). Despite the difference between father and son, however, the poet suggests that continuity between them is maintained by language. By using his father's word he is carrying on family tradition, but he also reveals his inability to escape from it. The private word *quoof* is a mark of personal authenticity derived from familial tradition. More particularly the lineage goes from father to son, so that the father's personal history infuses the son's identity – gives him his particularity. In this sense the word is, as Muldoon has said, a shibboleth, a test for inclusion or exclusion from the tribe. Here, however, it is the family which is the exclusive group. The word can be used to enlarge the familial circle, or to set boundaries around it.

The relation between octet and sestet in this poem is almost maddeningly oblique. We are offered a snapshot, a still, of the poet and a girl in one of the strange beds – on this occasion in New York:

> An hotel room in New York City
> with a girl who spoke hardly any English,
> my hand on her breast
> like the smouldering one-off spoor of the yeti
> or some other shy beast
> that has yet to enter the language.

The eroticism of the encounter is signalled in the 'smouldering' hand, and the exoticism of the unknown beast, so that we almost forget that his hand is being compared to the print of an animal. But what are we to do with this scene? Does the fact that he is with a girl 'who spoke hardly any English' symbolise the difficulties of crossing the boundaries of the tribe, since communication cannot take place? What, then, of Muldoon's exaggerated display of his own command of English ('an hotel'), his affected and unnatural use of the phrase 'New York City', despite (or perhaps because of) his Irish heritage. Alternatively, does the fact that the girl wouldn't have understood the phrase 'hot-water bottle' any more than the word 'quoof' suggest a need to revise the sentiments of the first stanza? In this reading the couple are liberated by the impossibility of verbal intercourse into the pleasures of physical communication. It is precisely because the two are so alien (like the yeti), because their association has yet to enter language, that the burdens of the tribe can be sloughed off.

Yet this reading is, of course, as arbitrary as another. The poem doesn't allow for a definitive interpretation, offering instead of a narrative, an oblique relation between scenes. Muldoon alludes to many narratives but refuses to elaborate on any of them. Family, childhood, the past's 'many lovely heads', the New York encounter, all are tenuously held together by rhyme, half-rhyme and internal rhyme: word and sword, or city, yeti, yet to. The reader has to track the poet through this scenery like the unknown yeti. Characteristically in this poem we see not the beast, but the sign of the beast, and the fact that the spoor is smouldering suggests that we have just missed it. This is an emblem for the poem's own evasiveness, for a more elusive poem would be hard to imagine. The final lines of the poem direct us towards the future, towards something which has yet to happen (the sentence has 'yet to' have a main verb). But this suggestion of forward movement is in itself a remarkable achievement for at the same time these are among the most arrested lines in contemporary poetry. There is no verb in the sestet, which reads like a freeze-frame. Like 'Why Brownlee Left' the poem equivocates between movement and stillness – it looks towards the future yet is without issue.

In 'Glanders' Muldoon approaches this moment of suspension and indeterminacy from a different angle. He raises the question of poetic efficacy and purpose, which is an undercurrent throughout the book, by relocating the magician-healer figure in the rural Ireland of his childhood. Like 'Quoof' the poem sets up an intimate relation between language and the body, as it considers the healing of physical hurts:

> When you happened to sprain your wrist or ankle
> you made your way to the local shaman,
> if 'shaman' is the word for Larry Toal...
>
> He would conjure up a poultice of soot and spit
> and flannel-talk, how he had a soft spot
>
> for the mud of Flanders,
> how he came within that of the cure for glanders
> from a Suffolkman who suddenly went west.

Glanders is another name for farcy, the horse disease which preoccupied the father in 'The Mixed Marriage'. Larry Toal, the local shaman, is a home-grown version of a magic healer, skilled in cures for such local difficulties. He is also, clearly, a figure for the poet – like the poet he is given his position by the trust placed in him by the local community. Like Muldoon's earlier poem 'The Cure for Warts', 'Glanders' sets up an image of the poet as witch-doctor, suggesting that while he may not be able to perform miracles, he may make us see things in a different light. In this sense the poem is about the differences (and similarities) between a physical and a linguistic cure – 'flannel-talk' may be mere hot air (like poetry), but (like poetry) it has a certain efficacy nonetheless. Like so many of Muldoon's poems, 'Glanders' reveals a mastery of ambivalence and equivocation. The shaman is trusted for his curative powers despite the fact that he is a sham; the poem plays on the irony that he has built his reputation on failure, on not quite having a cure. If the poem is about how to cure hurt, the answer is that talk both does and does not work. Poetry is both cure and symptom, part of the problem.

This equivocation between an apparently ineffectual faith and genuine healing, between movement and constraint, is central to Muldoon's concerns in this book. He reflects on entrapment within the body, language, the home, the prison, within Northern Irish culture itself – and on how to go beyond it. Both 'The Right Arm' and 'Quoof' counter visions of stillness and entrapment with a sense of promise – the promise of breaking out of entrapment which has 'yet to' happen. To some extent the promise of something yet to come in the book points forward towards the long poem at the end where Muldoon experiments with both the creative and destructive aspects of poetic transformation. In contrast to the poised lyrics of the first part of the volume, the disorientating narrative of 'The More a Man Has' explores ways of evading entrapment or imprisonment through form. Like the shaman's tricks of evasion, poetry may be able to find ways out by breaking down and breaking out of forms. Herein lies the significance of Muldoon's repeated use of the sonnet form in this book – he is experimenting with the number of different ways he can transform and deform the sonnet. Yet as he acknowledges in his analogy between poet and violent, self-destructive revolutionary, the results can be cruel and baleful as much as productive.

The correspondence between poet and revolutionary is perhaps clearest in 'The More a Man Has the More a Man Wants'. A sequence of 49 sonnets (very loosely defined), the poem follows the wild, brutal, often hilarious fortunes of Gallogly, a terrorist/ mercenary, and Mangas Jones:

> an Oglala
> Sioux busily tracing the family tree
> of an Ulsterman who had some hand
> in the massacre at Wounded Knee.

'Loosely based on the Trickster cycle of the Winnebago Indians', according to the jacket note, the poem's plot is almost impossible to unravel. The trickster cycle follows the actions of a supernatural shaman figure who is able to transform himself in size and shape at will. His activities are destructive and creative in equal measure, and wholly without moral purpose. Muldoon's poem mirrors the trickster's sudden transformations, as the scene shifts between Belfast, the orchards of Armagh, the mountains North of Boston (in one of many allusions to Robert Frost), and the inside of a Northern Irish prison. Gallogly (a 'gallowglass', or mercenary, and the trickster figure in the poem) is mixed up in the shady world of terrorism in various ways: he seems to be responsible for various explosions and at least one assassination in Ireland, and he also assumes guilt for the murder of a woman in North America when on a visit to buy arms. During the course of the poem he rapes and murders a woman, is shot by a housewife, in turn shoots the woman's husband (a UDR corporal), blows up a consignment of gelignite, is caught and imprisoned and subjected to a strip-search, escapes, and finally merges with the vengeful American Indian to be blown to pieces at a petrol station. Yet this narrative of destruction occurs within some of the most creative lines in contemporary poetry. The use of the trickster myth allows Muldoon to break all sorts of rules of consistency and narrative purpose. In this sense the shaman's tricks are pragmatic; they constitute a means of escape for Gallogly, and a means of evasion for the poet.

Metamorphosis is central to this poem, as to the volume as a whole. Characters merge with one another, change shape, die violent deaths only to reappear transformed. Not only does Gallogly have shamanistic powers, including the ability to change shape at will, but he also shares with the poet a creative streak, as well as, significantly, a particular love of the Armagh countryside – to which he returns during the course of the poem. Yet it is perhaps his ability to transform himself which most clearly allies him with the poet, and it is this which allows him to evade his pursuers. At one point, having been arrested following an explosion by a 'snatch-squad' of paratroopers, he turns himself into a beaver in order to tunnel himself out of prison:

> Gallogly, Gallogly, O Gallogly
> juggles
> his name like an orange
> between his outsize baseball glove
> paws,
> and ogles
> a moon that's just out of range
> beyond the perimeter wall.

He works a gobbet of Brylcreem
into his quiff
and delves
through sand and gravel,
shrugging it off
his velveteen shoulders and arms.

The image of Gallogly as a beast perhaps signifies the bestial, nihilistic origins of violence. Gallogly is forever hungry, greedy for food and sex, without responsibilities or allegiances, driven by desire. On the other hand the metamorphosing Gallogly is also an image of everyman. At one point the poem interpellates its male readers, only to suggest that Gallogly has assumed their identity – he is wearing 'your' jacket:

All a bit much after the night shift
to meet a milkman
who's double-parked his van
closing your front door after him.
He's sporting your
Donegal tweed suit and your
Sunday shoes and politely raises your
hat as he goes by.

But metamorphosis is equally important to the form of the poem. The seemingly endless possibilities of change and transformation lend tremendous energy to this work, and there is a striking contrast between 'The More a Man Has' and the relatively composed nature of Muldoon's previous sonnet sequence, 'Armageddon, Armageddon'. Here the language is supple and plastic, and the sonnet form itself is entirely transformed. It may be helpful to think of the sonnet form itself as a body which can change shape. It can expand to include an analogy between the wounded Gallogly, Picasso's Cubist attempt to represent the horror of the Spanish Civil War in Guernica, and the life and work of Knut Hamsun (himself a hunger artist). Or, like a hunger-striker, it can become thin – one stanza is comprised simply of fourteen words (two lines from a popular verse). For the most part Muldoon's sonnets are fourteen-line stanzas employing intermittent rhyme and half-rhyme, with a measure which both attends to and enhances the measure of colloquial speech. Muldoon juxtaposes dialect, colloquial diction, brand-names, references to eighteenth-century Irish revolutionaries and modernist artists and writers, quotations from literature and popular song, complex syntax, extended metaphors, scenes of sex, drugs and violence.

Though the magical metamorphoses performed by the poet may be linguistic rather than corporeal, the poet too is a shapeshifter, breaking through desensitisation, prejudice, cynicism. And Muldoon implies that the poet's tools for transforming one thing into another – metaphor and figurative language in general – can be violent as well as creative. In part this can be understood as a continuation of Muldoon's preoccupation with the question of poetry's purpose – his rejection of the idea of poetry's task as one of reconciliation or resolution, the imagining of future, peaceful, possibilities. If poetry brings about change, Muldoon implies, that change is as much dependent on destruction as creation – a principle embodied in the 'destructed' sonnets which form the narrative of 'The More a Man Has'. The correspondence between poet and revolutionary therefore serves in part as a meditation on poetic form, which, Muldoon suggests, can be "explosive" in its methods.

Rather than a straightforwardly Romantic view of the poet's revolutionary role, the poet as rule-breaker and fugitive from the law, Muldoon highlights the violence, anarchy and social breakdown which are the other side of revolution. While revelling in the creative possibilities of poetic transformation, the poem also works in part as a violent satire on lawlessness, not least because when the revolutionary is in jail his violence becomes turned in on himself. Gallogly is able to escape capture through much of the poem by shape-shifting, but he nonetheless self-destructs at the end – and it is this link between the creative tricks of self-transformation and a tragic self-destructiveness which is at issue for Muldoon in the prison protests.

As I have mentioned, Muldoon has said that in writing this poem he wanted to 'purge himself' – to cleanse himself of the corruptions of language and thought. Purging is also, traditionally, one method of curing disease. Is Muldoon suggesting that such poetry might be the beginning of a cure for sickness? To think in this way is to fall into the trap of believing that poetry can 'make things happen', a trap which Muldoon is wary of. He is clearly suspicious of claims for the magic, healing power of poetry, yet at the same time he is drawn to them. The poems in *Quoof* constantly offer contemplative epiphanies, as if poetry does lead to insight, a deeper truth. Yet set against these attempts at transcendence (the small triumphs such as the protected trifle) is the wholesale negation of visionary possibility. This ambivalence about the purpose and power of poetic transformation is familiar from Muldoon's earliest work, but if anything *Quoof* sees him more totally divided on the issue. Like the mixed marriage between earth and stars in *Mules*, and the circular journeys in *Why Brownlee Left*, *Quoof* includes a symbol for this equivocation between the transcendent and the earthbound – the pebble of quartz brought to Northern Ireland by the American Indian, Mangas Jones, in 'The More a Man Has'. This piece of rock appears in many guises throughout the volume, not least as a sweet which the child Muldoon likes to eat in 'The Right Arm'. It assumes tremendous importance in part because it is the only thing to survive at the end of the book. The final lines of 'The More a Man Has' focus on a 'hairy / han' wi' a drowneded man's grip / on a lunimous stone no bigger than a ...'. The luminous stone has, in fact, travelled from a very specific American location. It is the equivocal shining thing which appears in Robert Frost's poem, 'For Once, Then, Something'. In this poem the poet is found looking for insight into the bottom of a well. Usually his gaze his met with his own reflection (rather like Muldoon's worries about poetic self-absorption), but once, he recalls, he saw something else: 'What was that whiteness? / Truth? A pebble of quartz? For once, then, something.' It is impossible to tell whether what was experienced was a moment of transcendence, or an instant of ordinary vision, and the moment now can never be recovered. Muldoon's use of the image allows him to suggest the possibility of visionary transcendence, while at the same time undercutting that possibility by using a very material image (it is the pebble of quartz and not truth which is brought into Ireland).

The pebble of quartz is many-sided, reflective, luminous, yet material rather than transcendent. But set against this 'hard-edged' image of the poetry is the soft, malleable body, able to change shape, evade capture, escape from imprisonment, but also to be destroyed. In the last piece of clove-rock, Muldoon offers us an image of something hard and soft as the same time. The arm sleeved in glass grasping the rock is another version of the dismembered hairy hand left holding the luminous stone at the end of the book. Unlike the hard mineral, clove-rock is sweet, it dissolves, it can be ingested. Muldoon seems to be saying that the only truth we're going to get in the volume is a personal truth – the waste products of his own digestive system, his own body, his own childhood. And we are left with the suspicion that insight is as much compromised as enhanced by this passage through the body. Poetry as purgation is as much symptom as cure.

CHAPTER FIVE

The Wishbone and Meeting the British

If *Quoof* evidenced a turn to narrative as a possible way out of entrapment, metamorphosis as a means of escape, that narrative turn is brought to a halt in Paul Muldoon's next book. In representing the poet as a Trickster figure, transforming himself as a pragmatic means of evasion, Muldoon's interest was in metamorphosis as a way of moving the narrative on, having more alternatives, having a place to go without necessarily having a clear direction. One year later Muldoon published twelve short lyrics in a limited edition pamphlet entitled *The Wishbone*. On the face of it the poems collected in *The Wishbone* could not be more different from the narrative twists and turns of 'The More a Man Has' – here narrative is arrested, and development interrupted. Even the minor narrative cohesion of the sonnet form (eight of the twelve poems are sonnets) is broken up by asterisks signalling breaks and omissions. The pamphlet is dedicated to Muldoon's lover, the artist and printmaker Mary Farl Powers, and several of the poems deal with the failure and ending of their relationship – but their tone is very different from the poems in *Why Brownlee Left* which touched on the end of Muldoon's marriage. Muldoon has said of *The Wishbone* that around this time he was trying to write poems 'that brought to its logical conclusion the idea of leaving, that were treading a very thin line between what you can put in and what you can leave out'.[1] The idea of leaving here implies both departure and omission (leaving out); the poems experiment with how what is put in can signal what is left out, and at the same time how people and objects can be gone and yet maintain a ghostly presence. The poems reflect on failure, on malfunction, on endings but also on how things continue despite their end. For Muldoon's concern with leaving is also with what is left after life has ended. His 'mother's dying words', the legbone of a priest from 'a long-abandoned mission', the carcass of a chicken eaten for Christmas dinner – what can be made of such remains?

The remains of people and animals are littered throughout the book, as are the signs of their recent or ghostly presence – the claw prints of wolves in the forest, an 'invisible waitress', the 'would-be children' of men long dead. The opening poem 'Wolves', a loose translation of a poem by Alfred de Vigny, offers a useful image for Muldoon's poetic practice in this book. The hunters follow tracks in search of their prey in much the same way as the reader must interpret signs and signals in order to follow the writer's meaning. (Muldoon is continuing the experiments with enigmatic signs and lateral interpretation which marked his earliest poems such as 'Thrush'.) The wolves, like the pandas and bears of other poems, also a point to a concern with species and forms of life near extinction. These animals survive now only in captivity and pandas barely manage that, as Muldoon's poem wryly acknowledges. The death of wild animals, the destruction of their habitat, the consumption of animal flesh – all represent stages in the demise of the relationship between Muldoon and Powers, which is described in terms of sexual betrayal, emptiness and lifelessness. One of the ways Muldoon conjures an aura of lifelessness and inertia is through images of frozenness (or perhaps frigidity) – a frozen chicken, a grandmother frozen to death, two streams frozen over, or two huskies which 'lie at the foot / of our bed / in a death-embrace.'

There is a wintry feel even to those poems which don't explicitly refer to snow and ice. In 'The Ox' the couple travel to the Burren, an area of natural beauty on the west coast of Ireland, to see the orchids in bloom. (Once again, the orchids are a species near extinction, a rarity.) But they miss the wild flowers by arriving too early in the year. Spring has not yet arrived and, in the language of *Quoof*, the orchids have 'yet to' bloom. Parking in front of a butcher's shop, the couple decide to find a room:

> They reversed away from the window.
> To the right hung
> one ox-tail,
>
> to the left one ox-tongue.
> 'What's the matter? What's got into you?'
> 'Absolutely nothing at all.'

Instead of the wild orchids they are confronted with the dismembered body of an ox (an animal both wild and domesticated). The missing carcass of the animal perhaps represents the missing ingredient in their relationship (the nothing). A gruesome emptiness impossible to see from up close, it requires distance and perspective. Paradoxically 'nothing' in this poem carries a great deal of meaning. Absence is palpable – it can get into you.

Missing bodies are also at issue in the title-poem of the pamphlet, which describes father and son spending Christmas Day alone. Muldoon's sister and brother are abroad, his mother is dead, and Mary is also gone, though her absence remains unspoken:

Maureen in England, Joseph in Guelph,
my mother in her grave.

                    *

At three o'clock in the afternoon
we watch the Queen's
message to the Commonwealth
with the sound turned off.

                    *

He seems to favour *Camelot*
over *To Have And Have Not.*

                    *

Yet we agree, my father and myself,
that here is more than enough
for two; a frozen chicken,
spuds, sprouts, *Paxo* sage and onion.

                    *

The wishbone like a rowelled spur
on the fibula of Sir —— or Sir ——.

This poem is about spectres. Like the Queen whose Christmas
message to the Commonwealth – always broadcast at three o'clock
– is seen but not heard, the absent family members are both there
and not there. (The Queen is a ghostly presence in more ways
than one, since her status as queen is denied by those in Northern
Ireland who wish for a 32 county Irish Republic). The poem
reflects on the strange state of having and not having, being there
and not there at the same time, and sets up a contrast between
this spectral present and the wish-fulfilment offered by the story
of Camelot and the quest for the Holy Grail.

Certainly this is a bleak celebration. The relationship between
the two men is mediated by the television, with a hint of underlying
disagreements; although there is literally enough for the two of them
to eat, something is missing, some ingredient which might raise the
food from its convenient packaging to the level of festivity. This
sense of something missing is reinforced by the unusual use of
'here' rather than the more conventional 'there' in the line 'here is
more than enough for two'. The 'here' conjures the absent there,
and therefore the ghostly presence of all that is not here.

Although the meal provides enough for two, a problem arises
with regard to the wishbone, in that only one of them can have their
wish. The wishbone is something to be fought over, and therefore
recalls the battles between Arthurian knights for the Holy Grail. The
end of the poem graphically illustrates the concern with missing

elements, for these are nameless knights, long gone, their history
and identity impossible to recover from their bones. Glancing
back to the cannibalism and flesh-eating motifs in *Quoof*, this
glimpse of human bone may seem gruesome and macabre, and
suggest too the pointlessness of striving for the grail, doomed to
be thwarted by death. Yet at the same time there is a suggestion that
the meal's leavings, the bones of the chicken, are able to conjure
almost magically those who have left, the dead and departed.

The poem beautifully illustrates how missing elements maintain
a presence – mentioning Maureen, Joseph and Muldoon's mother
introduces them into the world of the poem just as securely as
they inhabit the inner world of the two men. Paradoxically, not
mentioning Mary Powers – in a pamphlet dedicated to her and
charting the end of their relationship – just as stongly points to
her powerful absence. Formally too the poem suggests the presence
of more than is actually there. The sonnet is set out as though it
were a curtailed longer poem, with the asterisks indicating what
has been left out, breaks in the narrative. On the other hand the
story of this Christmas afternoon makes perfect sense without the
need for additional material, and the rhyming couplets signal an
almost exaggerated completeness. The poem is all there but something is still missing.

The poems in this pamphlet continue *Quoof*'s interest in metamorphosis and in the body. As much as ghosts, 'The Wishbone' is
also about what you can do with old bones, about the power of
imaginative transformation, about how to make a Christmas out of
so little. A companion poem 'The Lass of Aughrim' similarly
reflects on the way something 'long abandoned' may still have
power, on how remains, transformed in the imagination, may
become relics. In a surreal scenario, on a tributary of the Amazon,
the poet comes across an Indian boy playing a flute:

> Imagine my delight
> when we cut the outboard motor
> and I recognise the strains
> of *The Lass of Aughrim.*
>
> 'He hopes,' Jesus explains,
> 'to charm
> fish from the water
>
> on what was the tibia
> of a priest
> from a long-abandoned Mission.'

'The Lass of Aughrim' is a traditional Irish ballad which laments
the end of an affair and the betrayal and death of a young woman

and her child. The ballad is central to James Joyce's short story
'The Dead', where it reminds Gretta Conroy of the delicate young
man who once loved her in the West of Ireland ('I think he died
for me'). Just as the song conjures the dead man for her, so it
causes her husband momentarily to understand his own insignificance
both in relation to his wife's past, and to the dead all over Ireland.
(Winter enters this poem too, through the Christmas setting of
Joyce's story: 'Snow was general all over Ireland.') In Muldoon's
poem the narrative of sexual betrayal, and the abiding presence of
past love, is a subtext, with the weight of 'the dead' placed on the
dead Irish Missionaries, whose legacy lives on in Irish music, in
the naming of the guide Jesus, in the faith invested in the magical
power of the missionary's bone.

A lighter version of this preoccupation with ghostly bodies
occurs in 'Emily'. In this poem the poet awakes at night to find
that his arm, on which his lover sleeps, has gone numb, it is 'a
knotted, phantom limb':

> I called you by another's name:
> Emily.
>
> You looked at me no less knowingly
> than Matt the Hoople
> through a tree
>
> long before he ever swung his axe:
> 'This one's bird's-eye maple,
> good for fiddle-backs.'

The phantom limb, like the other lover, is both there and not
there, a third party which interrupts the relationship between the
lovers. But the couple are also haunted by the future, the 'would-
be children' of 'Pandas' , the orchids which have yet to bloom. In
Meeting the British this preoccupation with an untapped future is
described as 'the couple we never quite became'. Like many of
the characters in *Why Brownlee Left* they are caught between past
and future, haunted by both.

In 'Emily' the felled tree is transformed into a musical instrument, like the priest's bone which becomes a flute in 'The Lass of
Aughrim'. Such images signal a preoccupation with the process of
making music (poetry) out of the remains of the past, out of whatever is no longer alive. These remains are the signs not merely of
individual deaths, however, but of the extinction of races, species,
settlements. Throughout the pamphlet Muldoon hints at the dangers
inherent in taming the wild (the wolves hunted near-extinction, the
tamed pandas unable to reproduce) each implies that domestication

destroys – a possible comment on the Muldoon's relationship with Mary Powers. The destruction of the wild continues Muldoon's preoccupation (since 'The Year of the Sloes, for Ishi') with the colonisation of America and the fate of the American Indians, but here annihilation comes as a result of disease rather than outright warfare. Muldoon alludes to the decimation of Indian tribes through smallpox, but also to the failure of colonies such as the 'long-abandoned mission' in 'The Lass of Aughrim', or the 'prominent men' wiped out by cholera in 'Pandas'. Such images recall Muldoon's previous interest in the failure of colonisation, such as the use of Raleigh's failed settlement at Roanoke as a metaphor for personal loss and failure in 'Promises, Promises'. Indeed in its haunting image of 'the blue in an Indian girl's dead eye' – something which is there but can't be reached – this poem also set up an ambivalent relation between presence and absence similar to the ghostly bodies of *The Wishbone*. Again and again Muldoon represents the sexual relationship between two people as a relation between cultures. And as in the poem 'Quoof' or the long narrative poem in Muldoon's later book, *Madoc – A Mystery*, which takes up the theme of Raleigh's failed settlement once more, there are dangers of colonisation and extinction for both parties.

The final poem in *The Wishbone*, which was to become the title-poem of Muldoon's next collection *Meeting the British*, draws together these concerns with betrayal, disease and extinction in a narrative which refers enigmatically to an episode that occurred during the North American French-Indian Wars of the 1760s. The chief of the Ottawa Indians, Pontiac, led a rebellion against the British towards the end of the war, which was defeated after the British reputedly succeeded in infecting the Indians with smallpox. Muldoon sets his poem at the moment of truce between the American Indians and the British, as the two sides talk. 'Meeting the British' is an arresting but difficult poem, especially in the context of a group of poems which seem to be dealing with the ending of Muldoon's relationship with Mary Powers. As many critics have noted, the title encourages us to think in terms of the political relationship between Britain and Ireland, but the poem offers the reader no firm political ground to stand on. The question of 'sides' is a complicated one, not least because the speaker in the poem, the poet figure, bridges the gap between the warring parties by 'calling out in French' to his enemies. Through his role as spokesperson he becomes party to the betrayal of his people.

> Neither General Jeffrey Amherst
>
> nor Colonel Henry Bouquet
> could stomach our willow-tobacco.
>
> As for the unusual
> scent when the Colonel shook out his hand-
>
> kerchief: *C'est la lavande,*
> *une fleur mauve comme le ciel.*
>
> They gave us six fishhooks
> and two blankets embroidered with smallpox.

The characters in this poem, since they speak in French, are quite literally parleying. But the language is used as a disguise for real intentions (it is, as the last line suggests, embroidery). Again, this is a poem is about something unseen (not there), something virtual which turns out to be deadly. It's about communication which is really communicating something else – treaty and trade which turns out to be murder and betrayal. There is another sense in which this poem is about unseen bodies however, for it is haunted by the spectral bodies of other writers. The first lines of Muldoon's poem ('We met the British in the dead of winter') echo the beginning of W.H. Auden's elegy for W.B. Yeats:

> He disappeared in the dead of winter.
> The brooks were frozen, the airports almost deserted,
> And snow disfigured the public statues...

The ghosts of the previous writers (both Auden and Yeats) are both there and not there. Indeed Muldoon's slyly allusive poem seems to embody Auden's proposition in 'In Memory of W.B. Yeats' that 'the words of a dead man are modified in the guts of the living'. Thus this poem continues the theme of making poetry out of old bones – out of the remains of the past. But it is also in 'In Memory of W.B. Yeats' that Auden famously argues (contra-Yeats) that poetry makes nothing happen. Muldoon had debated this question in both *Why Brownlee Left* and *Quoof*, in the figures of Joseph Mary Plunkett Ward who was 'making things happen' in 'Anseo', and the metamorphosing Gallogly in 'The More a Man Has'. Here the question of the relationship between poetic language and politics seems dangerous, to say the least, as communication leads to betrayal and death. The poem plays on the connections between communication, trade and circulation. The circulation of words from one writer to another, though productive of new meaning, is at the same time analogous to the handing on of disease through the 'gift' of blankets. This is, I think, a development of Muldoon's continuing interest in the conflict between the desire for isolation and self-containment, and the consciousness that it is only by opening onself up to external influences that new meanings can occur. In early poems such as 'Wind and Tree' and 'Thrush', the dangers were of personal hurt or harm; here the consequences of trust and openness are devastating. This idea of 'passing on', in the sense of handing things on, bequeathing objects and bits of language, but also passing on in the sense of dying, and of moving on, forms the core of Muldoon's next volume *Meeting the British*.

The period after the publication of *The Wishbone* was a time of great personal change for Muldoon. In 1985 his father died. Soon afterwards, in January 1986, Muldoon left his job at the BBC and lived for a period in Dingle, County Kerry, with his new partner Jean Hanff Korelitz. The following year he taught creative writing at Caius College, Cambridge and the University of East Anglia, before his move to New York and marriage to Jean Korelitz in the summer of 1987. *Meeting the British* was published in the autumn of 1987 (and much of it was therefore written before his migration to the States). It is a volume which furthers the concerns with endings and disappearance, and the meditation on remains which informed *The Wishbone*. This is of course partly because five poems from the pamphlet are carried over into the new volume ('The Mist-Net', 'The Marriage of Strongbow and Aoife', 'The Wishbone', 'The Lass of Aughrim' and 'Meeting the British' itself). But Muldoon's continuing interest in remains also reflects the impact of the death of his father, and Muldoon's subsequent decision to leave Northern Ireland, as he returns to the theme of departure which had haunted him in *Why Brownlee Left*.

Meeting the British is dedicated to his father's memory, and he is movingly elegised in several poems which continue *The Wishbone*'s preoccupation with animal life and death. In 'The Coney', 'The Fox' and 'Brock', Muldoon turns from pandas, bears and wolves to these less exotic wild animals, native to the Irish countryside. In 'The Fox', the poet, staying in the family home, is woken by the cries of geese from a nearby farm. Startled by the alarm, he looks out of the house, towards the graveyard where his father has been recently buried:

> You lay
> three fields away
>
> in Collegelands
> graveyard, in ground
> so wet you weren't so much
> buried there as drowned.

That was a month ago.
I see your face
above its bib
pumped full of formaldehyde.

In a surprisingly material image, Muldoon imagines he can see into the grave, to the preserved body of his father within. The word 'bib' implies that the father's body has been laid out in his best clothes (best bib and tucker), but of course it also suggests a baby's bib and therefore carries with it connotations of innocence (and perhaps even of old age as a return to infancy). The father reassures his son that the noise of the geese is nothing to be alarmed about:

You're saying, *Go back to bed.*
It's only yon dog-fox.

At ease with the threat of the wild, and the inevitable death of the geese, Muldoon's father imparts knowledge and understanding to his son. (Though the father can write only 'painfully' he has other kinds of expertise his son lacks.) An opposition is set up between the wild and the domestic, and perhaps also between rural and urban existence, with the implication that the poet is unused to the countryside and therefore afraid of it. The father's untroubled acceptance of violent death (and the naturalness of being *eaten*) perhaps acts as a consolation for his own death. But the poem also suggests that *unlike* the geese the father's body will be preserved – he is exempted from physical destruction. Formaldehyde is a preservative, but also a spirit (a type of alcohol). Despite the material image, therefore, the father becomes a protective spirit, a type of guardian angel.

Like 'The Wishbone', 'The Fox' is about what remains after death, but the movement of 'The Fox' is almost exactly opposite to the earlier poem – there the ghostly presence of the absent family members appeared in the empty spaces around father and son. In 'The Fox', with extraordinary delicacy, Muldoon evokes an overwhelming sense of loss by imagining his father's continuing, unchanging presence. In part Muldoon seems to be reconsidering his own identity in relation to his family now that both parents are dead. Once he is no longer tied to the family home, where does he belong? This question of belonging is highlighted in other poems in the book. In a clear echo of the drowned body in 'The Fox', in 'The Toe-Tag' Muldoon alludes to the practice, in the seafaring islands on the west of Ireland, of knitting clothing in a particular family pattern, so that the bodies of the fishermen could be identified after an accident: 'The intricate, salt-stiff / family motif / in a month-drowned Aranman's geansai'. Importantly the pattern

denotes not personal but familial identity; it states not only to whom
the body belongs, but who can claim it.

If 'The Fox' hints at Muldoon's difference from his father, and
worries about belonging, such concerns are more clearly present in
'The Coney'. The poem presents a surreal and disturbing vision,
as the poet meditates on taking his father's place. Since he has
been too ill to work his farm over the winter, Muldoon must take
on the necessary task of mowing the ground before planting. Like
'The Fox', the poem begins with Muldoon disclaiming knowledge
of his father's skills:

> Although I have never learnt to mow
> I suddenly found myself half-way through
> last year's pea-sticks
> and cauliflower-stalks
> in our half-acre of garden.

In a bizarre transformation in the second stanza, the whetstone
which Muldoon uses to sharpen the scythe (it 'would dull / so much
more quickly in my hands than his') disappears and in its place is
a 'lop-eared coney' who confronts the poet from 'one particular
plank / beside the septic tank'. In the context of Muldoon's lack
of expertise with the scythe the coney becomes a kind of embodiment of the difference between father and son. Yet the weird Bugs
Bunny character also points up their similarity:

> 'I was wondering, chief,
> if you happen to know the name
> of the cauliflowers in your cold-frame
> that you still hope to dibble
> in this unenviable
> bit of ground?'
> 'They would be *All the Year Round*.'
> 'I guessed as much'; with that he swaggered
> along the diving-board
>
> and jumped. The moment he hit the water
> he lost his tattered
> bathing-togs
> to the swimming-pool's pack of dogs.
> 'Come in'; this flayed
> coney would parade
> and pirouette like honey on a spoon:
> 'Come on in, Paddy Muldoon.'
> And although I have never learned to swim
> I would willingly have followed him.

The coney either mistakes Muldoon for his father (implying that
they are more alike than he thought), or perhaps he understands

correctly that Muldoon is now the chief 'all the year round', since
his father's illness has left him unable to take charge of the farm.
In an almost unbearable final stanza the father's illness and death
is visualised in the flaying of the coney, his being eaten alive by
'the swimming-pool's pack of dogs'. There is a surreal Disney element is at work here, as the bunny miraculously survives while
being torn apart. The cartoon comedy mood is accentuated by the
use of exaggerated rhyming couplets – the rhythm of the lines
falls on the rhyme word, creating an effect very different from the
imperfect, half-rhyme more characteristic of Muldoon's poetry.
The poetic measure is rounded off and completed, but this child-
like formal patterning is at odds with the poem's intense emotional
charge. Feeling, so far from being reined in by the poem's rhythmic
pattern, seems always in danger of overwhelming the lines. The
profound sadness of the poem derives in part from this contrast
between its jaunty tone and its distressing vision.

The last lines echo the first in their denial of knowledge and skill
('Although I have never learnt to swim'), but this time Muldoon
doesn't take up the challenge. To enter the water unable to swim
means death – a death which is transposed onto the father figure
in the poem. At the same time the lines imply that he can't follow
the coney because he is not his father – he is not Paddy Muldoon,
and therefore the call to death is for another person. But there is
also the strong suggestion that he *would* have followed had he been
Paddy. In other words the call is attractive. There is surely an
echo here of the equivocal invitation to enter another world in
Robert Frost's celebrated poem 'Come In'. In this poem the poet
hears 'thrush-music' within the dark woods:

> Almost like a call to come in
> To the dark and lament.
>
> But no, I was out for stars:
> I would not come in.
> I meant not even if asked,
> And I hadn't been.

In 'The Coney' too there is an 'almost' call, which is almost res-
ponded to, but not quite.

Beyond its evocation of his father's death, 'The Coney' surely
alludes to Muldoon's decision not to listen to the call of home – to
sell the farm and move to England and later America. Given Muldoon's decision to leave Ireland, the series of poems about the death
of Patrick Muldoon may be an attempt to reassure himself that despite
his own and his father's absence from the farm, there is still some-

thing there – they create a ghostly presence akin to the preserved
body in 'The Fox'. The poems meditate on what happens to things
and people when they disappear, and at the same time reflect on
various methods of preservation. One way to keep things going, to
halt decay, is to pickle them, as in 'The Fox'. But another method
of preserving things – and one perhaps more attuned to Muldoon's
poetic method – is to turn them into something else. Another way
to stop the body rotting is to strip it of flesh. There are, indeed, a
remarkable number of animal skins in this volume – 'kid gloves',
upholstery made of 'the hides of still-born calves', even the flayed
coney reappears in another poem as the 'three-quarter length
coney-fur' worn by an ex-colleague of Muldoon's at the BBC, who
is elegised in 'The Soap-Pig'. Like the bones in *The Wishbone*,
preserved animal skins are a sign of death, but also a macabre
form of continuity.

This process of preservation is analogous to the "eternalising" role
of poetry. It was a feature of the traditional sonnet in particular,
but also of elegy, that the beloved attain an unchanging presence in
literature, in contrast to life's processes of corruption and decay.
The poem acts as a protection against both age and death. Yet as
with animal skins (or the fiddle made from a tree, the flute from a
bone), artistic preservation involves initial destruction. So the
reflection on bones and dead flesh is not only about how poetry
can be made out of dead things, but how poetry kills in order to
use things for its own purposes.

The link between death and artistic representation is a familiar
preoccupation in Romantic and post-Romantic lyric verse, and has
been a particular concern for Muldoon since his earliest work. In
'The Waking Father' he reflected on the monumentalising and
aestheticising role of poetry as he suggested that artistic beauty
requires the stillness of death. Running through his early poetry
was an implicit logic whereby poetry protects from or 'cures' emotion by transforming it, or burying it within the aesthetic work (as
in 'Dancers at the Moy' or 'Wind and Tree'). What is interesting
in this later work is Muldoon's search for an alternative to poetic
burial. In *Meeting the British* the poet is surrounded by part-objects
from other lives, both human and animal. In addition to skins and
bones, the volume features all sorts of animal flesh, from the conger
eel in a fishmonger's window, to exotic and luxurious dishes such
as lobster, sushi, spider-crab, and 'medallions of young peccary'. If
flesh is there to be eaten, however, it is also there to be destroyed.
The volume is preoccupied with violent death, and in particular
with corpses. One poem images Kennedy at his assassination as

'the dead weight / of a grouse / flaunted from an open car', another considers the black plastic body bags used to transport corpses away from the scene of a crime, a terrorist attack, an accident. Like pickled flesh and animal skins, black plastic is associated with death and decay, but also with preservation and protection. In 'Christo's' the black bags hung out as flags during the hunger strikes become one with the yards of black polythene protecting 'mounds of sugar-beet, / hay-stacks, silage-pits, building sites, / a thatched cottage even – '. Like the emotions surrounding the hunger-strikes, the farmland can be held down but not buried; plastic can keep things 'under wraps' but it can't put them away entirely. The dead and the passions they provoke are still there, undecayed, threatening to break out again.

But if dead and discarded bodies can disrupt the surface of things, they can also be disturbed, as in this passage from '7 Middagh Street' in which 'Wystan' Auden recalls an encounter during the Sino-Japanese war:

> They arranged a few sedimentary boulders
> over the body of a Japanese
>
> spy they'd shot
> but weren't inclined to bury,
> so that one of his feet stuck out.
> When a brindled pariah
>
> began to gnaw
> on it, I recognised the markings of the pup
> whose abscessed paw
> my father had lanced on our limestone doorstep.

Throughout the volume the violence of death is imaged in terms of dogs and their indiscriminate appetites – there is the dog-fox, the pack of dogs which attack the coney, the dog-eat-dog of life in the metropolis, and in 'Christo's' there are dogs which 'spritz the hotel refuse sacks' (black bags again) – they defile unburied waste. As Wystan suggests, to be dead is to be food for dogs. (This is perhaps one reason for the father's calm in 'The Fox', for he is protected from the dog-fox in the grave.)

The danger of not being properly buried is that the body will become food for scavengers. At one level all this may articulate a concern about the poet's indiscriminate use of remains – refuse, decaying flesh, what will the poet not recycle? We might compare here the preoccupation with food and waste in *Quoof*, where Muldoon suggested that poems were created from human waste. But in *Meeting the British* he also seems to be trying to write about the consoling aspects of that which remains after death. For while

there may be something disturbing about the way that dead bodies
don't just disappear and can be re-used or re-made for other purposes, there is also something comforting – that which is lost is
not also gone.

One poem which meditates on how a burial isn't a burial is
'Chinook'. The poem reworks the scenario of 'The Waking Father',
but this time the son is out fishing alone. Rather than catching fish
to eat them, the poet's aim is to 'micro-tag' them, to 'give each
brash, / cherubic / face its number'. This will not only serve to
track them, it will also provide information about when their time
(their number) is up. In a sense micro-tagging the fish enables the
poet to let them go while still holding on to them. But confusion
and lack of certainty enter the poem as Muldoon finds he can't
hold on to the meaning of his activity, or even to the meaning of
his own words: '*Melt*-water? These were sultry / autumn / fish hang-
gliding downstream. // Chinook. Their very name / a semantic /
quibble.' (In addition to a type of salmon, the word denotes a North
American Indian tribe, a seasonal wind and a military helicopter.)
The poem sets up a contrast between this semantic slipperiness and
the way that events and emotions are given definition by departure:

> The autumn, then, of *Solidarity*,
> your last in Cracow.
> Your father
>
> rising between borsch
> and carp,
> relinquishing the table to Pompeii.

These last two stanzas offer, instead of elusiveness, the consolations of solidity (and Solidarity). Unlike the equivocal semantics
of the first part of the poem, we know what these words mean.
Solidarity, Cracow, borsch and carp have definitive connotations: a
political movement, a Polish city, a Russian soup, a fish (although
'carp' shares with 'chinook' a certain semantic duplicitousness,
since it also means complaint or argument). The time and place of
these events concerning 'your father', in Poland in the 1980s, are
unmistakable. As important as these definitive meanings, however,
is the reason why the verbal slippage is brought to a stop – for the
end to movement comes from moving (departure from Poland). The
final lines offer an image of a world frozen in time – although stasis
is imaged paradoxically as a result of the intense heat of volcanic
dust, which 'freezes' the moment. The time and place of departure are etched in the memory; all that is lost remains unchanged
in recollection. So that loss (in this case the loss of life in Poland)
is, paradoxically, retained. Of course the language of departure

and loss has other valences. Ostensibly this poem is about someone else's father, but it is impossible, I think, to ignore the connotations of the image of a departing father for Muldoon personally.
With subtlety and delicacy Muldoon alludes to his dead and departed
father by writing of another departure and another loss.

Like the burial in 'The Fox' the image of the table at Pompeii
is an image of a burial that preserves, that avoids corruption and
decay. But perhaps just as important is the way the lines try to
capture process, movement. Muldoon has said that one of his preoccupations in this book was with 'the inability to capture a moment
except in the archaeological sense – well that's even a metaphor for
the capturing of a moment, you know, seeing the dog curled with
its litter under the table at Pompeii'.[2] The difficulty is that the
poet, like the rest of us, can only capture the past, not the present.
Poetry shares something with the medium of photography, only
ever able to create an image of the past. Through 'micro-tagging'
the poet tries to hold on to life as it moves, and the poem sets this
up as a contrast with the stilled picture of the table in Cracow or
Pompeii. A clear image can only be created through stillness,
departure or death. Yet at the same time the use of present parti-
ciples in the final lines offer the father a kind of eternal present. He
is forever rising, forever relinquishing, forever in the process of
leaving. Like the endless subtle shifting of the feet in the final lines
of 'Why Brownlee Left', this is an image of perpetual movement.

One of the central concerns of this book is with how to articulate
change, how to capture process rather than burial, dying rather than
death. Throughout the volume ghostly bodies and the preserved
remains of the dead jostle for space with things in the process of
departing, disappearing and changing. Muldoon's preoccupation
with metamorphosis in *Quoof* becomes in this book a process of
endless movement, variation and modification as meanings slip and
words mutate (developing his already skilful use of half-rhyme),
and Muldoon reflects on how to keep this movement going. In a
sense he is experimenting with how to overcome the boundaries
of the poem itself, as in the quasi-sonnet 'Something Else':

> When your lobster was lifted out of the tank
> to be weighed
> I thought of woad,
> of madders, of fugitive, indigo inks,
>
> of how Nerval
> was given to promenade
> a lobster on a gossamer thread,
> how, when a decent interval

had passed
(*son front rouge encor du baiser de la reine*)
and his hopes of Adrienne

proved false,
he hanged himself from a lamp-post
with a length of chain, which made me think

of something else, then something else again.

This is a poem about how to represent movement and change, but not just any change – at issue is the change that occurs at the moment of death. Just as the lobster's colour will change when it is put in boiling water, so 'madders' and 'fugitive' inks – colours which fade – are reminders of disappearance, departure, things which do not last. Here, as in 'Chinook', Muldoon is trying to represent the activity of departure, or the process of losing rather than the loss itself. For that which is lost is already in the past, and can therefore only be captured in an archaeological sense, dug up from memory.

Formally the poem experiments with ways of articulating movement, the slippage from one state to another. Here, if there is such a thing, is a fifteen-line sonnet, made up of a single sentence, which follows the seemingly random thoughts of the poet. The movement of the poem is precipitated by association, as the poet's thoughts move from his companion's lobster (about to be cooked) to Nerval's lobster (kept alive) to Nerval's love and death. These associations are held together as though by a gossamer thread, which links them, but also allows them to slip into one another. As much as analogy and thought association the poem moves because of its rhyme – for example 'woad' comes to mind in part because of thoughts of colour, but also because it is a half-rhyme with weighed. Muldoon is expert at using half-rhyme as a way of opening up connections, and keeping thoughts going – an alternative to the perfect closure of proper rhyme. However the most striking aspect of the poem is its ending. The poem seems to find it difficult to end, as the rhymes push the lines on beyond their alloted time. As Muldoon has said, 'I remember thinking it was quite good from a technical point of view, the way it fiddled around with the sound.'[3] In order to complete the traditional sonnet rhyme scheme *abba cddc eff geg*, the rhyme which is being looked for at the end of line 14 is 'else'. Instead 'think' refers back to 'tank' and 'ink', allowing the poem to have another go at ending. Even then things remain precarious, since the fifteenth line shoots beyond 'else' in order to offer 'something else again' (forming an internal rhyme with 'chain' as well as picking up on reine and Adrienne, and suggesting another ghostly half-rhyme scheme for the sestet: *eff eef*). At one level the poem is about ways of keeping your mind off thoughts of death. But as I have suggested it is also about how things continue despite their end. In this poem, what we think will be an ending, turns out not to be. As well as suggesting a comforting duration, this implies that it's impossible to tell where the end is. How can you pinpoint the exact moment of death, in the small modifications of the spectrum?

'Something Else' is a poem about an end which also effects a continuation. Like 'Chinook' it is also a covert elegy for Muldoon's father. In 'The Soap-Pig' Muldoon has written a more formal, recognisable elegy – this time for an ex-colleague at the BBC, Michael Heffernan, who died of heart disease. This poem again meditates on movement and departure, and on how to maintain identity while things change and slip away. The soap-pig is a kind of body, at once fragile and enduring, which becomes symbolic not only of the body of Michael Heffernan, but of the friendship between him and Muldoon. A present from Heffernan to Muldoon ('this was Heffernan / saying, "You stink to high heaven." ') the soap-pig at first seems to stand for permanence. It survives the changes which have marked Muldoon's life, as he moves from house to house and from relationship to relationship:

> they'd given him a tiny, plastic valve
> that would, it seemed, no more dissolve
>
> than the soap-pig I carried
> on successive flits
> from Marlborough Park (and Anne-Marie)
> to the Malone Avenue flat
> (*Chez Moy*, it was later dubbed)
> to the rented house in Dub (as in *Dub*-
>
> lin) Lane,
> until, at last, in Landseer Street
> Mary unpeeled its cellophane
> and it landed on its feet
> among porcelain, glass and heliotrope
> pigs from all parts of the globe.

In contrast to Muldoon's 'flitting', Heffernan, despite his ill-health, appears firm and constant. He is 'steadied' through illness by his wife Margaret, suggesting that unlike Muldoon his relationships endure. But of course this permanence is an illusion, and the soap-pig, like Heffernan himself, is vulnerable. At one point Mary flings it into the yard and Muldoon rescues it, unpicking 'the anthracite shards / from its body'. In a sense, however, it is the pig's very fragility which underlines its constancy, just as Heffernan's physical frailty (having twice undergone heart surgery) points up his remarkable endurance.

This faith in the body's enduring presence is shattered with the news of Heffernan's death, which prompts Muldoon to reflect on what exactly it was that endured through all those moves – what essence of physical or personal identity remains constant through the various departures? During the course of the poem we learn that Michael Heffernan's favourite word was '*quidditas*' – the real nature or essence of a thing, that which makes a thing what it is:

> For how he would delib-
> erate on whether two six-foot boards
> sealed with ship's
> varnish and two tea-chests
> (another move) on which all this rests
>
> is a table; or this merely a token
> of some ur-chair,
> or – being broken –
> a chair at all: the mind's a razor
> on the body's strop.
> And the soap-pig? It's a bar of soap,
>
> now the soap-sliver
> in a flowered dish
> that I work each morning into a lather
> with my father's wobbling-brush,
> then reconcile to its pool of glop
> on my mother's wash-stand's marble top.

Ostensibly the problem being debated here is where identity lies. Should the boards and tea-chests which Muldoon is using as a table be referred back to their origin, or to their present state? A similar uncertainty haunts Muldoon's sense of himself – despite his many departures, the last lines interpret his identity in terms of his origins – his father (a little 'wobbly') and his mother (a monumental, unchanging presence). The permanence of the marble memorial is clearly at variance with the spirit of the transient soap – particularly since Muldoon decides to use the soap-pig rather than preserve it as a memento. He washes away the body of the pig as he washes (and shaves) his own body. As well as emphasising the body's vulnerability through nakedness (the poem begins with Muldoon in the bath and ends with the ritual of shaving), we can understand this, I think, in terms of Muldoon's professed dissatisfaction with the archaeological method of capturing the moment, which is based on preservation – instead he decides to experience the soap. As he does so, as the soap-pig is 'worked' into a lather, so Michael Heffernan is worked into the poem. While one body disappears, Muldoon creates a new body to endure. He builds a monument which at the same time acknowledges movement, loss, the process of things slipping away. On the other hand, we could understand the act of shaving as a way of trying to stay the same (physically), of trying to arrest growth. Is there an implication that the cost of remaining the same is the gradual erosion of other people – of Michael Heffernan, of Muldoon's father? Both men's objects, the brush and the soap are being worn down in the service of Muldoon's shaving.

As 'The Soap-Pig' makes clear, Muldoon's interest in movement and process is in part a way of reflecting on how to define personal (and also national) identity. Are we to understand ourselves in relation to our origins (in Muldoon's case his parental home, the small farm in Armagh), or through the journeys we take away from our beginnings? Muldoon's father's death is pivotal to this meditation: his departure from this life is at once an end, and a beginning for Muldoon's own series of departures – it allows him to move on. Thus the question of remains is not limited to the remains of the dead, but concerns also how much of Muldoon's identity remains tied up in the Armagh countryside, preserved in the soil along with the body of his father. How far can we ever leave our origins behind? Remains, then, are what you leave behind you, but also what you take along with you on your journey. One of the ways Muldoon gestures towards this paradox in *Meeting the British* is through the recurring image of the cargoes carried by different vessels all over the world. Through this image he suggests that individuals are freighted, rather than rooted, by their pasts. In 'Profumo' the snobbish mother figure censures her son for forgetting his superiority over his thirteen year old sweetheart: ' "Haven't I told you, time and time again, / that you and she are chalk / and cheese? Away and read Masefield's *Cargoes*." ' As Muldoon has said, Masefield's poem, a favourite in children's anthologies, 'is essentially about one idea: the distinction between the colour, beauty, possibility of the imagination that we associate with far-off lands and the down-to-earth ordinariness of our day-to-day world of dirty British coasters'. To a certain extent Masefield's poem confounds the mother's message of hierarchical difference as it gestures towards the overwhelming power of fantasy. But at the same time the mother figure succeeds in linking the cargo, the burden carried across the world, to social origin and familial background.

The image of a personal cargo is reiterated several times in the final long poem in *Meeting the British* – a poem which at first seems to have little in common with the concerns of the book as a whole. Despite many differences in tone, style and form however, '7 Middagh Street' continues Muldoon's preoccupation with personal and social origin, departures, cargoes and remains, but places these concerns in the context of a discussion of poetry's purpose in time of war. The poem is constructed as a sequence of seven linked monologues spoken on Thanksgiving Day, 1940, by the inhabitants of a house in Brooklyn, New York, which was rented at the time by the poet W.H. Auden. The monologues are spoken by Auden, his lover Chester Kallman, the novelist Carson McCullers, the striptease artist Gypsy Rose Lee, Benjamin Britten, Salvador Dalí, and Louis MacNeice. The poem is, in effect, a series of ventriloquisms, or, as Muldoon has said, an attempt at 'verisimilitude' of the characters' speech. He has not attempted ventriloquism at the level of style however, except perhaps in 'Wystan' where Muldoon employs a characteristically Audenesque octosyllabic line. (It is worth noting, perhaps, that '7 Middagh Street' again explores the possibilities of the sonnet form; the verse forms in each of the seven monologues are various, but all are based on the number seven. The poem includes sonnets, reversed sonnets – in which the sestet precedes the octet – repeated sequences of a couplet followed by three quatrains, and rhyming couplets in multiples of seven.)

Each speaker offers a different perspective on their journey to New York, on their life there, and on the role of the artist in wartime. This is an intensely "literary" poem, the product of a considerable amount of research on Muldoon's part, and dependent on substantial knowledge on the part of the reader. Muldoon draws on literary biographies (in particular on Humphrey Carpenter's 1981 biography of Auden), as well as on the creative work and autobiographical statements of the artists. The poem was criticised by some for a certain academic dryness and for relying too heavily on a body of literary knowledge (although the use of source texts is negligible compared to Muldoon's next major poem 'Madoc – A Mystery'). Certainly readers hoping for a repeat of the narrative extravaganzas of 'The More a Man Has the More a Man Wants', or even 'Immram', were disappointed. This is a meditative rather than a dynamic poem, little interested in plot or story except as stories enter in the form of life histories of the characters. The poem seems a long way from Muldoon's experiments with process and poetic movement in the rest of *Meeting the British*. Here the action is retrospective, as each character recounts their journey, physical and mental, to the present of 1940. Rather than a concern with narrative alternatives and new directions, the alternatives represented here are those of approach and attitude, and importantly these attitudes have already led to certain decisions. Rather than a meditation on roads not taken, this is a poem about

explaining (and excusing) decisions which have already been acted on
– and the most important of these is the decision to leave Europe
for the United States.

'7 Middagh Street' begins with 'Wystan' Auden's reflections on
his departure from England for the United States (with Christopher
Isherwood) some time before the beginning of the Second World
War, for which they were accused of betraying Britain. The poem
deals explicitly with the question of the poet's political responsibility,
framed in terms of the characters' involvement (or lack of involvement) with the World War and the Spanish Civil War. (One could
argue that the centrality of the Spanish Civil War in this poem is
in itself a political statement on Muldoon's part. It inevitably suggests an analogy with civil unrest in Northern Ireland, with all the
attendant political implications of referring to the Troubles as a
war.) In terms of the debate about the poet's responsibility the
most important sections of the poem are those spoken by 'Wystan',
'Salvador' and 'Louis'. Each offers a different perspective on the
role of the artist in wartime: Auden's disillusioned rejection of the
rhetoric of war, and insistent claim that 'poetry makes nothing
happen'; Dalí's surrealist emphasis on the need to disregard both
'moral and aesthetic considerations / for the integrity of our dream
visions', and his refusal to take sides in the Spanish Civil War;
and MacNeice's Northern Irish perspective on civil war and his
Yeatsian belief that social responsibility begins with poetry.

Yeats is central to this poem – the characters repeatedly quote
(or misquote) him, in a graphic embodiment of Auden's comment
in 'In Memory of W.B. Yeats' that the words of a dead man are
modified in the guts of the living. Indeed, quotation and allusion
are fundamental to the meaning of this poem, which cites or refers
to a wide array of writers from the 1920s and 30s, including Masefield, Crane, Beckett and Lorca. Auden's poem is a focal point for
the debate between the inhabitants of 7 Middagh Street on the
role and purpose of poetry. His own views on the relation of art
to politics and history had changed radically with his religious
conversion. The move to the States was interpreted by many as a
rejection of the association of literature and politics that had been
the mark of the 1930s (particularly with reference to the Spanish
Civil War). Auden rationalised his move as a rejection of the link
between the writer and his community; his removal to a country
where all were 'equally isolated' exempted him, he felt, from any
need to speak for a community. As Samuel Hynes has pointed
out, 'In Memory of W.B. Yeats' was a first statement from Auden
of his new outlook:

Auden and Isherwood arrived in New York on 26 January 1939. That
same day Barcelona fell, and with its fall the last hope of the Spanish
loyalists ended. Two days later there was another kind of ending – the
death of Yeats. Auden must have begun at once to write his great elegy,
'In Memory of W.B. Yeats', in which he made these three endings
merge into one vast human defeat: the old poet dead, the young poet in
retreat from his lost causes, the city conquered seen as a single historical
occasion, the end of the 'thirties'.[4]

In Muldoon's poem these sentiments are presented as a rejection
of Yeats's overweening pretensions to a political role:

As for his crass, rhetorical

posturing, 'Did that play of mine
send out certain men (*certain* men?)

the English shot…?'
the answer is 'Certainly not'.

If Yeats had saved his pencil-lead
would certain men have stayed in bed?

For history's a twisted root
with art its small, translucent fruit

and never the other way round.

Auden seeks a new "origin", in Oregon, without social class, hierarchy, or difference. A counterview is offered by Louis MacNeice,
who emphasises the impossibility of breaking away from social
origins. His own views are the fruit of his background in Northern
Ireland (he even interprets Dalí as an Irish 'O'Daly'). He suggests
not that poetry must be read politically, but (quoting Yeats again,
'In dreams begin responsibilities') that it is through poetry, through
the imagination, that real political thought occurs.

For poetry *can* make things happen –
not only can, but *must* –

and the very painting of that oyster
is in itself a political gesture.

The temptation in reading '7 Middagh Street' is to identify Muldoon's position with MacNeice's – not only are both from Northern
Ireland, but the poem ends with Louis's monologue, as though
bringing the debate to a conclusion. However, rather than a linear
development the form of the poem is cyclical – each monologue
leads on to the next through the repetition of phrases, and 'Louis'
ends with the first words of 'Wystan', bringing the reader full circle.
Muldoon surely also sympathises with Auden, not least because
his own decision to leave Europe for marriage in the States parallels Wystan's erotic fulfilment (he calls it marriage) with Chester

Kallman. And he also seems to sympathise with Dali's refusal to take sides in the name of aesthetic integrity. Indeed Muldoon challenges us to decide where he stands in relation to this debate, teasing us with a glimpse of 'the back door of Muldoon's' in the final sonnet.

The cyclical form of '7 Middagh Street', in which each speaker "hands on" lines to the next, is in part a continuation and development of Muldoon's interest in circles – the cycles of history and those of the revolutionary activity which attempts to change history, as well as the circles, tangents and new directions to be found in poetic form. (The next time he will experiment with the handing on of lines is in his verse-play about an IRA cell, *Six Honest Serving Men*, published in 1995. The play is comprised of thirty-six short scenes, through which Muldoon weaves a sonnet sequence and a double-sestina. As the six remaining members of the cell try – through innuendo, accusation and counter-accusation – to discern which of them was responsible for having 'The Chief rubbed out', lines are passed on from one scene, and one character to the next, becoming wildly distorted in the process. Here revolutionary activity is dramatised as a cycle of confusion, brutality and murder. Each of the characters seeks vision, but we remain as far as possible from any form of enlightenment. The repetitive patterns of the play establish a sense of entrapment, an enclosed world of darkness and ignorance where there are questions but no answers, as the play's title, loaned from Kipling, implies.) But the cycles of '7 Middagh Street' also reflect Muldoon's interest in *Meeting the British* in the notion of circulation in general. Throughout the book Muldoon explores communication's dependence on circulation or trade, as objects and bits of language are re-used and re-made by being taken out of their original context and placed in new ones. For as much as about political responsibility, the debate between the characters in '7 Middagh Street' is about art's relation to its origins. In part, these are literary origins – the remains which haunt Muldoon throughout this book become in the final poem the remains of other writers which are circulated or passed on in language. Quotation is in a sense analogous to making use of the old bones of other writers; the poet may be no more than a dog consuming the bodies of his predecessors. Can he make something new of them, like the kid gloves or calf-hide upholstery?

At one level Muldoon's interest in this book can be understood as a continuation of the bodily concerns of *Quoof*: how can the body (and its most personal and intimate relationships) be transformed into art. So a tibia becomes a flute, an instrument with which to 'charm'; but one thing to note about artefacts such as kid gloves and calf-hide upholstery is their luxury. The metamorphosis of the body is repeatedly associated with increased monetary value, with opulence and indulgence. So for example the remnants of a relationship between two lovers turns up at auction in the guise of a set of Venetian goblets in 'Gone'. Muldoon seems to be asking, what is the price of bits of people's lives, and who has the right to trade in them? This question of the trade value of goods is crystallised in the different cargoes of Masefield's poem, but it is in the poem 'Meeting the British' itself, where what the Indians 'buy' is smallpox, that the real costs of trade – and communication – are brought home.

Here the old world is destroyed to make way for a new one, but the traffic between old and new worlds is an issue for many of the characters in the book – people who are in transit away from their origins, like the emigrés in '7 Middagh Street'. As much as literary origins this poem, and the book as a whole, is also preoccupied with biographical origins and how to move away from them – or let them go – while still holding on to them. At one level '7 Middagh Street' can be understood as a rewriting of 'Lunch with Pancho Villa', in its concern with political responsibility measured against the importance of home. In the light of his decision to leave Northern Ireland, Muldoon seems to be asking how departure might affect this relationship – what happens to the cargo you bring with you? Are 'the things of childhood washed overboard'? Have the artists and writers living at 7 Middagh Street lost their identity with their move away from their homelands, or have they found it? While none of these questions is answered in this book, it may be, as 'The Soap-Pig' suggests, that a move away from origins is necessary in order to find out where the essence lies.

CHAPTER SIX

Madoc – A Mystery

Paul Muldoon's emigration to the United States in 1987 could almost be described as a case of life imitating art. The difficulty of knowing what to take with you, as well as how to leave things behind, which he had explored throughout *Meeting the British*, took on a new personal urgency as Muldoon contemplated transporting his poetry to unfamiliar territory. How was he to develop his work in new directions, while still maintaining his links with the past? While it would be a mistake to see a radical break in Muldoon's poetry and poetics after his move away from Ireland, his departure did open up new possibilities in his work.

Inevitably, the relation between the old and the new worlds becomes a central concern. And in his next book *Madoc – A Mystery*, this concern is reflected not only in the volume's subject-matter but also in its poetic style, as Muldoon explores ways of making connections between Ireland and America, the familiar and the unaccustomed. Unsurprisingly for a poet who insists that nothing is ever entirely new, but always a transmutation of something else, *Madoc* doesn't turn its back on Muldoon's abiding concerns. But it does present them in unfamiliar ways. His preoccupation with origins, entrapment, repetition and fate, and the search for new directions, is projected onto a different stage – one that requires a new language and an original form. I want to take this opportunity, therefore, to draw back a little and consider briefly the development of certain central ideas in Muldoon's career so far, in order to understand better where he takes them after this turning point.

I have touched several times on the importance in Muldoon's work of movement, change, and by implication, stasis. Muldoon's early work is preoccupied with the tension between alternative possibilities, the pull of opposing forces. His early poems continually strive towards balance and equilibrium, but a balance which has nothing to do with stillness or a state of being at rest. The equivocal hand gesture at the end of 'Armageddon, Armageddon', the shifting feet at the end of 'Why Brownlee Left': these images beautifully illustrate moments of indecision which are also – of necessity – moments of change. The ambivalent inbetweenness of *Mules*, the perpetual forwards and backwards movement of *Why Brownlee Left*, develop in his later work into a more thoroughgoing concern with ways of making poetic lines encompass indeterminacy – to both complete and open up a way of thinking. Throughout *Quoof* Muldoon explores a state of things being whole and at the same time unfinished; the lack of verb in the final lines of the title-poem prompts the reader to wonder 'has the poem ended?' Again and again we are encouraged to look forward to an event which is 'yet to' occur, and which can never occur – because the poems are complete, the 'yet to' is always yet to come. Such incompleteness is graphically embodied in *The Wishbone* and *Meeting the British* in the gaps in the poems which point to the ghostly presence of absent beings, the unburied dead. Above all, these poems try to articulate the incompleteness of death, and other kinds of ending; they conjure states of suspension or indeterminacy which are the logical extension of the concerns of *Mules*.

One way of grasping Muldoon's preoccupation with states of ambivalence and suspension is in terms of his schooling in practical criticism. Set in this context Muldoon emerges as a master of Empsonian ambiguity, deploying in an exemplary way the formal techniques beloved of the New Critics, and exploring forms of balanced ambiguity, rather than fragmentation. There is undoubtedly something to this view, which interprets Muldoon's formal poise in the light of certain familiar modernist poetic ideals – the isolation of the poetic image from external contingencies, the elevation of the poem to the condition of a thing. My description is reductive yet serves, I hope, to indicate certain aspects of Muldoon's relation to his modernist heritage. His exploration of states of movement and suspension can in part be understood as a way of resolving the post-romantic dilemma concerning the relation between poetic language (with its formal patterning) and the particularities of experience. In his poetry the conflict between the generalising and abstract aspects of poetic form – sequence, lineation, rhyme, temporal duration, and connections of all kinds – and the unique moment of experience is, as it were, "resolved" on another plane, that of the imagination. Muldoon's interest is in how poetic language can articulate the imagination's capacity to encompass contradiction, to hold alternative possibilities in suspension, to arrest choice. Yet as I've suggested in my discussion of Muldoon's work so far, these moments of imaginative resolution are continually disturbed or upset by niggling or residual elements which won't quite fit the poetry's balanced structures. The poems keep pushing us towards that which has 'yet to' come, revealing an openendedness at odds with enclosed, iconic modernist form.

While we can interpret this quality of disturbance and inconclusiveness within the loose framework of "postmodern" stylistic technique, and in particular its narrative turn, Muldoon's pre-occupation with future temporality is more than an issue of poetic form. It is also an important thematic concern, one which at its most basic level may derive from a kind of heightened *fin de siècle* historical consciousness. In general, our modern awareness of time is continually confronted with the question of our problematic relation to the past and to the future. Our need to break away from the past, in order to move forwards into a "better" future, is con-stantly counterbalanced by a sense that we are losing touch with the past, and thus losing the very source of our identity. Thus contemporary advertising oscillates between a nostalgic evocation of traditional virtues and the presentation of products as the most "scientifically advanced", the latest thing. Yet even when we try to acknowledge our sense of the past, this is all too often expresssed in the synthetic form of "costume drama", "interpretive centres" and the whole apparatus of the heritage industry. In this context, Muldoon's concern is to explore the ways in which we are indebted to, and indeed held in the sway of the past, without either senti-mentalising or repudiating it. Above all his poetry conveys an abiding sense that the past is not yet the past. At the risk of over-simplification I want to suggest that much of Muldoon's concern with motion and arrested motion is driven by a sense of entrap-ment within time – what the poem 'Lull' calls an 'eternal interim'. Put bluntly, the problem for Muldoon is that if the past hasn't ended, then the future can't begin.

The problem of when things end (and when something else begins) is a philosophical one, and also, as we saw in *Meeting the British*, a problem of personal identity (if the father's death is not final what does this mean for the son?). It is also a problem of poetic tradition – how is one to find the appropriate balance between old and new forms? Muldoon's relation to literary history is of course eclectic – he finds seventeenth-century, romantic and modern poetry equally varied and accommodating, and draws on aspects of each in order to drive towards the future. But as a poem such as 'Lull' suggests, the question of the relation between what we inherit and what we carry forward has particular relevance to Irish history, and to the search for a possible future. It is, I think, in this light that we need to interpret Muldoon's increasing interest in historical analogy, as well as historical fantasy, in his later work. From '7 Middagh Street' onwards Muldoon's interest in states of temporal and spatial sus-pension focuses more and more on specific moments of world his-tory, whether the debate about art and politics in 1930s Europe in *Meeting the British*, the poetic movements and political events of the 1790s in *Madoc – A Mystery*, or the eighteenth-century battles over republicanism in South America in *The Annals of Chile*. Given Muldoon's relocation to the United States in the late 1980s it is perhaps no coincidence that each of these moments becomes in Muldoon's hands an exemplary instance of traffic between the old and new worlds, as well as a way of reflecting once more on historical repetition and the possibilities for change.

Muldoon, then, has always been preoccupied with the ways in which the historical past haunts the present. Often, the relation of present to past seems to be one of repetition, even if unintended repetition. In *Why Brownlee Left*, for example, the cyclical movement in which the past is replayed over again conveys Muldoon's sense of the ineluctability of fate, both personal and collective. Of course, no such cycle is ever a perfect repetition of what has gone before, but this very fact poses the question of beginnings and endings, and of transformation, in a particularly acute form. How can we be sure that something new is commencing, and that we are not simply repeating the old? How can we know that a break is truly a break? Muldoon's circular narratives stress the omnipresence of repetition. But at the same time the notion of circulation conveys other undertones. It suggests those forms of metamorphosis, of trade and exchange, in which one thing can become another. Thus in *Meeting the British* Muldoon imagined the connections between past and future, origin and destination, in terms of the cargoes and merchandise which circulate between cultures. And this in turn continued the preoccupation of *The Wishbone* with the ways in which remnants of the dead, the traces of extinct lives, can become the basis for new possibilities (just as the forces of life can be lost, or turned into something deadening). Understanding the connections between past, present and future has thus always been crucial for Muldoon, and his emigration to America posed this question of connections with renewed force. For here was a move which genuinely did look like a break from the past, a linear – as opposed to a circular – movement. Might it offer the chance to leave fate behind with place, to break out of the cyclical traps which haunt the poet in 'Anseo', or 'The More a Man Has the More a Man Wants'? Or, since the past is enabling as well as constraining, might it instead be the occasion of an irrevocable loss? The question of what remains, in the sense not only of what is left behind but also of what stays with us, and indeed of what we need to keep with us, becomes in this context more urgent than ever. Of course, for Muldoon, the question of the historical relation between Ireland and America looms behind his personal experience of emigration, suggesting that, however it might feel, his move isn't really something new – he's repeating history after all.

In his sixth book, *Madoc – A Mystery*, these questions of historical continuity and discontinuity, and of the unpredictable impact of new environments, are taken up in a new way. Connections, or more properly the difficulty of making connections, are once more fundamental, as Muldoon explores the possible conjunctions between Europe and America, fact and fiction, literature and politics, poetry and philosophy, romanticism and contemporary poetry, and between lyric and narrative. This last relationship is crucial, since Muldoon's experiments with the long poem are taken to an extreme in this book. The volume reverses the relation of long to short poems – seven short lyrics serve as a kind of introduction to the title-poem, a fantastical narrative stretching over 246 pages, and comprised of 233 lyrics, each "surtitled" with the name of a Western philosopher. The "story" of 'Madoc – A Mystery' is suspended between fact and fiction, past and future, Europe and America. Like '7 Middagh Street', the poem makes use of biography and historical source material, but here the relation between history and fantasy is far more involved. 'Madoc' presents a bizarre narrative detailing, among other things, the imaginary exploits of two Romantic poets, Robert Southey and Samuel Taylor Coleridge, as they set out to fulfil their dream of founding a utopian community in post-independence America. In reality, of course, the two poets never left Europe, but Muldoon takes the actual historical events surrounding their lives – marriage and family life, the publication of poems, letters and journal entries, the births and deaths of Coleridge's children – and mixes them with quite another history, that of republican expansion and the federalist conspiracies of the early nineteenth century in America. Muldoon uses historical documents both to retain and at the same time transform the 'facts', projecting the demise of the poets' radical, democratic and republican youth onto an American stage. Interwoven with the narrative of the imagined utopian project are other contemporary historical events. These include Aaron Burr's conspiracy against Jefferson (Burr tied with Jefferson in the presidential election of 1800, but was only awarded the Vice-Presidency by the House of Representatives), the Louisiana Purchase, and the expedition of Lewis and Clark, who Jefferson ordered to find a land route to the Pacific. Muldoon goes further than simply referring to this complex history; he includes in the poem extracts from contemporary writings such as the journals kept by members of the Lewis and Clark expedition, the writings of artist George Catlin, and poems by Tom Moore, Byron, and Coleridge and Southey themselves. Muldoon refuses to draw distinctions of role or significance between different kinds of text, so that 'Madoc' gives equal weight to – for example – the memoirs of the publisher Joseph Cottle, poetic fantasies such as Byron's *The Vision of Judgement*, and historical fictions such as Gore Vidal's *Burr*. Thus historically recorded events frequently occur in the poem, but they undergo various kinds of dislocation, often being literally transferred somewhere else. On one level the imagined fate of the poets' 'pantisocratic' scheme offers a structure through which to reflect on the efficacy of poetry, the relationship of poetry to politics (and to nation-building in particular). But if Muldoon's use of a historical parallel inevitably suggests an analogy with the concerns of poetry in contemporary Northern Ireland, it also offers a way of exploring the possibilities of new knowledge. 'Madoc' is a poem which explores, in surreal and outlandish ways, the relation of history not only to the present but the future, the relation of history to imagination, and how to make history differently.

All these preoccupations are viewed through the prism of the volume's central concern with finding a new poetic language appropriate to altered circumstances. In this respect the shorter poems serve as a kind of methodological preface, providing sly advance warnings of the kinds of subversion of the reader's poetic expectations which the dominant poem in the volume will undertake. Not only do they introduce questions of form, style and subject-matter relevant to our understanding of the long poem, but they too turn on the issue of the connection between the old and new worlds. Teasing us with our desire for an interpretative framework for 'Madoc', Muldoon entitles the first poem in the book 'The Key'. This prose-poem recounts an anecdote, as Muldoon recalls an encounter with another Irish emigrant, a 'foley' who is at work on a 'remake' of a film, *The Hoodlum Priest*:

> Foley was working on a sequence involving a police line-up, in which the victim shuffled along, stopped with each suspect in turn, then shuffled on. At a critical moment, she dropped a key on the floor. Foley was having trouble matching sound to picture on this last effect.

The key, it turns out, is a problem. Like so many of the wayward elements in Muldoon's poetry it is out of synch. Foley's problem is one of timing, but also one of connection, and the implication is that these are problems for Muldoon too. As readers we are being warned that we may encounter similar difficulties making connections in the long poem to follow, itself a 'remake' of a poem by Robert Southey. But the poem also introduces us to other difficulties for Muldoon – those of language, nationality, race and subject-matter. In a clever parody of a passage from 'Brock' (a poem in

Meeting the British), the Muldoon figure cautions Foley to remember his roots. (In a characteristically witty passage he articulates this warning literally, through instruction on the linguistic roots of the Irish language.) But Foley rebuffs him:

> *Still defending that same old patch of turf?*
> *Have you forgotten that 'hoodlum' is back-slang*
> *for the leader of a San Francisco street-gang?*

> He flounced off into his cubicle. Though this, our only exchange, was remarkable for its banality, Foley has had some profound effect on me. These past six months I've sometimes run a little ahead of myself, but mostly I lag behind, my footfalls already pre-empted by their echoes.

This is a poem about the relation between an Irish past and an American future, about the need to find a 'fit' between Irish concerns and American idioms. Foley warns the poet of the need to move on from 'that same old patch of turf', a warning which surely reflects Muldoon's own awareness of the need to find not only new subjects now that he has left Ireland, but a new language with which to express them. Importantly the poem suggests that in doing so he will be moving forwards towards his 'own' identity, since 'hoodlum' is (nearly) Muldoon backwards. These lines imply that the poet doesn't need to invent connections between Ireland and America – they are already there. Muldoon's 'new' language will in fact depend on a prior history of international cultural exchange, a web of historical connections which is already in place. As we will see, Muldoon adopts a similar approach to the parallels between Ulster and the struggles of the new American republic which are the burden of 'Madoc'.

There are clearly autobiographical concerns at work here. Muldoon, recently moved to the United States, is caught between an Irish past and an American future, with his new wife. At a very basic level the style and form of *Madoc – A Mystery* reflect Muldoon's concerns about having recently arrived in America. Quite simply, what was he going to write about? 'The Key' reflects his need to find a way of writing which would neither reproduce in nostalgic fashion the language and forms of his poetry from Northern Ireland (that same old patch of turf), nor approach American culture from the bland, detached point of view of a tourist. The outlandish nature of the long poem can thus be understood as a response to the foreignness of American culture, and Muldoon's position as a foreigner within it.

If we read 'The Key' as an introduction to 'Madoc', it prepares us for a book which will be concerned with belated versions, with the difficulty of making connections (between cultures, and between past, present and future), with the problem of what language to use. It should prepare us too for a book in which language, as much as story or event, will be the object of interest. While this is of course true of all poetry to a greater or lesser extent, what is distinctive about 'The Key' is the almost parodic use of symbol and metaphor. For a poem which is about how language and meaning, sound and echo, sound and image fit together poorly, the exaggerated clues and keys which the poem offers are remarkably – oddly – neat. With the introduction of the 'identity parade', the question of linguistic roots, and of course 'the key' itself, Muldoon seems to be winking at the reader with an almost slapstick obviousness. These are the deadest of dead metaphors – they obtrude by virtue of their very lack of "poetic" ornament, their leaden "literalness". Furthermore, Muldoon draws attention to the brazenly clichéd or corny aspects of the poem by using italics and quotation marks. These are all very evident ways of holding the 'exchange' at a distance, and highlighting the linguistic aspects of the event. While the poem ostensibly relays an anecdote, the meaning comes not from generalisation or abstraction from the particular experience recounted in the poem, but from the literal (and also lateral) meanings of words. As the quotation marks should alert us, this is above all an experience in language – and as such it prepares us for the way meanings are created in 'Madoc'. Certainly it augurs an irreverent attitude to poetic language, bizarre ways of making connections, a certain renunciation of the lyric voice, and perhaps in particular it foreshadows the tone of the poem – jokey, parodic, full of apparently nonsensical wordplay and sound repetition.

At the same time, even as the seven lyrics in Part I of the book introduce some of the images, themes and linguistic games of 'Madoc – A Mystery', they also indicate the direction that Muldoon has decided not to take in that poem, as he explores different ways of making connections between worlds. Muldoon has described one of these lyrics, 'The Panther', as 'the classic poem of the new immigrant'. Here again, he presents us with an anecdote – though this time a historical rather than a personal one. The poem turns on the fact that the 'last panther in Massachusetts' was killed near the house in which Muldoon and his wife are living, and 'hung by its heels from a meat-hook / in what is now our kitchen'. The house itself Muldoon describes as 'something of a conundrum, / built as it was by an Ephraim Cowan from Antrim' – in other words a Scots-Irish settler. Like 'The Key' the poem tries to make connections, in this case based on the motifs of colonisation and civilisation (the destruction of the wild), and what these mean for the present occupiers of the house – but there's something missing:

I look in one evening while Jean
is jelly-making. She has rendered down pounds of grapes
and crab-apples
to a single jar
at once impenetrable and clear;
'Something's missing. This simply won't take.'

The air directly under the meat-hook –
it quakes, it quickens;
on a flagstone, the smudge of the tippy-tip of its nose.

The jelly (an American term for jam) is clearly an image for the
poem, but – again – one so knowingly presented that we should be
suspicious. The poem is supposed to be able to take the wealth of
experience, to 'boil it down' into a condensed symbolic form, both
'impenetrable and clear'. But something has gone awry – this poem,
Muldoon is saying, won't set. Is it that there is something wild, untamed in the air, which resists the genteel devices of the European
lyric tradition? Or is it rather that everything has been too domesticated – the panther 'brought to justice', like a character in a B
Western, and turned into a dangling soft toy (with its 'tippy-tip').
Either way, the reader is in difficulties, not knowing how to take
these lines. We could read the poem 'straight' – with Muldoon and
his wife implicated in colonisation, and the ghost of the panther as
the spirit of disturbance, an untamed or wild presence which per-
sists inside the house. But this is to accept the terms of the poem,
which Muldoon has warned us won't work. The reader is put in an
impossible position, unable to accept the only narrative on offer.
    Muldoon is suggesting that there's something missing (another
dead metaphor) from the traditional lyric distillation of experience,
which makes this an inappropriate way to come to terms with his
new environment. But why is it exactly that the lyric will no longer
function? The final poem in Part I of the book, a sonnet dedicated
to Seamus Heaney and entitled 'The Briefcase', hints at Muldoon's
dissatisfaction with the established ways of making connections
between Ireland and America even more clearly – but has, I believe,
been poorly understood. The poem alludes to a passage in Seamus
Heaney's 'Lough Neagh Sequence'. In 'Beyond Sargasso' Heaney
contemplates an eel which has 'drifted / into motion half-way /
across the Atlantic', to make its way two hundred miles inland in
Ireland. By contrast Muldoon's poem is about an eelskin briefcase.
Rather than Heaney's living 'gland', Muldoon's eel has been killed
for luxurious decoration. But like the panther it comes back to life;
the Manhattan streets become suddenly flooded with rain and in a
surreal moment the briefcase begins to quicken, threatening to travel
east from New York City (and thus necessarily across the Atlantic

to Ireland). Muldoon imagines this journey as crossing to the underworld (there seems to be a likely allusion here too to Louis MacNeice's
poem 'Charon' which similarly sets the River Styx in an urban
setting, though in MacNeice's case it is London). Muldoon doesn't
want to set his briefcase down:

> to slap my pockets for an obol –
>
> for fear it might slink into a culvert
> and strike out along the East River
> for the sea. By which I mean the 'open' sea.

At readings the ending of the poem is often greeted with a gasp, as
though something very profound has been said. But perhaps a giggle
would be just as appropriate. Look, for instance, at the way Muldoon
draws attention to the final statement – he is manipulating the reader
into believing in its profundity but (as in 'The Key') the use of
quotation marks should alert us to something odd going on. After
all, what other kind of sea is there, especially east of New York City?
    Muldoon is being characteristically double-edged here – he both
allows the statement to stand, and at the same time undercuts it
(again, through the use of quotation marks). The quandary over
whether to giggle or gasp is indicative of a real uncertainty – are we
to take this seriously? Muldoon challenges us to decide how far he
is really behind this distinction between a nostalgic return to Ireland
and open American forms. Of course distancing the poetic voice by
the use of a persona is a familiar modernist convention, so common
indeed that it sometimes hard to see. But what's different about
Muldoon is that the voice both is and is not his own, both is and
is not sincere. He wants us to be impressed, but also to distance
himself from any too earnest show of personal feeling. I think this
is what lies at the heart of accusations that Muldoon's poetry is
too self-aware (in the words of one eminent critic, 'tricky, clever,
tickled by its own knowingness').[1] But what these criticisms miss is
a sense of Muldoon's debate with himself about poetic voice and
style. 'The Briefcase' clearly points to a real concern both about
voice and about form. Like 'The Panther', it seems to suggest that
the lyric voice, the language of private response, is the wrong way
to go about drawing together past and present, Ireland and America.
Instead Muldoon needs to find a way of writing which does not
seek to authorise itself through personal experience and testimony.
As several critics have noted, the rhyme scheme of 'The Briefcase'
is entirely self-reflecting and self-contained (*abcdefgfgedcba*), but
the poem is also about how there is 'something missing' from this
closed form. The poem suggests that its own style has to come to

an end in a kind of stasis or closure – and that we will be out on the open sea in the poem that follows.

Of course experiments with the possibilities of the long poem are not new for Muldoon, whose sense of being constrained by the temporal and spatial limitations of lyric verse clearly did not begin with his emigration to America. Even in his earliest books he experimented with ways to overcome the boundaries of the lyric through the design of the volumes, as increasingly the poems commented on and questioned one another. In one very often quoted comment in early interview (from 1980) Muldoon explained how he had 'become very interested in structures that can be fixed like mirrors to each other – it relates to narrative form'.[2] The juxtaposition of ideas and images across poems allowed Muldoon to open up the possible meanings within individual lyrics. The logical development away from poems which relate to one another across the volume is the poetic sequence. Frustrated by the limitations placed on movement and tension in the short lyric, Muldoon experiments more and more with the possibilities inherent in the long poem. However, the narratives which emerge are far from being linear and seamlessly integrated. Rather they are refracted through a sequence of discrete, interlocking sections – Muldoon's long poems aren't about making things clearer, but about adding further layers of possibility, more directions. To revert to the image of the road not taken, the longer poems offer a way of increasing openendedness, of exploring further avenues rather than leading the reader somewhere directly.

'Madoc – A Mystery' is an immensely complex and ambitious poem, one that explores, among other things, the possible extent of 'openness'. It is, clearly, a narrative poem. However, the narrative cuts across what could be construed as a residual lyrical structure, since the poem is divided into 233 sections, each of which has a title (albeit a title in brackets – a problem to which I'll return) which gives it a certain autonomy. On the other hand, scarcely any of the sections is recognisable as a lyric. Some of the individual 'poems' consist of diagrams, one-line repetitions of the same nonsense word, quotations from other poems, or verbatim extracts from historical journals and memoirs. Significantly, the poem was regarded as too weird and outlandish for many critics who had followed Muldoon's career with approval up to this point, while the poetic avant-garde did not regard it as experimental enough. Certainly it may be that for poets and critics at home with the radical redefinition of poetic language associated with the L=A=N=G=U=A=G=E group (including experiments with arbitrary formal constraints and fragments of 'found' discourse, the refusal of reference, and the rejection of the

convention of poetic voice), Muldoon's poem remained too much in
thrall to Romantic and post-Romantic literary tradition. Not only
does an understanding of the poem's plot depend on an in-depth
knowledge of literary history, but so too does its style; the surreal
humour of 'Madoc – A Mystery' is largely directed towards send-
ing up lyric seriousness, rather than rejecting the lyric outright, as is
the parody of poetic conventions which was foreshadowed in 'The
Key' and 'The Briefcase'. More than ever, Muldoon delights here
in the sheer vitality of language as such. He plays with outrageous
rhymes, jokes, semantic puns and puns on sound, not to mention
rhythms: in a gesture which is both exuberant and mocking he
alludes to the role of poetic metre in the recurrent 'de dum, de dum'
of a horse's hoofbeats, in fact the mount of the villain of the piece.

'Madoc' is impossible to categorise in terms of genre, mixing
futuristic science fiction, the western, the historical novel, detective
fiction, adventure story, as well as philosophical history. It's not even
easy to say whether it is set in the past or the future (or indeed the
present). The poem begins and ends somewhere around the middle
of the twenty-first century, 'Half-way between Belfast and Dublin,
near the present site of Unitel West'. Ireland has become home to
the headquarters of an international police state, where we witness
the attempted escape of a character we come to know as South. He
is recaptured and, somewhat the worse for wear from his struggle,
linked to a 'retinagraph' – a machine which is able to replay the
images recorded on the back of the eye. South therefore becomes
our unwilling narrator, 'though it may seem somewhat improbable, /
all that follows / flickers and flows / from the back of his right eyeball'. Even for a poet given to all kinds of distancing and deper-
sonalising effects, this device is extraordinary. In a kind of materi-
alised pun on the convention of the poetic 'I' (reminiscent of the
play on words in 'The Key'), the poem's narrative is presented
through the 'eye' of a character. 'Madoc' thus renounces poetic
'voice' altogether; rather than a story grounded in experience we
are presented with a series of unconsciously projected images,
retrieved by a machine. This then is a mechanised voice, as far as
possible from a voice of feeling. Perhaps no other element in the
poem more clearly indicates Muldoon's concern to remove himself
from the poem. Whereas in his earlier work he had tended to offer
emblematic versions of his own autobiography, often containing
wry comments on collective history, South's 'voice' is the voice of
history – although as we shall see the history it speaks is coloured
by somewhat personal concerns and obsessions.

The story is a fragmentary series of "images", and also a projection back in time. The main action of the poem begins in 1798 as Coleridge and Southey, along with their wives Sara and Edith Fricker, Coleridge's sons Hartley and Berkeley, and other pantisocrats make their way along the banks of the Susquehanna. They are accompanied by their Scots-Irish guide, Cinnamond, and (another guide of sorts) Southey's talking horse Bucephalus, picked up by the party during a stop over at an Irish port on their sailing to America. Although it's not easy to say exactly what happens, the poets' plans go dreadfully awry when they are betrayed by Cinnamond, and the alliance between Coleridge and Southey breaks up. Sara disappears in the middle of the night. (Herein lies one puzzle – is she abducted or does she go of her own free will?) The mystery as far as Coleridge is concerned primarily concerns her whereabouts. He spends much of the poem trying to find her among the Seneca tribe of Indians, before he falls in with the Lewis and Clark expedition, and moves with them further and further west. The poem is full of elaborate 'clues' to the mystery, many of which pick up on the clues and keys offered in the first seven lyrics, but none of which help much to unravel the narrative enigmas. There are several discoveries of 'a belt of blue beads, and a bow made of horn', endless recurrences of a 'teeney-weeny key', and a valise, scraps of paper containing codes such as A-R-T-I-C-H-O-K-E-S, or CROTONA, a pair of earrings given to Cinnamond. Meanwhile Southey travels east to wreak his revenge on Cinnamond. He tracks him down to an ale-house in Carthage, New York: 'Cinnamond frowns // in disbelief, then squawks and squalls / as Southey rams the sheaf of goose-quills / into his eyes.' Cinnamond consequently leads a raid on the Pantisocrats' settlement in Ulster, Pennsylvania, in which several of the party are killed; Edith is raped (by Cinnamond, we are given to understand), and subsequently gives birth to a child who is named 'South'. This character, it seems, is the ancestor of the South linked to the retinagraph, making this a family history of sorts. Feeling betrayed on all sides and increasingly isolated, Southey builds a stockade around his settlement and lives in a state of siege. Much of the narrative concerns his increasingly desperate, autocratic attempts to maintain a separation between his tiny fiefdom ('Southeyopolis') and the outside world. But as Bucephalus points out, his community is already under siege from within:

> September, 1799. They're putting the finishing touches
> to the maze of dykes and ditches
> beyond the live-oak palisade.
> The stone blockhouse is proof against a mortar-blast.

Its roof is of ten-inch-thick sheets of slate
hauled here by mule-sled.
For a weekly ration of grog and a few gew-gaws
Southey has enlisted fifteen disaffected Cayugas.

One of whom guards Edith. She rolls over in her hammock
and twiddles a newly peeled, sharpened osier
from the bundle by her side. A hummock

under her chemise. Its occasional jitter-jolt.
Her recurrent dream of a shorn and bloody hawser.
And, as always, Bucephalus, niggling; 'Who *owns* the child?'

Questions of cultural exchange and assimilation are fundamental
to this story, as Muldoon returns once more to the history of the
conquest of Native American peoples. The poem revolves around
relations between the would-be poet settlers and local American
Indian tribes. While Southey attempts to maintain an ideal of cultural integrity and to instil deference and discipline in the Cayugas
through physical punishments such as flogging, Coleridge investi-
gates the possibilities of cultural integration. He is entertained to
tea and scones by the anglicised Indian Joseph Brant, and spends
time with the Iroquois chief, Handsome Lake, who – at a time of
growing crisis for the tribes in constant contact with European
settlers, decimated by smallpox, the steady whittling away of land,
and the corrupting influence of whisky – advocated a form of
accommodation with certain Christian beliefs and with the Quaker
farming lifestyle. Ironically, while the Seneca tribe are moving
towards a more European, settled lifestyle, Coleridge becomes more
and more influenced by the drug-induced visions of shamanistic
religion: 'Coleridge is himself the blossom in the bud / of peyote',
and 'his familiar is a coyote made of snow'.

But below this surface narrative level assimilation and colonisation
turn up in many other guises. The fortunes of the poets' utopian
scheme are shadowed throughout by the mysteries surrounding
previous attempts at British colonisation. As I've mentioned Muldoon's poem is, among other things, a 'remake' of an epic poem
by Southey about the fortunes of Madoc – the legendary Welsh hero
who, disillusioned by feuding and tribal warfare at home, left his
native Wales to sail westwards and reputedly discovered America in
1169. There are clearly resonances here with Muldoon's own decision
to leave behind the violent civil strife in his native Northern Ireland.
'Madoc' is thus in part the latest incarnation of Muldoon's interest
in westward voyages, such as those of Bran or Mael Duin, or the
voyages to the Isle of the Blest. But unlike the fantastical voyages
of Irish myth, the Madoc legend is more clearly bound up with

the history of colonisation. The legend fuelled expansionist rhetoric from the age of Elizabethan imperialism onward. It served to legitimate a prior British claim to the Americas, pre-empting the Spanish claim backed by the landing of Columbus – and led to the launching of the first Virginia colony (Raleigh's Roanoke settlement). Moreover the Madoc legend was also used to justify imperial claims on Ireland. As Gwyn Williams argues in tracing the history of the myth, 'Whatever his original provenance and character, Madoc first effectively entered history as an instrument of imperial conflict. His story henceforth was to follow the ebb and flow of imperialism, trade rivalry and colonial settlement with hypnotic precision.'[3]

Several of the narratives which Muldoon weaves into his own are directly bound up with the search for the descendants of Madoc: the lone journey of the Welshman John Evans in search of the lost tribe of Welsh Indians; the Lewis and Clark expedition (Jefferson spoke of his Welsh heritage and instructed Lewis and Clark to find the Welsh Indians). In '[Cooper]' Muldoon quotes from Southey's preface to Madoc of 1805:

> Strong evidence has been adduced that Madoc reached America, and that his posterity exist there to this day, on the southern branches of the Missouri, retaining their complexion, their language, and, in some degree, their arts.

The belt of blue beads and the bow made of horn are each offered as clues as to whether there might be white Indians, but the most important clue lies in language. In '[Schelling]' Muldoon quotes from a journal kept by Whitehouse, one of the men with the Lewis and Clark expedition:

> These Savages has the Strangest language of any we have ever Seen. They appear to us to have an Empediment in their Speech or bur on their tongue. We take these Savages to be the Welch Indians if their be any such.

Were the Welsh colonisers destroyed, or did they assimilate to their new culture and become 'savages'? Is there, indeed, much difference between these two poles? In one sense assimilation is the only hope of success for the colonisers, yet it can also be understood as the mark of failure. Perhaps Madoc's settlement succeeded so well that his descendants are now indistinguishable from other natives, apart from 'a bur on their tongue'? Here Muldoon returns to issues which had already preoccupied him in 'Promises, Promises' in *Why Brownlee Left*. Indeed, he makes this connection with the earlier poem explicit, since 'Madoc – A Mystery' also purports to investigate the mystery of Raleigh's failed settlement, on the evidence of the

Roanoke rood, the piece of wood inscribed with the letters CROATAN found at the site of the lost colony. These letters are thought to represent the name of a tribe, but South glosses them as C[oleridge] RO[bert Southey The S]ATAN[ic School] – thereby making poetry the 'key' to an unsolved mystery.

It is worth pausing for a moment to consider what is really at issue here. In 'Madoc', as in so many of Muldoon's earlier poems, the question of the success or failure of colonisation is inextricably bound up with the question of intercourse – both sexual and social. In many early poems he used the analogy of colonisation as a way of representing personal relations, imaging desire as predatory but also damaging to the integrity of the self. So in 'Promises, Promises', the 'blue in an Indian girl's dead eye' is not only a symbol of un-fulfillable desire and loss, but a sign of assimilation – and there-fore continuity of a sort – through intercourse, a 'mixed marriage'. In 'Madoc' Muldoon returns to issues which have preoccupied him since the beginning of his career – those of identity, isolation, and contact, the need to open up to others for survival and growth, and the dangers of doing so which he has explored in poems as different as 'Wind and Tree', 'Quoof' and 'Meeting the British'. In 'Quoof' both sexual and social, or 'tribal' elements are clearly in play, but 'Madoc' makes these connections even more explicit. Sex is represented again and again in inter-racial terms, as some-thing which breaches the boundaries between the white settlers and Native Americans. While it is often associated with violence (as well as danger, hinted at in the disease which ravages the body of the horse 'Busyphilis') it is also, of course, a source of enjoy-ment. The poem revels in the pleasures of assimilation, one of which is the pleasure of intercourse between languages and cul-tures, and all the linguistic and semantic possibilities it offers.

If all this gives some idea both of what happens in 'Madoc', and of its range of references, it is perhaps harder to say exactly what it is *about*. Undoubtedly, in one sense it can be read as a political poem – though even that doesn't get us very far as its politics lead in many different directions. Partly, Muldoon is reflecting on the political hues of early romanticism. As the poets' democratic, republican ideals decline to narrow dogmatism, Muldoon quotes liberally from Byron's attacks on Southey in 'The Vision of Judge-ment' (he 'turn'd his coat – and would have turn'd his skin'), as well as Southey's denunciation of Byron and the Irish poet Tom Moore for their 'Satanic spirit of pride and audacious impiety'. But beyond these literary invectives, the poem is interested in politics more generally – in utopian politics, the relation between politics and violence, and in particular the politics of intercultural encounters. The intersection of fictional, historical and mythical or legendary material enables Muldoon to explore these issues from a variety of perspectives at once. Thus one consequence of 'relocating' the history of Romanticism to America is that the connections between poetry and the politics of imperialism and nation-building are high-lighted. Although they begin committed to rationalist and utopian ideals, the pantisocrats' 'experiment in human perfectibility' rapidly degenerates, as they succumb to the prejudices of imperialist ideo-logy and become involved in the machinations of the various groups competing for power in North America. Not only do the poets get caught up with the search for white Indians, but they become mixed up in political battles between republican and monarchist groups.

A further political dimension of the poem is suggested by the parallels between the colonisation of North America and that of Ireland. This was, of course, a well established theme in Muldoon's poetry prior to 'Madoc', but here it returns with added vigour and complexity. Historically, the colonisation of Ireland served as a template for subsequent British settlements in America. In both cases the colonisers' claim was that what was being occupied was in fact "virgin land", and the analogies between the dispossession of Indians and the Irish in the seventeenth and eighteenth centuries seem unavoidable. But Muldoon also undermines any simple par-allel, as he draws attention to the role played by Irish emigrants in the destruction of Native America. Alexander Cinnamond, the un-savoury Scots-Irish scout whose betrayal of Coleridge and Southey's enterprise is central to the narrative, has no qualms about mani-pulating the native population for his own purposes. By stressing the colonialist designs of Irish emigrants (including the ultra-nationalist Bucephalus, who is preoccupied with proving the Gaelic derivation of certain American place-names!) Muldoon por-trays a tangled relationship between Ireland and Native America. He undercuts simplistic distributions of good and evil, resistance and oppression by representing them not simply as parallel, or analogous cultural situations, but as connecting.

Ireland figures in the poem in many different ways. The whole poem is "set", as I've said, 'half-way between Belfast and Dublin' – therefore somewhere around the border between North and South? (or possibly in Muldoon's home-county of Armagh?) But of course by far the most obvious narrative connection with Ireland is the pantisocrats' attempt to set up their utopian society in 'Ulster' (significantly located downriver from 'Athens', the heart of demo-cracy). It may well be that this particular connection is so blatant that the reader is in danger of overlooking it, becoming absorbed instead by the intricacies of the narrative. But however absurdly obvious the connection may be at one level, Muldoon certainly does not wish us to ignore it for that very reason. He has stated, 'I don't want to belabour the point, but the fact that much of the poem is set in a place called "Ulster", and that one of the main characters is a particularly unwholesome Scots-Irish scout, Alexander Cinnamond, whose "theme music", as it were, is the "de dum, de dum" we hear throughout the poem, is scarcely an accident: though I think of *Madoc – A Mystery* as being a ripping yarn with a strong humorous element, I certainly don't discourage its being read as a political poem.'[4]

Like Madoc's putative colony, or Raleigh's Roanoke settlement, 'Ulster' is an unsuccessful colony; it fails because the terms in which it is set up are invalid – it cannot be maintained without violence. At one level this seems to be a comment on eighteenth-century republican ideals. The date of the colony's inception in the poem, 1798, sets up an obvious link with the United Irishman Rebellion in Ireland in the same year. (Indeed there are further narrative connections since 'Smith', alias Cinnamond, is an ex-Unitedman 'in the service of Aaron Burr'.) It is possible to read the poem as, at one level, an allegorical tracking of the decline of republican ideals and dissenting tradition in Ireland – their degeneration into the disabling provincialism and siege mentality of the contemporary Northern loyalist community. So Southey attempts to create a British cultural island in Ulster – fearful of a loss of cultural integrity he refuses to assimilate, yet the boundaries between his settlement and the outside world are breached nonetheless. Like the besieged Protestant community in Northern Ireland, Southey finds himself building walls in 'Ulster' to protect the illegitimate progeny of an Englishwoman raped by an Irish mercenary. The development of Southey's increasingly "unionist" mentality, and his fear of the surrounding natives, is thus directed as much at the Ulster politics of the 1980s as at the failure of the ideals of 1798.

There is however something slightly embarrassing about enumerating these political analogies – these connections are so blatant, where is the mystery? In contrast with the oblique treatment of Bloody Sunday in 'The Year of the Sloes, for Ishi', or of the hunger-strikes and dirty protests in 'The More a Man Has the More a Man Wants' (both poems which also draw on American Indian material), the political allusions in 'Madoc' are comically obvious. The reader is hardly likely to miss the point, given that Coleridge and Southey's colony is called 'Ulster', or the principal "narrator"

'South'. Is Muldoon poking fun at the very temptation to read political analogies into poetry? Or, perhaps less honourably, is he unwilling to stand behind his own political statement, so has to make it half a joke? It would perhaps be more plausible to take Muldoon as suggesting that the fundamental "politics" of the poem can be found as much in the exploration of language as in the overt possibilities of cultural analogy, or obvious historical parallels.

I want to return here to the issue of connections between old and new worlds, and between past and future, with which I began this discussion of Madoc. So far I have been investigating the possible meanings which lie behind a variety of connections, many of them political but not all – connections between eighteenth-century and contemporary society, nationalism and imperialism, Irish colony and American colony, past and future, myth and history, fantasy and fact, sound and picture. This list could be extended, but – rather than doing so – it may be worth focusing once more on the problem connection itself. 'Madoc' highlights this problem in several ways. As we have seen, it sometimes makes the connections so obvious that it becomes difficult to take them seriously. But at other times it draws attention to its own open nature – to the difficulty of interpretation, and of drawing conclusions from juxtapositions. The clearest example of this is provided by the philosophical history which "organises" the poem.

'Madoc' offers a bizarre take on the history of Western Philosophy – each of the poem's 233 sections is "surtitled" with the name of a philosopher. What are we to do with these titles? In one sense the chain of philosophical names, suspended in their protective square brackets above the frenetic verbal activity on the page below, suggests the impartiality and detachment of the philosophic point of view. But at the same time the philosopher's name, or the doctrine associated with that name, can scarcely be regarded as encapsulating the poetic insight expressed in the relevant section of 'Madoc'. On the contrary, the links between philosopher and poem are often of the most bizarre and tenuous kind. Connections are made through biography, etymology, philosophical argument, and sometimes all of these. Sometimes the reference is biographical (so '[Augustine]' is set in the hamlet of Carthage in New York, a reference to Augustine's birthplace), sometimes philosophical ('[Kant]': 'it stands to, well, "it stands to reason" '), sometimes the philosopher's name is the same as one of the characters in the poem (Moore, Burnet, the Seneca), and at other times the connection is built upon word-play (so '[Bacon]' features a boiled ham, as well as a reference to the way Bacon met his end, and '[Paine]' seems

to refer to the pain felt when 'Burr sends a ball through the kidneys /
and milty spleen of Alexander Hamilton'). The point about these
links, of course, is their recognition of the arbitrary, the contingent.
Philosophy gets hooked up with history in the most unpredictable
ways, which often seemed based on sheer linguistic accident. But
Muldoon's deeper point may be that history and linguistic accident
may not be so easily separated.

Poetry and philosophy, Muldoon suggests, are parallel realms
(but also connecting). Poetry offers a different form of knowledge
from philosophy, since it is able to tolerate and even pursue these
wild, apparently meaningless connections into the tangle of history
while philosophy remains suspended above it. At the same time,
poetry is different from history too, since – by cutting back and
forth between fantasy and reality, future and past – it can open us
up to new possibilities of meaning and interpretation. And the
ultimate 'key' to these possibilities, what enables us to make the
unexpected connections, is language itself.

One way in which Muldoon makes this point is through the
various writing and transcription machines which occur throughout the poem. Most obviously, there is the retinagraph which
transforms the images stored on the retina into the verbal narrative of the poem itself. But there is also the polygraph machine
invented by Jefferson which

> will automatically
> follow hand in glove
>
> his copper-plate 'whippoorwill'
> or 'praise' or 'love':
>
> will run parallel to the parallel
> realm to which it is itself the only clue.

This image of a multiplication of languages reflecting or mirroring
each other is central to the poem – it occurs again, for example, with
the backwards writing of the motto 'TOUJOURS GAI' on Merry's
seal in '[Bentham]'. The poem, Muldoon seems to be suggesting,
is a device or machine for generating such parallels, and for introducing ever further possibilities of meaning and interpretation.

Whatever else 'Madoc' is, it is an epic of language, a story told
not just through, but about language. The many connections
which the poem plays with, though they may be cultural, political,
aesthetic, are at the most basic level linguistic. Hence the mad
puns on philosophers' names, and the comically overt use of lead-
en metaphors, but also the delight in linguistic variety. It would
scarcely be possible to overstress the extent to which 'Madoc' is a

celebration of language as such. First of all, 'Madoc' makes use of a wide range of vocabularies and types of discourse. The language of the poem embraces Ulster-Scots, Irish American, and Native American, as well as eighteenth-century period discourse, the jargon of science fiction, futuristic techno-language, and Sara Fricker's private language: ' "Where's my stumparumper? My confabulumper? / My maffrum? My goffrum? My swarnish pigglepow?" ' As this example shows Muldoon evinces a pleasure in the sheer sound of language, and its capacity for precise denomination which, on several occasions, he reduces to its barest statement, the catalogue:

> Southey rests on a wannigan. Cams and cinches.
> Sprags and sprockets.
> Parakeets.
> Finches.
>
> Wrens and whimbrels.
> Tups and wethers.
> Laverocks. Leverets. Levers.
> Tumbrils.
>
> Tricoteuses and sansculottes.
> Red-shanks. Her spackled cambric.
> Ox-head. Dithyrambic.
> Tups and wethers. Boars. Sows. Gilts.
>
> The pike and carnelian sturgeon
> that will rise to this, as to every, occasion.

This is a sonnet propelled by sound, by the pleasure of language for its own sake. It reveals an intense delight in words, in the vastness and precision of vocabulary itself. We could think of the poem itself as a sort of wagon train, containing everything needed for the moment of Westward expansion in America, but also perhaps as a repository for all those words and objects which are in danger of being lost for ever. For this poem, like so much of Muldoon's work, is again preoccupied with the cyclical nature of creation and destruction, wittily imaged at one point as a woodchuck which 'has had occasion / To turn into a moccasin'. In his opera libretto *Shining Brow*, written soon after *Madoc*, Muldoon makes this point explicitly as the architect Frank Lloyd Wright philosophises, 'For everything that's built / Something is destroyed.' (The libretto is in part a send up of these notions, and the place where Muldoon finally signs off on his American Indian concerns: 'So much, then, for the domain / of the Ottawa, the Ojibwa, the Omaha Sioux, / the Potawottoman'.)

The nineteenth-century westward expansion led to the destruction of the American Indians, but it was also a moment of contact which brought new languages and knowledges, and a new vocabulary to all the protagonists. Although 'Madoc' might be regarded, from one perspective, as an elegy for the American Indians, it is impossible to ignore the new energies which are released by the clash of cultures, languages and verbal styles which occurs throughout the poem. In one sense, the characters of the poem seem to be caught up in a doomed historical process, where utopian ambitions are compromised and undermined, turning into repression and destruction. But Muldoon also hints that these cycles are never just cycles, that the energies which language itself can release prevent any such closure. Perhaps the most obvious example of this is '[Vico]', the section of 'Madoc' which Muldoon has chosen to anthologise, and one in which – for once – the thought of the presiding philosopher really does find expression in the poem:

> A hand-wringing, small, grey squirrel
> plods
> along a wicker
>
> treadmill that's attached
> by an elaborate
> system of levers
>
> and cogs and cranks
> and pulleys
> and gears…
>
> …to a wicker
> treadmill in which there plods
> a hand-wringing, small, grey squirrel.

Here the dreary, despondent cycle really does seem closed. But at the same time the exuberance of the language belies this closure. The cycles of conquest and colonisation which Muldoon explores in 'Madoc', stretching from the mythical past to the science-fiction future, might give us good reason to lapse into cynicism. Yet, all the time new energies are being released and there is a forward movement of creation which cannot be captured in circular terms.

CHAPTER SEVEN

The Prince of the Quotidian
and The Annals of Chile

To what extent can poetry can 'help us to live our lives', as Wallace Stevens suggested it might?[1] The experiments in style and form which have marked successive phases of Paul Muldoon's poetic development are, in one sense, different ways of posing this question. One answer might be that poetry helps us by offering an exemplary response to our own historical and political situation. Muldoon quotes approvingly Czeslaw Milosz's comment in *The Witness of Poetry*, 'I do not doubt...that posterity will read us in a attempt to comprehend what the twentieth century was like.'[2] But while he is willing to acknowledge its role as 'witness' to history he is clearly suspicious of any claims for poetry's ethical force, its ability to offer respite and consolation – a suspicion he puts down in part to a reaction against his religious upbringing ('all these ideas of "solace" and "succour", never mind "restitution" and "redemption" '). One of the aspects of Muldoon's work I've focused on throughout this book is the repeated failure of his poems to "add up" – to arrive at some final insight or revelation. Perhaps the most moving instance of this lack of confidence in poetic enlightenment comes at the end of 'Armageddon, Armageddon', a poem which pushes the capacities of the lyric to the limit with its tale of apocalyptic breakdown – the crisis in Northern Ireland and his mother's death. Death above all is an event beyond the control of the poet, or anyone else. In the context of the failure of religious forms of solace, the poem yearns for a different kind of consolation, yet knows such poetic resolutions are equivocal and illusory.

In Muldoon's more recent work this lack of resolution is played out in other ways. His long poems in particular are like large canvases on which a perplexing variety of elements are aggregated or juxtaposed, generating unpredictable, apparently contingent connections. It's as though the poem must register or be witness to everything, but this very inclusiveness destroys the possibility of a perspective which could bring all the elements into a subjectively meaningful order. This may indeed be the difference between poetic whim and poetic subjectivity. Just as there is no self which organises the poem (in 'Madoc' this absence is encapsulated in the way the poem is retrieved from the back of an eyeball), so there is no revelation to

be arrived at. Yet as I have discussed, this openendedness is counterpointed by a real sense of purpose and pattern – a poem like 'Madoc –
A Mystery' *is* in one sense tied up through its elaborate internal
mirroring and cross-connections. Each element provides a key to
another, creating a self-reflexive system which nonetheless resists a
state of equilibrium. It is, if you like, the expectation of a purpose
set up by such patterning that makes the lack of resolution in these
poems so acute.

The two books Muldoon published in 1994 once more take up this
question of how poetry can help to us live our lives, what it can "make
happen". In many ways the books could not be more contrasting,
but the tension between a fundamental lack of resolution and the
possibility of enlightenment or revelation is central to both. One, *The
Prince of the Quotidian*, published by the Gallery Press in Ireland,
is a sequence of lyrics written over the thirty-one days of January
1992 (the fruit, apparently, of a New Year's resolution to write a
poem a day). Among other things, the sequence charts the gestation
of his child (who was born in July of that year) as well as the first
inklings of his long poem 'Yarrow', which appears in the second
volume, *The Annals of Chile*. This is Muldoon's seventh major collection, and includes several of his most important poems to date:
'Incantata', an elegy for his former lover Mary Farl Powers, who
died in March 1993, and – another elegy of sorts, this time for his
mother – the long poem 'Yarrow'.

Both the diary sequence and the larger volume are more open,
lyrical collections than Muldoon has produced for some time, and
it is tempting to connect this with the powerful feminine presence
in the books, and to the fact that these are, among other things,
narratives of birth and death. The stimulus for the various reminiscences of the long poem is a sprig of yarrow which Muldoon plucks
from a 'funerary vase' while 'in a den in St John's, Newfoundland'.
Despite the temporal and geographical distance then, the poem
returns to the terrain of 'Armageddon, Armageddon' and his mother's
death. In the final lines of the poem Muldoon explicitly declares
himself to be at a loss, and in its tone 'Yarrow' recalls the failure
of poetic consolation of the earlier poem. To some extent this may
be because unlike his other long poems, where Muldoon was able
to determine the narrative according to his whim, there's a real
narrative behind 'Yarrow'. Real life stories don't lend themselves
to neat conclusions. Reviewing *The Annals of Chile,* Mark Ford
suggested that 'Yarrow' articulates, 'a much more organic understanding of origins and terminations than other Muldoon volumes'.[3]
We might compare for example the circular narrative of '7 Middagh

Street', a poem which begins and ends with the same line, like a serpent with its tail in its mouth. In 'Yarrow' there's a failure of articulation, something is missing. In contrast to a conventional elegy, where recovery is at play in a double sense – as the retrieval of the past, and as the healing of the bereaved person through this retrieval – in these poems there is an overwhelming sense of the failure of remembrance to preserve the past and thereby heal its wounds: poetry fails to achieve the consolation or revelation which can no longer be delivered by faith.

But beyond the specific form of the elegy, Muldoon seems to be asking what it would mean to "make sense" of one's life through remembrance, even in a tentative way which no longer offers solace and reconciliation? 'Yarrow' is built upon the idea of revisiting or replaying the past in an attempt to understand it. Despite its lyrical and elegiac tone, there is a complex architectural form underlying the reminiscences, modelled on the strict repetitive rhyming structure of the sestina. Muldoon has admitted that the poem, 'uses repetition in a way that wouldn't have occurred to me before *Shining Brow*',[4] his opera libretto based on episodes in the life of the architect Frank Lloyd Wright. The long-range, 'architectural' sense of rhythm and reiteration which Muldoon strove for in the libretto appears again in the form of recurrent phrases, and recurrent episodes, whose significance shifts from context to context. In one sense we could think of this underlying structure as more natural or organic than the repetitions and parallel worlds of 'Madoc', for example; it grows out of the work of memory and Muldoon's basic sense of temporality as repetition and return. In its search for enlightenment through a return to the past, the poem could almost be thought of as a version of the therapeutic talking cure.

The language of cure is explicit in *The Annals of Chile*. At a fundamental level the volume is about healing, and the failure to heal. The two long poems are elegies for women who died of cancer. In them the search for a cure – through conventional medicine or herbal remedies – is indistinguishable from the search for consolation and relief from suffering. Each of the characters in these poems clings to a different form of consolation: sex, drugs, fatalism, God. Indeed, in terms of the mother's strongly held Catholic faith, religious consolation and eventual relief from suffering (through death) are the same. But the notion of a cure involves ideas of improvement or making progress as well as the achievement of an encompassing perspective, and Muldoon is suspicious of both. Instead he seems to be looking for ways of returning to the past which are not based on notions of discovery and development. Just as in *Quoof*

the cure took the form of a violent purging, so here Muldoon is
concerned to maintain rather than resolve the contradictory pull
of events, to allow the past its ineluctable weight, without transforming it into myth, a nostalgic history of origins. Annals might
seem the perfect vehicle for a poetry which resists a narrative of
discovery. Annals preserve or record historical events but they do
so in an impassive way, in the form of chronicles; they are narratives which trace time rather than offer an interpretation of the
past, and an integrating perspective.

But Muldoon is not just thinking abstractly about what kind of
perspective we can have on the past. He is concerned with how
poetry can best measure up to the contemporary world. Both *The
Prince of the Quotidian* and *The Annals of Chile* reflect on the impact
of a global culture in which television, video and news broadcasts
can make events on the other side of the world as immediate, if not
more immediate, than those at home; in which the very notion of
home as a place of return is put into question. One of the questions
Muldoon is asking is how it is possible to withstand this total disorientation of the senses, without appealing to notions of an inner
stability or authenticity, or relying on ways of organising experience
which could overcome its incoherences. If Enlightenment notions of
technical and scientific progress have led to this jumbling of temporal and spatial relations, then a poetry which is to respond to this
cultural confusion can't simply reproduce, in its ways of returning to
and retrieving the past, the narratives of progress which led to the
dislocation in the first place. But nor is Muldoon happy simply to
mirror this confusion in his art. How, then, to write a poem which
is "up to" our channel-surfing universe, in which we have access to
everything and nothing at the same time? We might recall here
Wallace Stevens's insistence that the pressure of reality in the modern
world requires of the poet the creation of a new relationship between
the imagination and reality. 'The pressure of an external event or
events on the consciousness to the exclusion of any power of contemplation' is resisted not by the wholly idealistic 'noble rider'.
Rather 'it is a violence from within that protects us from a violence
from without. It is the imagination pressing back against the pressure of reality.'[5] Stevens was writing during the Second World War,
which first made the world a global theatre, and which launched
the era of telecommunications and mass consumption. Muldoon's
work begins from the conviction that if poetry is to 'make things
happen' it's not by overcoming hurt or shoring up a kind of mythic
integrity – instead it needs to create a form of healing that doesn't
gloss over the violence from within. The pressure of reality cannot

be combatted by an idealised inner harmony, but only be an equal and opposite force. Clery's trick at the end of 'Twice' ('Two places at once was it? Or one place twice?'), suggests that the special power of poetry to evade the normal constraints of identity and location may be the best counter to the chaos around us.

The overlapping and redoubling of time and space, the entanglements of history and geography, are explored in both these books in terms of connections between Ireland and the Americas, between North and South, between the old world and the new. The link between Ireland and Chile first appears in the "diary" sequence, *The Prince of the Quotidian*. In many ways this book reads like a perverse repetition of the concerns of 'Madoc'; it isn't clear how far the parallel is intentional, but it is certainly marked. Both poems track journeys through the north-eastern United States, both feature a talking horse as guide, both meditate on emigration, on connections between art and politics, and between Ireland and America, both even set up eighteenth-century parallels. The exaggerated difference between them lies in the very personal, conversational tone of *The Prince*, as opposed to the elaborately distanced, mechanised voice of 'Madoc'. Muldoon's "January journal" differs from much of his work in that the poems are very clearly dealing with 'quotidian' encounters, events and actions, as well as exploring everyday rhythms of speech and thought. Muldoon writes about marking student essays, going to the opera, watching videos, deciding where to go on holiday, his concerns about his dinner guests. But he also touches on deeper issues. He considers, for example, the politics of Northern Ireland's culture industry ('the casuistry // by which pianists and painters and poets are proof / that all's not rotten in the state'), as well as the relation between his own experience living in the United States and the continuing violence in Northern Ireland.

This tension between the 'trivial' (as Muldoon terms it) and the important is mirrored in the composition of the sequence. Muldoon maintains a familiar balance between formal narrative patterning (including rhythmic and verbal echoes, as well as traditional verse forms such as sonnets, terza rima, couplets and so on), and an informal conversational style. Rhyme becomes an almost subliminal structuring element, as 'mulch' rhymes with 'Milosz', 'MLA' with 'homily', and 'parachute' with 'Saint Brigid'. The gossipy tone of the book, and in particular the liberal use of proper names, recall the work of Frank O'Hara (although Muldoon's sequence is far more formal and structured, less spontaneous than O'Hara's *Lunch Poems*). Muldoon obliquely signals his debt in the first poem, in which O'Hara appears, seemingly offering some advice on modes of transport, gleaned from his own death in a beach-buggy accident:

> Yet another wore a caul
> made from a beach-towel edged with a blue flower;
>
> 'Try,' he said, 'try not to confuse carrus, a cart,
> with carina, a keel...'

This piece of advice is offered as Muldoon and his wife drive out of Manhattan through the Holland tunnel. (Significantly perhaps they are leaving O'Hara's urban environment for the very different rural and suburban landscape of Princeton, New Jersey.) Within the tunnel under the river their vehicle is something between car and boat, or it floats between the elements, as another poem puts it, of 'surf and turf'. The question of what type of vessel to use on this narrative journey (or journey through 1992) is therefore crucial, and indeed this is only the first of several pieces of advice Muldoon is offered. (His other guides include a goldfinch and, of course, the by now ubiquitous talking horse.)

The image of a ship or keel (carina) is taken up several times during the sequence, raising the question of where and whether we are "anchored" in the contemporary world. In a related vein the sequence seems to ask how meaning is anchored or held firm in the context of an "everyday" poetry in which elements are gleaned from diverse contexts. Employing the characteristic Muldoonian trick of offering contradictory advice on how to read it, one poem offers an ironic apology for the 'trivial' nature of the sequence, and at the same time suggests that for some this randomness has purpose:

> none will,
> I trust, look for a pattern in this crazy quilt
> where all is random, 'all so trivial',
>
> unless it be Erasmus, unless
> Erasmus again steel
> himself as his viscera are cranked out by a windlass
>
> yard upon 'xanthous' yard;
> again to steel himself, then somehow to exhort
> the windlass-men to even greater zeal.

Even for readers used to Muldoon's habit of including learned references, this is a bizarre allusion, especially in the context of a conversational sequence. Here the Reformation figure Erasmus becomes anchored by his own intestines, suggesting that the body is indeed a vessel in which to undertake a journey – whether carrus or carina. This poem suggests that anchorage is physical and indeed physiological (even deadly), but the sequence as a whole reflects on the function of family and community in grounding the individual. Family connections are also partly physical of course, as the corporeal link with the mother reminds us. While *Annals* seems concerned above all with a reworking of the history of Muldoon's childhood (and to a lesser extent his more recent past), *The Prince of the Quotidian* takes on childhood in another fashion, in charting the gestation of Muldoon's own offspring.

Of course the body of a pregnant woman is indeed a vessel for another, and this theme is echoed in the poems in *Annals* which are concerned with the birth of Muldoon's daughter. In 'The Birth' the umbilicus becomes a form of anchor, and the nurses on duty during the caesarean section are 'windlass-women'. Here the question of being in or out of "one's element" is concentrated on the border between inside and outside the mother's body. In a more general sense the poems seems to be asking about "belonging". In what sense does childhood anchor you – give you an identity in the flux of contemporary global culture? How far do origins within a particular family, culture and national history determine the future? Undoubtedly, part of the spur to Muldoon's consideration of these issues is a fear of the repetition of familial history. In becoming a father will he reproduce not only a child, but the structure of his own childhood? Just as Muldoon suggests that the late twentieth century is not necessarily more enlightened than the eighteenth, here the related concern is about whether the contemporary father can become different, can progress.

The Prince begins with the borrowing of a bassinet, and the baby is increasingly "realised" throughout the sequence – as we are given the visual image of the foetus on an ultrasound scan, the prospective birthdate, and the fact that she is female. Later he 'can hardly refrain' from letting slip her chosen name, Dorothy Aoife, in a telephone conversation. It is in relation to the baby's due date that the idea of the relationship between a significant date in Northern Ireland's "replaying" of history and the 'Annals of Chile' is first introduced:

> That our child's due date is the Twelfth of July –
> the anniversary of the birth of Neruda
> but a red-letter day in El Norte
> rather than Chile –
>
> is an irony that won't escape
> the famous "Longalley" or the famous "Montagael"

The reference here is to the Northern Irish poets Michael Longley and John Montague, though of course this irony won't now escape any of us, since he so carefully points it out. The Twelfth of July is the most important date in the Orange marching season – the day when Northern Irish Protestants celebrate the victory of King William III at the Battle of the Boyne in 1690. It is the occasion

for a show of strength on the part of Unionists and a day traditionally dreaded by Catholic inhabitants of Northern Ireland.

The link between Ireland and South America, between poetry
(Neruda) and politics, must remind us of the teasing connections
Muldoon explored in *Madoc* – though the South American fantasy
has of course a much longer pedigree in his work, stretching back
to the hacienda in *Why Brownlee Left*, or Pancho Villa in *Mules*.
Connections between "North" and "South" are forged throughout
the sequence through the details of everyday life, as well as more
pointed historical markers. For example, one of the activities that
Muldoon and his wife are engaged in during January is leafing
through holiday travel literature on Louisiana and the Southern
States. Such reading (as well as visual images in still photographs,
film and video) serves to transport the reader across time and space.
At one point Muldoon is translated in another direction, to the
West of Ireland:

> As I coasted into the tunnel
> of the Pennington car wash
> I glanced at my copy of *Feis*
> By Nuala Ní Dhomhnaill:
>
> a wave broke over a rock
> somewhere west of Dingle;
> my windshield was a tangle
> of eel-grass and bladderwrack.

As in *The Annals* (where it's boy's adventure fiction, epic and romance), it's the very old-fashioned pastime of reading which makes the
world contract in this way. Reading – as well as more recent modes
of communication such as film and TV – can obliterate cultural
distances, but at the same time create experiences of tremendous
force and local particularity. Part of the point here is surely that you
can be anywhere in your imagination. Certainly for many emigrants
Ireland is a place they carry with them, but Muldoon goes further by
implying that imagination renders travel redundant. At one level such
fantasy transportations mirror the dissolution of geographical boundaries caused by modern global connections. Modern consumer society
creates a 'café of the world', in which anything available for experience anywhere. Muldoon is both delighted and troubled by this new
internationalism. The title-poem of the sequence is a celebration
of the almost surreal collisions and juxtapositions it throws up:

> 'Let him,' I heard, 'let him be one ignited by the quaint
>
> in this new quotidian: a mound
> of coffee beans in the 'Café du Monde';
> the New Orleans School of Cookery's
> okra-

monious gumbo; a dirigible of Paul Prudhomme
floating above the Superdome;
let the Prince of the Quotidian lead an alligator

along the *banquette* of Decatur
yet let him not, with Alejandro O'Reilly,
forget the cries of the bittern and the curlew.'

Written on the birth of his Irish-Canadian nephew, this is a picture of global Irishness, which Muldoon seems to be presenting as yet another version of the "real" thing. With international flavour part of his formative experience, the child's identity will not be defined by narrow national, ethnic or religious boundaries. (Is there an echo here of Wallace Steven's well-known lines: 'Let be be finale of seem. / The only emperor is the emperor of ice-cream.' – except that rather than a finale, Muldoon's poem sounds an overture for his nephew's life?) But what is the significance of the reference to Alejandro O'Reilly? The name looks like a joke version of a Spanish Irishman or an Irish Spaniard (like Dalí as O'Daly in '7 Middagh Street'), a comically obvious embodiment of the geographical connections between North and South. In fact Alejandro O'Reilly was an Irish mercenary who fought for the Spanish in the mid-eighteenth century, and was rewarded with the governorship of Cuba. From there he invaded Louisiana and annexed New Orleans on behalf of Catholic Royalist Spain. Is Muldoon suggesting that the Irish diaspora has anticipated the contemporary globalisation of culture? That "modernity", in the guise of dislocation and national fragmentation, has been an element of Irish experience for centuries? There is, I think, a more specific point at issue here. As Muldoon has repeatedly stressed, particularly with reference to Native American histories, the Irish diaspora cannot be understood only as a modern or postmodern condition, but needs to be placed in the context of its roots in the seventeenth and eighteenth centuries – hence his frequent gestures towards historical links between the old world and the new through trade, colonisation, exile, and of course the figure of the mercenary. O'Reilly appears as the latest in a long line of Muldoonian mercenaries, which includes Gallogly, from 'The More a Man Has', and Alexander Cinnamond from 'Madoc'.

As if that reference weren't cryptic enough, we still have to make sense of the bittern and curlew. These birds, like the corncrake, have tremendous resonances in Irish literature (and despite their international feel both *The Prince* and *Annals* are very bound up with old Irish literary texts). The cries here are those of 'The Yellow Bittern', an eighteenth-century poem which partly reflects the bitterness born of the experience of post-plantation Ireland.[6] Is it then that

O'Reilly, in becoming a royalist mercenary, has forgotten the political lessons – of repression and dispossession – that he should
have learned in Ireland?

There is undoubtedly something maddening about such references. It's not just that they are obscure, but that they are totally
idiosyncratic. Irish readers may be familiar with the resonances of
the bittern and the curlew, but at a loss compared with Americans
when it comes to 'Decatur' (while English readers possibly fare
worst of all). The references mirror not only the contemporary
cultural patchwork which is the subject of the poem, but the writer's
own obsessions. It's almost as though we are required to become
the poet in order to follow his logic fully. There's a sense in which
this tantalising obscurity lends the poetry a certain glamour (the
more outlandish the allusions, the more intriguing they become).
Yet at the same time such learned displays are provoking. Is he
merely showing off? It is perhaps the element of doubt about
Muldoon's technique which such allusions keep in play that is their
real value – it's almost impossible to gauge how to read them.

Retain the memory of your national history, even as you enjoy
the deracinated pleasures of the café du monde. It's far from clear
how far Muldoon stands behind this, the apparent statement of
the poem (he writes that he 'heard' it rather than thought it). And
given the density of allusion, its almost impossible to unpack the
subtleties, or pin the poem down. One of the ways you might choose
to read this emphasis on powerful anti-Republican Irishmen in the
new world, is as a criticism of an exclusive emphasis on the figure
of the Irishman or woman as victim or exile. And Muldoon certainly has things to say about this. In a characteristically double-
edged way, he offers as his epigraph for the book an extract from
a letter by the leader of the United Irishmen, Wolfe Tone, detailing his 'exile' in Princeton (where Muldoon now teaches). And at
the same time Muldoon rejects the suggestion that as a poet he is
exiled in the States, instead transposing the idea of exile to rural
Northern Ireland ('I'm not "in exile", / though I can't deny / that
I've been twice in Fintona.'). Again, partly what is at issue here is
a question of how the poet is grounded, what can and should be his
element. At the same time Muldoon undercuts the idea that exile
and alienation from the community comes only with travel and
geographic displacement. Fintona, a small town in County Tyrone
became renowned throughout Ireland in the 1950s following a
documentary film, made partly in secret, exposing organised discrimination against Catholics (particularly over housing). Being at
home, Muldoon implies, is not at all the same thing as feeling at

one with where you are. Imaginative escape is an obvious recourse for those who are made to feel their presence is somehow illegitimate, like Catholics on the 12th of July. Just as the emigrant remains at home in imagination, wherever he may be, those at home are already elsewhere.

There is a danger of over-reading *The Prince*; it is for the most part a light, even a slight work, and Muldoon is characteristically cagey about how impromptu and true to life the narrative really is. But whether the diary can be taken as literally true or not, the mood which comes across is one in which Muldoon still feels hugely connected to his past. It is surely significant that the book was published only in Ireland – is he still uncertain of his milieu? He meets Irish writers, hears news of murders in the Moy, imagines he's in Dingle when he drives into a carwash. At one level such encounters suggest that it doesn't matter where you are, since Ireland is a place in the imagination anyway. On the other hand it could be regarded as a rather troubling aspect of the book that all "real" news – as opposed to "trivial" events – is connected with Ireland, except for news about the baby. Where is Muldoon to seek his inspiration? Is it to be found in the past only, and in the Ireland of his imagination? At one point in the sequence Muldoon is assailed by 'the pressure of reality':

> I open the freezer. The blood-besmirched
> face of Kevin McKearney
> implores me from a hospital gurney;
> 'Won't you at least visit my grave in March?'

Here the power of imagination alone no longer seems adequate. Or perhaps we should say that the imagination points beyond itself, to a realm of ethical duties which must be allowed their own force. The murder victim suggests that a physical journey, a real return is required in order for the poet to fulfil his obligations to the dead. Yet the implication of these Heaneyesque lines is more complex than might at first appear. Even as they point to an ethical duty, an obligation to remember, which lies beyond poetry, they suggest that the power of the imagination to vault across time and space is central to our moral awareness.

Nevertheless these lines *are* a prelude to a real return, anticipating Muldoon's trip to Ireland in the Spring of 1992 (although the grave he visits is that of his parents, as the villanelle 'Milkweed and Monarch' records). *The Annals of Chile* is structured by this motif of return, which is entwined with the revisioning of Muldoon's relation to his mother. (The talking horse who appears in the final section of *The Prince of the Quotidian* insists: 'you must atone / for everything you've said and done / against your mother'.) The image of the mother, of course, has a particular resonance in Irish politics and culture. For generations of writers 'Mother Ireland' has stood for an essentially simple and untainted rural nation, dominated and despoiled by a ruthless neighbour. But Muldoon suggests that neither the mother nor the country can be understood in this way, in terms of an original purity resistant to alien intrusion. Thoughout *The Annals of Chile* his home in the Moy is associated with South America, the kernel of this fantasy being the pampas grass which grew outside the house. Pampas grass was introduced into Ireland by emigrants returned from Argentina, but it is merely one of the clearer examples of an exotic import. Things become more complicated when we think of the yarrow plant, an imported seed which colonises the farm in Muldoon's childhood fantasy. We might assume Muldoon was on safer ground in taking the potato as a mnemonic device in 'Incantata'. But when we consider that the potato, that plant most strongly associated with Ireland, was also introduced, this time by Walter Raleigh, then the notion of an uncontaminated origin starts to look decidedly suspect. The allusions to eighteenth-century Irish adventurers which appear throughout the volume also point in the same direction. It is not that rural Ireland was once pristine and self-contained, but has now been opened up to a global traffic. Throughout Muldoon's work home is less a secure point of departure and return than a place of elsewheres. The exotic – and the erotic – lie just below the suface of the familiar and the everyday.

'Brazil' is a poem deeply concerned with such questions of time and space, as well as femininity. The title conjures at once Brazil – the South American country, and Hy Breasil, the Isle of the Blest. Here, as in 'Immrama' and other poems in *Why Brownlee Left*, the land of the blest becomes associated with South America, but now it is the mother rather than the father who becomes imaginatively connected with it. Moreover while 'Immrama' offered the father's life in Brazil as an alternative to his life at home, here the worlds of imagination and actuality are one:

> When my mother snapped open her flimsy parasol
> it was Brazil: if not Brazil,
>
> then Uruguay.
> One nipple darkening her smock.
>
> My shame-faced *Tantum Ergo*
> struggling through thurified smoke.

This blessed land, the farm, the home is bound up with both maternal sexuality (the mother's body) and Catholicism (the thurified smoke, the font) with all its prohibitions. It is the concatenation of the two which embarrasses him. The poem charts an imaginative transformation of home into South America, the Far East, the South Seas:

> Later that afternoon would find
> me hunched over the font
>
> as she rinsed my hair. Her towel-turban.
> Her terrapin
>
> comb scuttling under the faucet.
> I stood there in my string vest
>
> and shorts while she repeated 'Champi...?
> Champi...? Champi...?' Then,
>
> that bracelet of shampoo
> about the bone, her triumphant 'ChampiÑON'.

Objects become 'exoticised': her towel a turban, her comb a terrapin. French mushrooms become Spanish (or possibly Portuguese?), signalling a similar process of "translating" words and concepts from the old to the new world. In keeping with this, the mother, and the home, are represented as opening out to the rest of the world. So far from being a restrictive influence the mother here acts as a route into the exotic, the far away.

The poem is in part a consideration of what things are and what they are not (though this is not Brazil, and not Uruguay it might have been – the imagination has the power to transform the everyday into the exotic). 'ChampiÑON' shouts prohibition, but the mother's body is an arena of desire nonetheless. (The bracelet of shampoo recalls Donne's bracelet of hair by which his love will be revealed even in the grave):

> If not Uruguay, then Ecuador:
> it must be somewhere on or near the equator
>
> given how water
> plunged headlong into water
>
> when she pulled the plug.
> So much for the obliq-
>
> uity of leaving What a Boy Should Know
> under my pillow: now vagina and vas
>
> deferens made a holy show
> of themselves. 'There is inherent vice
>
> in everything,' as O'Higgins
> would proclaim: it was O'Higgins who duly
>
> had the terms 'widdershins'
> and 'deasil' expunged from the annals of Chile.

It would be foolish to try to claim mastery over the interpretation of this poem – the enigma is part of the point. Nonetheless one element which emerges strongly is a concern with the relation of top and bottom, up and down, and with the descending movement from one to the other. The first two sections of the poem reveal glimpses of the upper body – the nipple revealed through the smock (presumably during breastfeeding), the boy's chest seen through his string vest. The last section suggests that such half-veiled nakedness (diaphanous substances abound here, from the flimsy parasol cover to the swirling incense at the altar) is far more revealing than one might expect: '*vagina* and *vas / deferens* made a holy show / of themselves'. This translation of top into bottom, breast to genitals, parallels the translation of North into South, which in turn suggests a position on the border, the equator, between the northern and southern hemispheres. Space is collapsed as, for a moment, the place which mother and son inhabit in this poem is neither north or south.

The final lines are extraordinarily oblique, piling layer upon layer of meaning. We are confronted with a puzzle – what's the connection between Muldoon's hair wash and Chile? Driven to the encyclopaedia we find that Bernardo O'Higgins, like Alejandro O'Reilly, was an Irishman "translated" into the southern hemisphere (or son of such a man, Ambrosio O'Higgins – who was both a mercenary fighting for Spain, and later Governor of Chile). O'Higgins was partly educated in England, where he became imbued with the ideals of republicanism and the Enlightenment, and later fought the Spanish to become leader of an independent Chile. He thus "translates" liberty into Spanish, brings it from the old to the new world. Clearly, O'Higgins represents an alternative to O'Reilly here, and also perhaps offers a blueprint for a son looking for a way not to reproduce in the image of his father. O'Higgins overturns the work of his father in the service of Catholic and Royalist Spain. He introduces Enlightenment ideals into the new Chilean Republic, even taking action against Catholic ritual and superstition. He bridges the gap between North and South, and thus, like the mother, embodies the fusion of the familiar and the strange.

But as well as the bridging or disappearance of the border, the poem also imagines the redundancy of left and right, as the circling of water in either direction is overridden by gravity. 'Widdershins' and 'deasil' mean turning to the left and to the right, against the sun and with the sun, and so anti-clockwise and clockwise. There is a link here with 'Yarrow', for, as Muldoon tells us in the long poem, the name of the local seed merchant Tohill's (which figures crucially in the poem) is the anglicisation of Tuathal, 'meaning withershins – with its regrettable overtones of sun worship'. But also lurking in this thicket of associations is the etymological sense of 'North' (tuaidh) and, not surprisingly, 'South' too (deiscart). The North is therefore associated with turning to the left and the South with turning to the right.

The stark moral struggle implied here is central to the meaning of the poem. Muldoon has suggested that that the world of 'Brazil' is 'seen from the point of view of an altar-boy…a world in which everything tends either to go straight up or, more likely, straight down',[7] where damnation and punishment, the road to hell, are only one false step away. As 'Yarrow' makes clear, the mother's concern is to keep her son on the right moral and religious track, to insulate him from the ungodly wrack and ruin she sees around her. But this very severity and repressiveness, particularly in sexual matters (Lear's 'But to the girdle do the gods inherit' is one of her favourite tags), intensifies the boy's embarrassment as the mother's body itself becomes exoticised and sexualised. The crucial point, of course, is that censorship and restriction are not the simple contrary of sinful imagination and sexual licence. It is the very veiling of the upper body which incites awareness of the sexual organs (that flimsy parasol put up to shield the breast-feeding mother itself quite literally turns "against the sun", leads the boy to sinful thoughts). The strict, repressive mother does not simply contain and control the child, but herself embodies an imaginative path towards the exotic and the forbidden. Indeed, it is this thought which holds together what seem to be the wildly disparate parts of the poem. For O'Higgins imbues the terms 'widdershins' and 'deasil' with intense imaginative force in the very act of excising them from the record. Expunged from an unwritten text, they become the sole marks of its ghostly existence.

'Brazil' like 'Twice' gives us a double vision – mother as erotic focus, and as source of moral and religious prohibition. Yet, as always with Muldoon, there is another level of allusion here, for 'widdershins' and 'deasil' are also words used by Yeats and Joyce. This is more than a nod at the power of Ireland's two great writers, however, for in some sense they represent alternative currents in Irish culture. Moreover both terms are introduced in connection with women. Yeats uses 'withershins' to describe the power of Lady Gregory to create an intellectual community in 'Coole Park, 1929'. Significantly, he imagines a form of progress and enlightenment which is not linear or teleological: 'The intellectual sweetness of those lines / That cut through time or cross it withershins'. Joyce

employs the term 'deasil' in connection with maternity and childbirth in 'Oxen of the Sun' – so this word too conjures a particular
relation between women and time, a form of cyclical reproduction
rather than paternal, linear succession.

Clearly we could carry on almost indefinitely tracking down
allusions in this way, and the activity has its own fascination. At
the same time it's important not to delude ourselves into thinking
that by following up the ramifying connections we will penetrate
ever more deeply into the heart of the poem. 'Brazil' has something peculiarly rebus-like about it, an elliptical compression which
resists rather than invites interpretation. In a way entirely typical
of Muldoon's poems, the associations seem to pull in many different directions, rather than converging towards a semantic core. The
terms widdershins and deasil, and their connections with femininity
and with circular movement are certainly not the "key" to 'Brazil',
but they can take us on an instructive journey through the volume
as a whole.

Take, for example, the thick lens of ice in 'Twice', a circle which
reveals a glimpse of a parallel world, and allows you to see double.
This perspective on the past is mirrored by the circular verse forms
which Muldoon employs throughout the volume: the villanelle, the
sestina, terza rima – all are based on repetition, doing things not
just twice but again and again. These circling forms, as Muldoon
employs them, are filled with the obsessiveness of powerful emotion.
One of the implications here is that it is wrong to think of formal
control as the antithesis of authentic feeling – indeed that tightly
controlled and "conventional" forms may be the best vehicle for the
expression of overwhelming feeling. But there is, I think, something
else at issue here – the question of memory as repetition. The fram-
ing narrative of 'Yarrow' has the poet idly watching television,
zapping the remote control. We are plunged into a channel surfing
universe, a violent disorientation of the senses, but the disordered
flow of images which passes before us, while far from from any
notion of recollection in tranquillity, is not just an assault on our
access to the past. The world of TV and video also structures and
sustains the narrative of the poem. The abrupt and arbitrary switch-
ing from programme to programme triggers a jumble of memories
of the last thirty years. But these scenes are less recollections than
a return of fragments of the past in which both poet and reader
find themselves immersed. There is an extraordinary vividness
and immediacy to the episodes – it is as though they are happening now, or happening again. Like Yeats's swallows, the circles of
the poem cut through time, enacting not return but repetition.

At the beginning of the poem the yarrow (mistakenly planted instead of vegetable marrow!) threatens to overwhelm the father's vegetable patch, giving rise to the fear that 'all would be swept away':

> Little by little it dawned on us that the row
> of kale would shortly be overwhelmed by these pink
> and cream blooms, that all of us
>
> would be overwhelmed, that even if my da
> were to lose an arm
> or a leg to the fly-wheel
>
> of a combine and be laid out on a tarp
> in a pool of blood and oil
> and my ma were to make one of her increasingly rare
>
> appeals to some higher power, some *Deo*
> this or that, all would be swept away by the stream
> that fanned across the land.

The pink and cream blooms are those of the plant yarrow. Muldoon has said that the poem was sparked off by the visit to his childhood home in March 1992, when he saw that, due to the changes which had been done to the house, all, bar the pampas grass in the garden in which he had lain to read as a child, had been swept away. The poem presents a kind of imagined foreknowledge of change (due in reality to the death of his parents and the sale of their house). Yet these lines are puzzling; for why should Muldoon suggest that all would be overwhelmed 'even if' his father were to suffer some terrible accident? The implication is that the mother's invocation of a "deus ex machina" will fail – this is to be an epic without gods. An additional irony is latent in the fact that being overwhelmed by yarrow is (in part) a positive, healing thing. Yarrow, or *Achillea millefolium*, is a curative herb, a plant for stopping nose-bleeds – so called because Achilles is reputed to have discovered its use. The healing yarrow is thus both the problem and the possible cure in a poem which asks how it is possible to express emotion without being overwhelmed or swept away by it – how to lose yourself, without becoming lost.

Though the gods may be absent, the poem is certainly epic in terms of its length (and it is almost impossible to give a real sense of it in a short space); but it is also a record of Muldoon's own epic journey back from his current life in the United States to the Ireland of his childhood, when his mother was still alive. That this is a modern epic is signalled by the fact that he is accompanied on his quest for understanding by a predecessor, 'my trusty Camoëns' (whose poem *The Lusiads* was based on the Portuguese voyages of discovery). The poem presents many bizarre and often

hilarious vignettes from Muldoon's childhood, all filtered through
his boyhood reading of quests, mysteries and adventures. Moreover
the poem is as weighted with literary allusions as 'Madoc – A
Mystery'. The poem is set up as a retrospective on the previous
thirty years of Muldoon's life, with the winter of 1963 as a central
focus (although 1973 and 1983 are also important dates in the
poem, dominated by the figure S- – for sex? – as much as by his
parents). The many literary allusions are sparked in the main by
the boy's reading (although the references to film and cinema going
are equally important, and some literary references, for example to
Sylvia Plath, are links drawn in retrospect, since she died in 1963).
Among the child's favourite authors are Rider Haggard, Sir Walter
Scott and Alexander Dumas (the conflict between supporters of
the Cardinal and those of the Queen in *The Three Musketeers* serves
as an imaginative displacement for battles between the UDA and
the IRB., with the spy Milady Clark playing a central role on both
sides of the ideological divide!). Then there are the narratives which
enable specific imaginative connections with South America, or
the South Seas: *Treasure Island*; Jack Shaefer's *Shane* (the story of
an enigmatic cowboy of Irish extraction, and a battle over land);
the story of one man's ride from south to north America with his
horses Mancho and Gato, *Tschiffley's Ride*. And despite the child
Muldoon's antipathy to the old Irish texts foisted on him by his
mother in the poem, his world is seen through the lens of medieval
epics such as *The Song of Roland*, Malory's *Morte d'Arthur*, and
(to add a Portuguese flavour) Camoëns's *The Lusiads*. The confusions generated by this plethora of films and books are compounded
by the child's fluid boundaries between reality and fiction. He is
forever transforming into adventurers in his imagination, as well
confusing the members of his own family with characters from
adventure fiction, epic and medieval romance.

One might think that a poem largely woven from travel fantasies
and imaginative journeyings would lose touch with any stable sense
of place or ground. But throughout its length 'Yarrow' keeps looping back to the family farm, and to the figures of the parents with
their contrasting roles in the life of the child. With characteristic
delicacy Muldoon sustains a sense of familiarity, of home as a site
of longing and return, while at the same time revealing how dislocation and displacement are at work long before any physical
emigration. Not surprisingly, the mother in 'Yarrow' bears a great
similarity to her counterpart in 'Brazil'. She is intensely religious,
obsessed with the ever-present danger of sin (the most pressing form
of which, for the young Muldoon, is masturbation), and almost

comically puritanical: 'hers is a sensibility so rare / that I'll first know Apuleius / as the author of *The Golden Beam*'. But repression leads to obsession: sex is everywhere in 'Yarrow', most obviously embodied in the figure of S-, the drug-addicted young woman whose story weaves through the poem, and whose very name may be a cipher for it. In some respects the figure of S- is an alter-ego, a perverse double of the mother. Both die, one from drugs and one hoping for a cure through drugs; both are obsessed with sex (as something to be strictly avoided or recklessly indulged in); S- even offers a perverse version of the mother's faith: 'should it happen / that he's lost his bit of Latin, / she would nevertheless have been understood by God / to whom she appealed at every twist and turn'. In short, the women circle 'widdershins' and 'deasil'.

The repressed and repressive mother's association with danger-ous sexuality is wittily, if obliquely, signalled in the recurring pic-ture we get of her ordering seeds by catalogue from the local seed merchants, Tohill's of the Moy. This is hardly the kind of activity you'd expect to give rise to dirty thoughts, except perhaps in one so practised at 'winkling the semen out of semantics':

> 'Wither' as in 'widdersinnes', meaning to turn
> against the sun: she ticks off 'carrots', 'parsnips', 'swedes'   .
> while I suffer
>
> the tortures of the damned, imagining myself a Shackleton
> frozen by fire;
> 'parsnips', 'swedes'; for, unless I manage to purge
>
> myself of concupiscent thoughts and keep a weather-eye open
> for the least occasion of sin, the Gates
> of Glory will be barred to me, not being pure of heart.

It's the economy of this representation which makes it so funny. In a few lines Muldoon presents us with a vivid and a telling pic-ture of family life. The boy's anxiety is comic not only because it's extreme, but because it's so inappropriate to the circum-stances. Muldoon achieves this in part through abrupt changes in measure, as the boy's racing thoughts (it's almost as though he's looking over his shoulder for the arrival of the avenging angel), are interrupted by his mother's regular, methodical activity – dependable, if somewhat stern. Then there's the tremendous clashing of registers, as parsnips and swedes rub up against over-heard moralistic clichés and nuggets of schoolboy wisdom. The jaunty tone of the lines comes across as almost self-protective or defensive, but it's also poignant, as Muldoon lets us see through this verbal screen to the boy's confusion.

For 'Yarrow' is also about confusion and loss. One of the central 'events' of the poem is the child Muldoon's loss of the carbon slip order for the seeds. The loss of this slip leads to further 'slip' as the child misremembers or confuses 'marrow' with 'yarrow', leading to an imagined agricultural nightmare in which he purchases not the vegetable seed needed for his father's market gardening, but the flowering plant, and the rogue seedlings then seed themselves across the arable land. The poem plays with the structure of a *bildungsroman*, or narrative of development, except that development never seems to occur. The child certainly loses innocence, he 'slips' from innocence into knowledge (imaged in the deshabillée white slip of his dreams). But at the same time as charting a loss of childhood innocence (and hence a gain in knowledge), the poem also circles around the loss of 'secret' knowledge. In part the poem is confusing because something is missing. As Muldoon puts it at the very end of the poem, something has been 'forgotten or disavowed' – would the retrieval of this repressed element clear up the confusion, make things fit, tender relief?

As Muldoon has stated, this is a poem 'about a deep-seated hurt', a hurt which may be at root spiritual but which is mirrored in physical pain. Violence and bloody noses (yarrow, we may recall, is a cure for nose-bleeds) are associated with the father in the poem, but at issue is not only the violence done to the father, but the violence done by him. The father appears in a very different light to that cast by Muldoon's earlier work, such as 'The Coney' or 'The Fox'. The tenderness and protectiveness of the son towards the father in these poems is displaced, as the father grows into a fearsome figure – firstly through the mutation of rhyming words. Towards the beginning of 'Yarrow', the father is 'quiet, almost craven'; this transmutes into Arthur Cravan, the 'poet-pugilist' lover of Mina Loy; this in turn transmutes into 'Artillutteur Ecrivain' – fighter writer; and then 'Agravain' – the fearful character from *Morte d'Arthur*.

The father's awful strength is first of all revealed on the occasion when:

> where my da took a turf-spade to poleaxe
>
> one of McParland's poley cows
> that had run amuck on our spread,
> bringing it to its knees by dint of a wallop so great
>
> it must have ruptured a major vein,
> such was the spout
> of, like, blood that hit him full in the face.

Later the blood on his face is his own when, in a manner reminiscent of Popeye, he loses his temper with his Protestant neighbour: 'all I remember was the sudden rush / of blood from his nose, a rush of blood and snatters'. Throughout most of the long poem however, the father is associated with a violence the son fears will be turned against himself. His father becomes 'Agravain of the Hard Hand', or even 'Agravyn à la Dure Mayn' – a fearful character who disapproves of the child's reading. As he travels on his imaginative journeys in and around the barn, his actions are punctuated by overheard statements, admonitions, and interruptions which mount up to a final "capture" by the father.

> 'I'd as lief,'
> Agravain was muttering, 'I'd as lief you'd stay and help me redd
> up after the bluestone barrels are scoured.'

One of the main tasks for the young Muldoon back in 1963 seems to be spraying the potatoes (like the imagined take over by the yarrow, various larvae have already infested the leaves of other vegetables). A version of the mother remonstrates against the child's unwillingness to help on the farm: 'What in under heaven / did we do to deserve you, taking off like that, in a U-boat, / when you knew rightly the spuds needed sprayed?' (although perhaps foolishly she fails to listen to her son's explanation: 'I've just lit the fuse / on a cannon'). The final sections of the poem focuses on the child's fear of the father:

> again and again I wedge my trusty Camoëns
> in the barn-door to keep it ajar
>
> lest Agravyn à la Dure Mayn
> mistake me for Ladon or some apple-butt dragon
> and come after me; even now I hear his shuffle-saunter
>
> through the yard, his slapping the bib
> of his overalls; even now he stops by the cattle-crush
> from which the peers and paladins would set out on their forays.

Soon the powerful Emir catches up with the Muldoon character in the barn: 'again and again they cry out, / "Open, Sesame."' The results of his 'mitching' are confusedly in evidence in the final tornada, where the young Muldoon is to be found leaving the farm 'with my arms crossed, click, under my armpits'. The click is one of remembrance or sudden realisation – his hands, which earlier in the poem were 'bandaged' with talc, are in pain from the beating with a 'freshly-peeled willow-switch' (this is a punishment we are familiar with from Muldoon's early poem 'Anseo' – where it was administered to another boy by the school-teacher).

While a painful past is in evidence here, the poem also enacts
the search for a cure for this hurt. Throughout the volume the
search for 'relief' is central; a recurring motif is the need for mitigation or assuagement, whether the turn to herbal remedies for
cancer in 'Incantata', the relief which S- seeks in drugs, the mother's
reliance on God, or the desire for nutmeg as sweetener for the endless repetetive diet of the Irish – which is imaged not only as the
gruel or porridge the mother eats in hospital, but also as conflict
and violence:

> That was the year there blew such an almighty gale
> it not only bent
> our poplars out of shape but downed one of the few oaks
>
> left standing after Cill Cais.
> We heated a saucepan of milk on a spirit-
> stove and dreamed of the day when we Irish might grate
>
> a little nutmeg over our oatmeal. The reek of paraffin.
> When we might sweeten out stirabout
> with *un petit soupçon* of nutmeg or some such spice?

Here Muldoon presents an mocking vision of relentless destruction:
from Cill Cais (an eighteenth-century lament for the destruction
of the Irish forests) to the trials of the present day, the Irish have
endlessly suffered, with nothing to vary their harsh diet. Clearly
this ultra-nationalist vision is being ironised here (the wit and
humour of this poem is itself a sweetener for such rigid views).
Here again the wry tone is in tension with a real sense of pain.
Muldoon's mother on her deathbed calls for nutmeg as relief for
her suffering. And at the same time the poem also charts Muldoon's
own search for relief, or for deliverance from an imperfectly understood personal past, from memories of paternal violence, and the
violence and destruction of the Troubles. Can the poem itself provide relief?

'Yarrow' concludes ambivalently as Muldoon suggests that the
traditional formal resolution of the sestina is in danger of breaking
down, and with it his hopes for some sort of redress. The end of
the poem implies that the overflowing of the 'stream' of curative
Yarrow will only ever be about to happen 'shortly', that the healing of loss and confusion has not taken place in the past and cannot take place in the present. As the poem repeatedly reminds us,
time is not a healer but the devourer of everything.

> In a conventional tornada, the strains of her '*Che, sera sera*'
> or 'The Harp That Once' would transport me back
> to a bath resplendent with yarrow

(it's really a sink set on breeze- or cinder-blocks):
then I might be delivered
from the rail's monotonous 'alack, alack';

in a conventional envoy, her voice would be ever
soft, gentle and low
and the chrism of milfoil might over-

flow
as the great wheel
came full circle...

The desire here is to go back in order to be 'delivered', but time (whatever will be, will be / The Harp that once) doesn't work like that. Instead the poet is left trying to figure out an 'indecipherable code', abandoned with 'no more relief, no more respite' than he experienced in the past. The precious cargo of ravensara (or nutmeg) is irretrievable – lost in a shipwreck in the poem's final lines. This poem can't resolve the hurt and confusion which are at its heart. Despite the complex architectural structure of rhyme and repetition which holds the dislocated parts of personal and national epic together, the elements cannot be reconciled because of a fundamental loss which cannot be brought to consciousness. What relief there is comes in the form not of promised integration, but in the humour, and the dissonances and disturbances of the poem itself.

Superficially 'Yarrow' seems to suggest that we are entirely boxed in by our past, so that a return to the past in order to find some understanding of our present situation, and therefore some possibility of a different future, is doomed to failure. Muldoon clearly believes that the contours of Irishness need to be rethought or reconceptualised in the present world order, but the repetitive and circling structure of *The Annals of Chile* suggests that a way out of the cycle of familial and national violence is not easy to find. Indeed he is tempted by the thought that time itself, and hence any notion of escape or advance, may be an illusion. Muldoon has signalled the importance to him, when he was writing *The Annals of Chile*, of Jorge Luis Borges's essay 'A New Refutation of Time'. Here Borges recounts a moment on a street in Buenos Aires which he experienced exactly as though it were occurring thirty years previously. On the basis of this experience of exact repetition across time and space, he maintains that time in the sense of succession does not exist (for if there is exact repetition then the experience is the *same* one, and not a recollection). If time is an illusion, clearly there can be no possibility of progress in the sense of linear development. Yet throughout the book Muldoon seems to be asking whether repetition brings its own form of illumination. Poetry offers us the chance not only to be in different places at once, but in the same place at different times – it doesn't require us to choose.

Throughout *The Annals* Muldoon poses this question: when is repetition not repetition, or reproduction, but the same. What's the difference between the real and the copy? In 'Yarrow' repetition occurs at every conceivable level, from the individual word to the looping story line. There is firstly the repetition of syllables: oscaraboscarabinary, lillibullabies, expiapiaratory. Then the repetition of phrases (often themselves having to do with time) 'That was the year', 'again and again', 'even now', 'all I remember'. Characters in the narrative repeat themselves: 'But to the girdle do the gods, / she repeats, but to the girdle do the gods inherit'. Even Muldoon's supper 'repeats on him'. Reference is made too to literary repetitions: Plath's 'poppies in July, October poppies'. Memory itself is triggered by the VCR, on which films, and sections of films, can be not only remade but also replayed: 'that same poor elk or eland / dragged down by a boblink; / the umpteenth Broken Arrow'.

Cycles and returns are also the basis of the structure of 'Yarrow', which Muldoon has described as 'twelve, intercut, exploded sestinas'. This is, in fact, a little misleading, for the twelve rhymed poems which form the templates of the sequence are not strictly sestinas, since they contain twelve, nine or six lines (there are thus ninety rhyme words in all, over a poem of more than a thousand lines). To take the poem of twelve lines which opens the sequence, this is repeated seventeen times, but with six variations on the order of the rhymes (as in a conventional sestina). The six variations themselves form a pattern throughout the poem, as at certain points the rhyme scheme is repeated without alteration. The whole poem follows an elaborate pattern, though a pattern which (significantly) seems to break down at moments. The order of the "sestinas" could perhaps best be described as a pattern with random elements, as increasingly the poems repeat preceding forms, often rhyming perfectly with the preceding poem (rather than offering a variation on the order of the rhyme words). After the central poem, which rhymes with the first, the sequence reproduces the exact order of all the preceding seventy-five poem forms in reverse, ending with a variation on the first poem.

What are we to make of this immensely complex structure? – is Muldoon always returning to the same (in which case time and succession, as Borges suggests, is rendered null), or does the poem progress through subtle variation? The tornada at the end of 'Yarrow', which repeats all ninety end-rhymes of the poem, suggests that progress cannot take place because something is missing. The nutmeg or sweetener, which would offer some 'relief' to the violent cycle of familial and national history has been lost. On the other hand the form of the poem itself, which does make headway despite always having to use the same elements, the same raw materials, suggests the possibility of a different future. Out of the ninety end-rhymes in 'Yarrow' come more than a thousand lines of poetry in which at least the beginnings of a new self-understanding seems to be attained. Importantly however, that future is not imagined in terms of linear progression or succession (the son supplanting the father) but as the circling, tentative, "homing" flight of birds which, like Yeats's swallows, can cut through time. 'Yarrow' creates a way of returning to the past which isn't based on development, discovery, revelation – a form of restitution which allows the past to breathe. The return to the past is neither the recovery of a lost origin which will tell us who we are, nor a therapeutic replaying of a "forgotten" trauma which will help to break its hold. If repetition is to bring about change, Muldoon suggests, it is not by taming the violence within, but by appropriating its force.

'Incantata' takes up these questions once more through an act of mourning. It is perhaps the climax of Muldoon's concerns with how poetry can help us live our lives, with what it can do in the face of violence and loss. The subject of this poem too is the search for relief – for a way of living in the knowledge of mortality, and for a balm to heal the dying body. An elegy for the artist and printmaker Mary Farl Powers, the poem is at once a lament for all the misery of past generations, and a reflection on the limits of poetic remembrance and aesthetic transfiguration. In part the poem is about what can be achieved through repetition – through the techniques of mechanical reproduction or repetition which Mary Powers used as an engraver, and through figures of poetic repetition such as rhythm and rhyme. The 'device' which structures the poem, for example, is a 'mouth' cut in a potato – a mouth which returns repeatedly, like the multiple images produced by potato printing. The repetition of this image (derived from the image of a cankered potato which appears in Powers' work) is mirrored in the rhythmic repetition of the poem itself. The constant recurrence of the same verbal patterns and grammatical structures gives the poem a magical "incantatory" aspect. In this sense, 'Incantata' can be seen as a successor to *Quoof*'s ambivalent representation of poetry as a shamanistic cure, a way to ward off evil.

Like 'Yarrow' the poem struggles with the possibility of change emerging out of the same; it wonders at what point repetition becomes difference. Entrapment by history and the power of fate are familiar Muldoon themes, explored in the circling revolutions of *Why Brownlee Left*, or the imprisoning circles and roundabouts of *Quoof*. These determinist intuitions are echoed by Powers herself in the poem, which depicts her seeking consolation in the thought that everything which happens does so in accord with a preordained pattern:

> Again and again you'd hold forth on your own version of Thomism,
> your own *Summa*
> *Theologiae* that in everything there is an order,
> that the things of the world sing out in a great oratorio:
> it was Thomism, though, tempered by *La Nausée*,
> by His Nibs Sam Bethicket…

Beckett appears 'again and again' in the poem. The potato mouth itself may have Beckettian resonances – recalling the mouth which strains for articulation in *Not I*. The difficulty of making the jump from inarticulate grunting to speech throws doubt on the power of poetry as a talking cure, the capacity of words to assuage suffering. But present here too are Beckett's creations: Krapp, Belaqua, Ham and Clov, Vladimir and Estragon. All are in one sense tragic figures, confronting a world bereft of any hope of betterment, let alone redemption. Their resilience, their ability to 'go on', is based on a kind of existential stubbornness, a refusal to give up their commitment to the routines and rituals of everyday life, despite the fact that all meaning seems to have been drained from them. This heroic persistence in the face of finitude, in a world which has lost all trace of the divine, is reflected in the poem's obstinate recording of apparently trivial everyday details.

Muldoon alludes several times to Powers' notion 'that nothing's random, nothing's arbitrary', and the poem itself seems a striking contrast to this. It appears to ramble wildly, gathering everything together without order or discrimination. Many of the references appear to be no more than a jumble of personal facts, a record of the tastes and idosyncrasies of one individual. But behind this lies a feeling that preserving the details of Mary Powers' tastes and habits might have some protective or sustaining value. It is as if the sheer specificity and repetition of the habitual contained some power of resistance against the threat of meaninglessness. Muldoon thinks, for example

> of how you called a Red Admiral a Red
> *Admirable*, of how you were never in the red
> on either the first or the last
> of the month, of your habit of loosing the drawstring of your purse

THE PRINCE OF THE QUOTIDIAN / ANNALS OF CHILE   183

> and finding one scrunched-up, obstreperous
> note and smoothing it out and holding it up, pristine and pellucid.

The sense of a pattern concealed in the disorder of such recollections, the tension between the chaos of trivial, quotidian events
and an elaborate determining structure is mirrored in the shape of
the poem itself. The verse form of 'Incantata' is based on Yeats's
elegy for Major Robert Gregory, but Muldoon uses the same ninety
rhyme words which he employed in 'Yarrow' (in the order in which
they appear in 'Yarrow', and then in reverse). An extraordinary
formal constraint is at work here. Repetition was a basic formal
principle of 'Yarrow', but there at least the rhyme words could
(initally) emerge from the material. Here the rhyme words are
imposed from elsewhere – generating a structure whose arbitrariness underscores the fatefulness of repetition.

At one point in the poem Muldoon jokes about his taste for
contrivance, suggesting that Powers

> ...detected in me a tendency to put
> on too much artificiality, both as man and poet,
> which is why you called me 'Polyester' or 'Polyurethane'.

The word 'plastic', of course, is applied not just to the artificial,
but to the fake and insincere. Muldoon is hinting here at the tension between the extreme artifice of the poem and its almost exaggerated display of overwhelming feeling, and acknowledging the
apparent imbalance between emotion and poetic means (which
Helen Vendler, for example, found so unsatisfactory).[8] Muldoon's
wry acknowledgement of the issue doesn't entirely dispel our doubts,
of course. Has he succumbed to sentimentalism with his use of
this unaccustomed rhetorical register? Muldoon's grief at the death
of Mary Powers becomes a mourning for the loss of a whole history, and entire worlds. The final lines of the poem suggest that
to have lost her is to have lost everything. He lists the things with
which the dead woman was associated in an epic drive to encompass and contain. The poet tries to relate everything (in both senses
of the word – to tell and to connect), from the more intimate
details of her personal preferences in food, clothing, and music, to
more public events – turning points in the Northern Irish crisis
such as the death of eighteen soldiers at Warrenpoint, and the
murders of Airey Neave and Lord Mountbatten. Yet, through the
image of the 'cankered potato', her death reaches beyond even the
specific memories enumerated here. The 'cankered potato' relates
the cancer from which Powers suffered to other blights – the
'army-worms' of her native Minnesota, and by implication also

the Irish potato blight. As if these instances of disease and destruction were not enough, Muldoon's lament (in a manner similar to the *caoine*, the Irish 'keen' or lament for the dead) encompasses the destruction of whole cultures and peoples, taking in the defeat of Scottish hopes at the battle of Culloden (which presaged the Highland Clearances), and the mass slaughter of Mexicans at Chickamauga. Here is a litany of catastrophe, grief, inconsolable loss. What can art do in face of such suffering?

> I thought again of how art may be made, as it was by André Derain
> of nothing more than a turn
> in the road where a swallow dips into the mire
> or plucks a strand of bloody wool from a strand of barbed wire
> in the aftermath of Chickamauga or Culloden
> and builds from pain, from misery, from a deep-seated hurt,
> a monument to the human heart
> that shines like a golden dome among roofs rain-glazed and leaden.

This appears to be a straightforward declaration of faith in the power of poetry – art may transform a 'deep-seated hurt' into a soaring golden dome – yet the very rhetorical excess of these lines exposes the fragility of such a vision. The soaring dome may well be a mirage. It contends with another, humbler figure for poetry – that of the healing herbs on which Powers relied for a cure, rather than conventional medicine. Despite the fact that in the end her conviction proved fatal, Powers' faith in the herbs invests them with almost magical properties, properties which become transposed onto the poem itself – can poetic incantation heal? Muldoon's poem remains exquisitely and painfully balanced on this question, both offering and refusing the conventional elegiac ending which witnesses the resurrection of the dead person. The poem lists a series of seemingly impossible possibilities, culminating in the final denial of the possibility of her regeneration, which suddenly seems possible:

> than that Lugh of the Long Arm might have found in the midst of *lus
> na leac* or *lus na treatha* or *Frannc-lus,*
> in the midst of eyebright, or speedwell, or tansy, an antidote,
> than that this *Incantata*
> might have you look up from your plate of copper or zinc
> on which you've etched the row upon row
> of army-worms, than that you migh reach out, arrah,
> and take in your ink-stained hands my own hands stained with ink.

Here Muldoon movingly articulates his ambiguous, tentative hope in the power of art 'to annoint and anneal', couched within a denial of that hope. The poem yearns for a redemptive vision which might transform the 'still, sad, *basso continuo* of the great quotidian', whilst knowing that there can be no definitive conquering or mastery of hurt. If any saving vision is to be found, it is nowhere than in an obstinate treasuring of the familiar, trivial details of life – a kind of heroic stubbornness, an affirmation, through repetition, of the rituals of the ordinary and the everyday.

Perhaps more than any previous volume, *The Annals of Chile* displays Muldoon's ability to move back and forth between past and present, between intensely private concerns and general issues of contemporary global culture. Indeed, his sense of the power of poetry is based precisely on this agility. Clery's trick in 'Twice' ('Two places at once was it, or one place twice?') becomes the volume's central image for the capacity of poetry not simply to recall or reduplicate, but to enable us to *be* in more than one time or space – Muldoon, as a child, dwelled not simply in the Moy, and as an adult he can be a child in the Moy once more, even as he lives his life in America. By preserving an imaginative arena for such repetitions and displacements, poetry may perhaps help us to live our lives in a world where we are bombarded by predigested narratives, or else by what feels like pure contingency and randomness. Such poetic repetition does not overcome the violence of the past, of course, or subsume it into some unambiguous story of development. But it can perhaps harness this violence, deflecting it against the encroaching pressure of a reality which would deny us access to the past altogether. The sense of temporality which Muldoon is struggling towards here is newly marked by the circular movement associated with femininity. And implicitly, the most significant cycle may be found in the birth of Muldoon's daughter. The gestation and gradual physical realisation of the baby throughout *The Prince of the Quotidian* and *The Annals of Chile* is paralleled by the father's own emotional realisation that in the child reproduction – repetition – is always the creation of something new: that the relation of the present to the past is also the outline of a future.

CHAPTER EIGHT

Hay

I began this book by attempting to define the 'Muldoonesque' – that elusive quality distinctive of Paul Muldoon's style. The fact that his idiom is unmistakable, that he sounds like nobody else, is a tribute to his work. Yet the achievement of a distinctive (and much imitated) style also has its drawbacks – not least the risk of self-parody. The need to move on and develop as a poet can bring with it the danger of losing one's distinctive voice. But a writer may also allow himself to be colonised by his own style, so that the new ends up as more of the same. The trick for any poet is knowing how to move on without leaving yourself behind. Muldoon seems very conscious of this dilemma in his most recent book, *Hay*. It's a volume which offers both something familiar and something new, often in the same poem. Like most of Muldoon's more recent books, *Hay* gives the reader the feeling of entering another world, which has its own unpredictable but consistent logic. There's a real sense of energy and pace to many of the poems in *Hay*, combined with a characteristic vividness – that unique feeling we get reading Muldoon that there are no holds barred, that the next surreal, startling turn of phrase could take us almost anywhere.

Hay shares with Muldoon's previous collections the long disorientating narrative poems, the literary and historical allusions, the fascination with repetition and metamorphosis, the cryptic references, the play with semantics and etymology. These are aspects of his style to which we have become accustomed. But there is also something different here. For a start, the established structure of his recent volumes is broken up in this book. Instead of a few short lyrics followed by one major long poem, *Hay* has several long or longish poems. It begins with a poem addressed to his wife in (half-rhyming) couplets, and ends with series of thirty sonnets; in the middle there's an extended poem about his father's childhood, a sequence of autobiographical poems on rock music, as well as something we could think of either as a long poem or a series of very short ones – ninety haiku which focus on glimpses of the natural world near his home in Princeton. The haiku sequence is just one example of what appears as a new interest in clarity, simplicity – and availability. Many of the lyrics are perhaps deceptively mild and modest offerings. Muldoon writes about his house, his garden, his cats – but perhaps most of all his backyard. There's a distinctively

Frostian tone to many of these quasi-rural poems, and a lyrical simplicity which seems as far as possible from the sprawling, allusive, "difficult" poems such as 'Madoc' and 'Yarrow' (several of the poems included in *Hay* were published in *The New Yorker*, a destiny unthinkable for much of the earlier work). As Muldoon said in an interview in 1994, in a comment one might have assumed to be ironic: 'What I want to write are beautifully pellucid, simple lyric poems.'[1] At the same time, Muldoon's technical experiments with form have become if anything even more wide-ranging and adventurous, moving beyond his ingenious renewal of the sonnet and the sestina. Along with the haiku, which clearly reflect the impact of a visit to Japan in 1994, we find a variety of poetic forms, many drawn from non-Western cultures – the Persian ghazal, the Malayan pantoum. But he also spans time, going back to the roots of English verse at one extreme (the Anglo-Saxon riddle) while trying out visual puns and versions of concrete poetry at the other. So the striving for simplicity is counterbalanced by a continuing concern with poetic artifice, a duality which is perhaps most clearly reflected in Muldoon's interest in Noh drama and in the haiku. For while the haiku seeks to capture a moment of spontaneous insight provoked by an encounter with the natural world, it is a highly constrained and rule-bound verse form. Muldoon's concern with the tension between poetic artifice and the natural and unpredictable could scarcely have found more condensed expression.

If I seem to be describing a middle path that isn't, I think, accidental. For this book is all about being in the middle – in the middle of life, and in the middle (or possibly muddle) of the family, but also perhaps in between styles. Muldoon hints at several points in the book that he is suffering his '*crise d'un certain âge*', that he is 'pausing in mid-career', even that he is at a 'turning point'. He explores this state in part through the conventional metaphor of life's journey (with a nod or two to Dante); he returns to ideas he had previously explored in *Why Brownlee Left*, the different paths or directions open to us and how these are inevitably narrowed by the choices we make (he returns too to the preoccupation with the father which haunts the earlier book). But he is also taken up with less traditionally poetic images for middle age – in particular his middle-aged spread (perhaps alluded to in the title of his recent lecture 'Getting Round'). The effects of eating and drinking, and indeed appetite in general, are a central theme of the book. Muldoon represents himself as an epicure and a gourmand; he takes an almost perverse pleasure in detailing his over-indulgence, gratifying tastes from the most popular to the most refined. From Heineken with

vodka on the side and throwing up in the toilet bowl, to Simi
Chardonnay and Muscadet de Sèvres et Maine, from a vanilla ice
cream cone to 'consommé, salad, and ray's wing braked // on a bed
of bockchoy'. The book is in part concerned with what happens
when such self-indulgence comes home to roost. One of the several
cat poems is both a backyard and a mid-life crisis poem too – if
crisis isn't too dynamic a word for the indolence represented in the
poem. 'Paunch' paints a picture of the poet as slob, turning to fat
and lounging in a garden chair, where he is approached by the
family's newly acquired stray kitten. The kitten:

> ventures across what might have seemed a great divide
> between her and me, had she not
> now begun to nag and needle
>
> and knead
> my paunch for milk. The bucket fills with human fat.
> The chair takes a dim view through a knot-hole.

The very first poem in the book, 'The Mud Room', establishes a
connection between food and the idea of life as a journey, through
the image of a 'wheel of Morbier'. This is a round of goat's cheese
which is (apparently) divided across the centre by a blue-green
seam of pine-ash, separating the curds made from the goats' morning milking, and that obtained from the evening milking ('that runs
like a schism / between bland dawn-milk and bland dusk-milk').
This image of drawing a line through the middle of the day, of
being suspended between dawn and dusk, returns again and again
in the poem, suggesting that Muldoon is somehow seeking to
draw a line through the middle of his life, to define its mid-point.
(Though the fact that it's impossible to tell where blue ends and
green begins implies that such definition is far from simple.)

The cheese becomes the terrain of a journey Muldoon undertakes with his wife through the French countryside (along a 'narrow track' through 'a valley in the Jura' and up an increasingly
steep mountain), an expedition which becomes ever more perilous,
at any rate for Muldoon. The couple are guided by a 'she-goat',
the latest in a series of unreliable guides to appear in Muldoon's
work. This, then, is yet another of Muldoon's quest poems – it
would scarcely be an exaggeration to claim that all his major poems
are structured round a journey, with guides ranging from sherpa
to horse, and including almost everything in between. Ever since
'Immram', however, a central issue has been the difficulty of trust-
ing the guide, along with clueless naivety of the protagonist. Muldoon's journeys are less pilgrimages from here to there, than a
record of chance encounters and discoveries; both poet and reader

are forever tripping up, stumbling on things. A goat seems an
especially uncertain guide. She can't be relied upon to take you
directly where you need to go (or she goes where you can't follow).
The goat here perhaps signals what Muldoon has referred to in
another context as the 'calculated capriciousness' of the poet. For
Muldoon is both follower and guide (at one point the goat is referred
to as a 'devotee', one version of the meaning of the name 'Mael
Duin'). With its nimbleness and agility, the animal is one of those
by now familiar 'stunt doubles' of the author, to which a later poem
in the book refers.

The French mountain journey merges with the repeated journeys which Muldoon and his wife make through the 'mud room'
of their house. A mud room is a kind of porch or cloakroom common in American houses, an area between the domestic interior of
the house, and the outside world, including the wilderness beyond
the yard. So called because it is where you leave your muddy boots,
in this poem the mud room also contains a mass of stuff which
finds no place in the house, but isn't ready to be thrown away
either. An in-between place, then, and therefore a fitting spot for
Muldoon's exploration of the merging of two lives; like the poem
about his mother and father in *Mules*, this is a portrait of a mixed
marriage, but forty years on and in another country. The mud
room is filled with the clutter of the life Muldoon shares with his
wife – everything from souvenirs of trips to Bogota and Kyoto, to
talismanic props from Muldoon's childhood (such as the bow and
quiver which has featured in so many of his poems), to less familiar
objects associated with his Jewish American wife's family life – all
are mixed up in the muddle of the mud room. This jumble is
reminiscent of his poems, where pattern struggles against disorder,
where meaning is pitted against confusion:

> Yet again I stood amid the drek
> and clutter
> of the mud room, the cardboard boxes from K-Mart and Caldor,
> the hoover, the ironing board, the ram's horn
> on which Moses called to Aaron, a pair of my da's boots so worn
> it was hard to judge where the boots came to an end
> and the world began, given how one would blend
> imperceptibly into the other, given that there was no fine
> blue-green line
> between them...

The tension between the need to keeps things distinct, and the
desire to let them flow into one another runs throughout this book,
recalling the channel-surfing kaleidoscope of events in 'Yarrow'.
Different trips to the mud room become jumbled together, just as

mountainside and domestic interior dissolve into one another (and a similar slippage between times and places occurs in many of the poems in *Hay*). In part this poem is about family life, about how you mix things up in marriage yet retain, or hold on to a sense of self. It's about holding a line. Both Muldoon and his wife bring something along with them on their journey, which seems to act as a point of orientation, a way of marking their separateness. But perhaps predictably these objects are themselves surreal and ambiguous hybrids, combining the living and the inanimate, ancient religion and contemporary ideology: 'I carried my skating rink, / the folding one, plus / a pair of skates laced with convolvulus, / you a copy of the feminist Haggadah / from last year's seder'.

The Passover seder is the first of many meals to occur in this book; the word 'seder' means order, and the meal itself is a time of separation. It is the occasion when Jewish families commemorate the exodus from Egypt (a story which includes that potent image of separation, the Red Sea parting for the Israelites). But preparation for the seder also involves separation, as a line is drawn between the mess of ordinary life and seder week: the house is cleaned and everyday food – especially anything made with flour – is boxed up and stored. In the same way the requirement to eat kosher food is all about purity, about not mixing things up (and certainly goat's cheese wouldn't be allowed at the seder table, since the main dish is a meat dish). But another kind of separation may be hinted at here too: the 1967 border between Israel and Palestine, which is known as the green line. In this case the separation is violently contested; the border is deadly, something to be battled over.

One of the subtleties explored by this poem is the fact that the middle is both a place of merging and a place of separation. The fine line drawn through the cheese finds it semitic counterpart in the afikoman, the middle of three cakes of matzo bread which is hidden during the Passover meal. The afikoman provides entertainment for children at the end of the meal when they look for it (and are offered a prize for finding it). But in this poem the afikoman is lost – hidden by the poet somewhere in the mud room at last year's seder, it was never found (suggesting a rather miserable occasion). An image, then, of an absent middle. The afikoman stands as the successor to the many lost objects which abound in Muldoon's poems, and which suggest a missing key or an elusive answer. It's not entirely lost of course, and Muldoon comes across it during his journey, carrying it with him as a kind of talisman. In one sense he can't escape the gravitational pull of the mud room, which he repeatedly revisits in memory. But finding the afikoman

suggests that, despite all the to-ing and fro-ing, some kind of progress can be made, that this journey proceeds precariously – two
steps forward and one step back.

Throughout his journey he's looking for a place to lay out his
skating rink, perhaps trying to create a domestic space free from
all that 'drek'.

> I, meanwhile, was struggling for a foothold.
> Even as I drove another piton to the hilt
> in the roughcast bag of Sakrete, the she-goat executed an exquisite
> *saut de l'ange* from an outcrop of shale,
> pausing to browse on a sprig of myrtle or sweet gale
> in the vicinity of the bow and quiver, down jackets, hoover,
> where I hid the afikoman last Passover,
> bounding, vaulting, never making a slip
> as I followed her, then as now – though then I had to schlep
> through the brush of skirts (maxi- and mini-)
> my folding rink plus my skates laced with scammony
> *plus* the middle of the three
> cakes of matzo-bread that had, if you recall, since gone astray.
> It was time, I felt sure, to unpack the Suntory
> into the old fridge, to clear a space between *De Rerum Natura*
> and Virgil's *Eclogues,*
> a space in which, at long last, I might inlock
> the rink, so I drove another piton into an eighty-pound
> bag of Sakrete and flipped the half-door on the dairy-cabinet
> of the old Hotpoint
> and happened, my love, just happened
> upon the cross-
> section of Morbier and saw, once and for all, the precarious
> blue-green, pine-ash path along which Isaac followed Abraham
> to an altar lit by a seven-branched candelabrum,
> the ram's horn, the little goat whirligig
> that left him all agog.

These lines capture the energy and verve of Muldoon's best work
– part of the pleasure of a poem like this *is* the muddle, as one
unlikely object follows close on another. It's a poem which asks
you to read it fast, allowing connections to happen, rather than
lingering over each image. The impression we get is of a person
increasingly crowded in and weighed down, struggling up a mountain in order (bizarrely) to get to the fridge. We might expect some
sort of revelation to occur on the back of the final "vision" (the
glimpse of the cheese) but if there's a discovery here it's a coded
one. Given the evident concern about being in mid-life, there may
be an allusion here to the 'whirligig of time' bringing in its revenges.
But what of the biblical story? The story of Abraham and Isaac
perhaps represents the fine line between killing your son and not
killing him, or between this world and the next. Certainly it's a

powerful image of willingness to sacrifice, and the idea of sacrifice, of giving something up or doing harm for the sake of some (possible) greater good, is one which resonates throughout the book.

The fact that this vision is 'happened upon' (a phrase which is also applied to the afikoman) tells us something important about the journey Muldoon undertakes in this poem. If this is a journey of discovery its outcome is at once predestined and unforeseen, 'a course of lucky events' (as Robert Frost suggests in 'The Figure a Poem Makes'). The most important 'finds', Muldoon seems to imply, are not those we are seeking, and perhaps all poetry can do is create a space, like the mud room, where unexpected connections can emerge.

The portable skating rink, where Muldoon can "cut a figure", is surely another example of a poetic space – a larger version of the circle of ice through which the poet peers in 'Twice'. Muldoon attempts to make room for his poetry between, on the one hand, the eclogue (the overheard speech of goatherds – pastoral, anecdotal and intimate but at the same time urbane) and on the other Lucretius's poem about the nature of the universe. *De Rerum Natura* is an explanation in poetry of the theories of Epicurus; it's a public poem, addressed to a patron, at the furthest remove from intimate talk. These contrasting responses to nature and the natural echo through the poems which follow: in the pastoral, agricultural register of much of the volume, in the Epicurean celebration of the physical variety in the world, even in the popular image of the epicure as one whose life is built upon self-gratification. At the same time Muldoon seems to be looking for something in between a totally private and a public register (and the mud room looks like a good half-way place – between inside and outside – if he can keep on top of the mess). It is in this context, I think, that we should interpret the distinctive mode of address of many of these poems. On the one hand the poems adopt a decidedly intimate register: 'my love', and 'my darling' – as though the poems were private talk which we are overhearing. How different this is from Muldoon's previous experiments with private language – the tentativeness with which the family word was offered up in 'Quoof', for example, seems miles away from this confident assurance that we are listening. (In the final line of the book Muldoon's address is to 'my darlings' – as though we readers have become part of his family by virtue of having reached the end.) But this pillow talk vies with an entirely different idiom, as the poems repeatedly address an unnamed authority figure with the words, 'you see, sir'. Is this cod Irish deference? A Lucretian address to a patron? Muldoon's mock homage to his guide and alter-ego?

Part of the point of the poem's address to 'my love' is surely
that she understands it; she can make sense of the muddle. To the
reader it may be no more than a mass of data, a pile of free-floating
associations, but to the family the significance of the objects is clear.
The mud room acts as a point of anchorage, a record of the shared
experiences, the entanglements and enthralments, which hold the
partners together. Another marriage poem, 'Long Finish' – a celebration of the Muldoons' ten-year wedding anniversary – continues
this image of marriage as a breakdown of distinctions between the
valuable and the ordinary, or even the rubbish. The title is a wine
term, describing the lingering, changing taste typical of a high
quality wine. Muldoon is thinking, then, about how things both
alter and endure. As in 'Brazil', the woman's body in this poem is
full of shifting analogies, which can never quite be pinned down:

> I glimpse the all-but-cleared-up eczema-patch on your spine
> and it brings to mind not the Schloss
> that stands, transitory, tra la, Triestine,
> between longing and loss
>
> but a crude
> hip-trench in a field, covered with pine-boughs,
> in which two men in masks and hoods
> who have themselves taken vows
> wait for a farmer to break a bale for his cows
> before opening fire with semi-
> automatics, cutting him off slightly above the eyebrows,
> and then some.

The patch of eczema might seem a surprising, even slightly distasteful sign of physical intimacy – a stark reminder of the muta-
bility of the body. To the poet it suggests not the privileged tower
in which Rilke wrote the Duino elegies but a scene of murder, a
'crude' and violent vision. Far from being a refuge from violent
reality, physical intimacy is a point of connection with the wider
world, and indeed opens onto the most cruel and horrific aspects
of it. The stucture of this poem consists of two intercut *ballades*, a
form whose envoi always begins with the word 'prince'. The final
lines of Muldoon's poem, however, twist the convention in order
to address his wife once more: 'Princess of Accutane, let's no more
try to refine / the pure drop from the dross / than distinquish, good
thou, between mine and thine, / between longing and loss'. Is this
tenderly mundane association of his wife with a prescription drug
intended to call to mind Gérard de Nerval's poem 'El Desdichado'
('*Je suis le ténébreux, – le veuf, – l'inconsolé, / Le prince d'Aquitaine
à la tour abolie*')? If so, the image is itself a brilliant fusion of the
pure drop and the dross. The allusion in 'accutane' is just as likely

to be to T.S. Eliot, who summons Nerval in the final lines of
'The Waste Land' ('These fragments I have shored against my
ruins'). Muldoon's poem is deeply sceptical of Eliot's belief that
we can refine some fragment, use it as a touchstone in the chaos
of twentieth century. It's a mistake to try to distinguish between
the pure drop and the dross, distil a pure essence, for the mixture
is what lends the marriage its distinctive taste – the long finish.
Though marriage may be a "middle", it is one pitched 'between
longing and loss', shot through with yearning. Put that way the
poem seems to be teetering on the brink of banality – it's the mixture of familiarity and change, the good and the bad, which sustains marriage, it seems to say. We could read the final lines as an
exhortation to take the rough with the smooth, or any number of
other platitudes about marriage. In fact the poem seems, quite un-
apologetically, to want to work with such clichés. Yet in the context of a poem about what makes marriage sustainable, the redness
of the patch of eczema – with all the associations of violence and
destruction it calls up – are a little unexpected, to say the least.

Like 'The Mud Room', 'Long Finish' suggests that family life
is shifting, disordered, various – far from being a sheltered domain,
it is open to the whole range of experience. In this sense marriage
is endlessly adulterous – it always leads to more, as the refrain
'and then some' implies. Both poems, in different ways, revolve
around an excess which cannot be contained, cannot be neatly
fitted into categories. Throughout *Hay* this indiscriminate mixing
up of marriage is compared to other forms of promiscuity, and in
particular the sexual promiscuity of the past. Many of the poems
return to earlier stages of Muldoon's life in which his wife played
no part, as though the security of entanglements in the mud room
allow him to risk revisiting painful or exciting moments from the
past. In particular these poems seem concerned to define what
made something the beginning ('Green Gown'), or the end ('Lag',
'Longbones') – in contrast to the middle. And as if to underline
the affinity of beginnings and endings they make use of forms such
as the sestina and the villanelle – recalling the circling repetitive
patterns of *The Annals of Chile*. One poem 'The Little Black Book'
(a ghazal) takes the repetitive structure and use of refrain to its
limit, while at the same time pushing at the boundaries of taste-
fulness. The poem is a list of sexual encounters, each one "new",
but at the same time barely different from the last:

> It was Niamh, as luck would have it, who introduced me to Orla.
> The lost weekend of a day-trip between *her* legs.

It was Orla, as luck would have it, who introduced me to Roisin.
The bramble-patch. The rosehip between her legs.

What ever became of Sile?
Sile who led me to horse-worship between her legs.

We could read this poem as a powerful denial of the idea that
through repetition we make sense of our lives. In contrast to
'Yarrow', where repetition was, at least on the surface, the path to
a form of enlightenment or insight, here apparent novelty looks a
lot like tedious reduplication, variety is difficult to distinguish from
monotony. It is of course the similarity between these encounters
which makes the list so repulsive – the constancy of his inconstancy.
Muldoon offers us a catalogue of sexual conquests whose focus is
almost laughably narrow ('between her legs'). This is a very different kind of crudity from the rawness of 'Long Finish'. The coarse-
ness of the poem goes much further even than the 'wild and wicked
poems in *Quoof*' (as Muldoon calls them in 'Sleeve Notes'). As
with the earlier volume we are clearly meant to find this vulgar
and in bad taste, so that to respond simply with shock would be
somehow to miss the point. Here again Muldoon seems to be playing on some of the most hackneyed ideas of male sexuality – embodied in this poem in the insistent refrain (though it's worth noting,
I think, that the women are differentiated in the least clichéd terms
imaginable, so that despite their serial similarity each one attains a
certain uniqueness). The poem ends as the narrator has the tables
turned on him – an afterthought in someone else's little black book,
'I fluttered like an erratum slip between her legs'. So called 'errata'
crop up again and again in *Hay*, and there is surely a suggestion
here that sexual promiscuity has its verbal parallel in catachresis,
the wilful misuse of words. Toying with language may be no less
irresponsible than toying with female affections – and in moving
from one word, one woman, to another the poet-lover could be
missing the essential, rather than getting to grips with reality.
Commitment enhances credibility, certainly in affairs of the heart,
where the would-be Casanova is unlikely to be trusted. There
may be something equally unreliable, it seems, about the poet's
cavalier way with words.

A poem like 'The Little Black Book' presents a far from pleas-
ant picture of the poet, nor is it meant to. We might console ourselves with the thought that at least these episodes belong to the
past (significantly, all the women's names in the poem are Irish).
But to make things worse other poems in the book suggest that
the poet hasn't changed, merely become less successful. 'White
Shoulders' offers a vision of the poet as hopeless middle-aged

voyeur (typically his opportunities for sexual excitement are connected with, even become confused with, the delights of food).
Once more the most personal and individual of sensations, sexual
desire, is at the mercy of chance verbal associations; the title plays
on another Irish name, Fionnuala, which means 'white shoulders':

> My heart is heavy. For I saw Fionnuala,
> 'The Gem of the Roe', 'The Flower of Sweet Strabane',
> when a girl reached down into a freezer-bin
> to bring up my double-scoop of vanilla.

This concern with ageing is also, of course, a poetic concern, as
Muldoon wryly acknowledges in 'Sleeve Notes', a sequence of
lyrics which again offer a version of his autobiography – using
music to chart stages in his life from school and home in the Moy,
through marriage, Belfast and the BBC, and finally to America
and family life again. The poems in the sequence are for the most
part light-hearted lyrics, deft encapsulations of time and mood.
But 'Bob Dylan: Oh Mercy' introduces us to a nagging anxiety: is
this paring down the prelude to new growth or a sign of the end?

> All great artists are their own greatest threat,
> as when they aim an industrial laser
> at themselves and cut themselves back to the root
>
> so that, with spring, we can never be sure
> if they shake from head to foot
> from an orgasm, you see, sir, or a seizure.

This poem, again, is concerned with beginnings and endings. Or,
more precisely, with the question of when an ending is a beginning,
and vice versa. Roots are, of course, "radical" in the etymological
sense. Muldoon may be hinting that being radical or, indeed, avant-
garde, is not a matter of advanced technique but of finding the
right way of moving on, even if this involves an apparent return to
roots (including the sources of English poetry, such as the Anglo-
Saxon riddle). It's hard to avoid the suspicion that this is a pre-
emptive strike on Muldoon's part: an attempt to forestall the suggestion that, with his new American pastoral simplicity, his middle-
aged slobbery, his poetry has lost its vital spark. Is the erotic shudder
the prelude to new life or does it presage its end? Is it merely the
muddle in the middle?

In bizarre literalisation of this concern, a number of poems in
Hay push his style to the limit. Take 'Symposium', for example.
The poem clearly announces itself as a modern successor to
Plato's *Symposium*, where the dinner guests discourse about love
during an all-night session of food and wine (and thus it's another
of the many drunken meals which feature in the book). At Muldoon's

dinner, however, there is no Socrates to wind up the discussion with his moralising philosophical wisdom. Rather 'Symposium' is a triumph of economy; the poem works by splicing together clichés and adages, exposing their arbitrariness and sententious absurdity at the same time as it generates its own surreal wisdom. In the inebriated confusion of the poem, a new kind of meaning emerges, as language itself has to make sense of the differing views.

> You can lead a horse to water but you can't make it hold
> its nose to the grindstone and hunt with the hounds.
> Every dog has a stitch in time. Two heads? You've been sold
> one good turn. One good turn deserves a bird in the hand.

Read as a comment on the topic of conversation at Plato's dinner party, the lesson of Muldoon's re-run appears to be (once more) that love is a muddle or a mixture. Here Muldoon's habit of revitalising the cliché by exposing its literal meaning is pushed to its logical terminus, for the poem is composed of nothing else. In a similar way other poems take Muldoon's experiments with repetition to furthest extreme, using insistent refrains and 'perfect' rhyme. The convergence of these techniques, the *nec plus ultra*, comes in 'They That Wash on Thursday', where the single rhyme word 'hand' occurs at the end of every one of the fifty lines, threading its way through a seemingly endless string of clichés and platitudes:

> She was such a dab hand, my mother. Such a dab hand
> at raising her hand
> to a child. At bringing a cane down across my hand
> in such a seemingly off-hand
> manner I almost have to hand
> it to her. 'Many hands,'
> she would say, 'spoil the broth.' My father took no hand
> in this. He washed his hands
> of the matter. He sat on his hands.

Here, in yet another retelling of his life story, Muldoon meditates (once more) on the relation between difference and repetition. It's not just that the rhyme doesn't vary – there's something banal and monotonous too about the story the poem tells. After all, he's told it so many times before, and this time he tells it in well-worn clichés. We could read this obsession with cliché, refrain and repetition as a linguistic version of the American backyard – in one sense the most dull and limited of places, but perhaps still capable of producing more ('and then some'). But beyond this, Muldoon seems concerned with the limits of expressive language. How can you use the exhausted language of cliché and at the same time maintain your distinctive idiom? Or, to put it another way, how can you take the ultimate in non-expressive language and put your own hand-print on it? 'They That Wash on Thursday' is comprised of little except worn-out phrases, yet it is unmistakeably Muldoon – it speaks with his voice. (It is worth noting here that hands in themselves are a Muldoon trademark, a recurring image from the severed and blown off hands in *Quoof*, to Agravain of the hard hand and Israel Hands in 'Yarrow'.) Like the well-worn boots in 'The Mud Room' a well-worn cliché has done lot of work, and it is precisely this which makes it indistinguishable from other things. But it may be that by wearing clichés, like the boots, beyond the point of usefulness, they can become expressive of something new.

Such exact repetition is at once the culmination and the end of rhyme, reaching towards a sterile perfection. Clearly it's not possible to take this any further, but what do you do after reaching the limit? 'Bob Dylan: Oh Mercy' suggests when you've gone as far as you can go you have to cut back to the root. Radical cropping involves damage, but brings with it the possibility of new growth, and this relation between destruction and renewal is fundamental to the volume, indeed is figured in the hay of the title. Throughout the book images of meadow grass, of mowing, of vegetation and new growth, serve to focus the question of whether the middle is a prelude to the end, or a new beginning.

Hay, of course, is a potent image for something in between, a product of the harvest which is laid up for winter and gets you through till spring. In a volume obsessed with food, hay is a suggestive image for fodder for the winter of your life. Muldoon offers us a figure for this relation between beginnings and endings in 'The Plot', one of two concrete poems in the volume, poems which are quite literally without a centre. The poem takes as its epigraph lines from a traditional ballad in which the 'gentleman' offers to help the 'maid' in the cutting of her hay, grass 'that's ne'er been trampled down'. The poem which follows is a witty representation of the consequences. It consists of the repeated letters 'alf' arranged across the page in a square: alfalfalfalfalfalfa. But this field or 'plot' of 'alfalfa' has a bit cut out of the middle, in which the word 'alpha' appears. Cropping the grass creates the space for a new beginning, but it is also an end, with the implication that the maid has lost her virginity (the idea of a 'fall' maintains a ghostly presence within 'alfalfalf'). After all what do plots need except a beginning, a middle and an end? Cutting down, and the loss of purity, the poem suggests, are painful but inevitable preliminaries to a new start. It's only in the aftermath (literally "after mowing") that things can begin anew.

In poetic terms this cutting back appears in Muldoon's recourse to the minimalism of the haiku: the series of ninety 'Hopewell Haiku' once more explores seasonal cycles, growth and decay. Given the affinities between Muldoon's sensibility and the characteristics of the haiku form, the wonder is that he hasn't turned to it before. Haiku typically embody a happy discovery – an accidental chiming or flash of thought, a fleeting insight or unexpected conjunction of images. The form shares with metaphysical poetry the startling connection of disparate ideas, the element of wit and a certain verbal trickery. But at the same time the haiku is far removed in tone from the abtruse and learned references of the metaphysicals. It seems an almost ideal embodiment of the simplicity and availability Muldoon is seeking in this volume – a confluence of accident and design guaranteed to attract him.

Classical haiku don't rhyme, yet conform to a very strict syllabic structure consisting of three sections, of five, seven and five syllables respectively. While this brevity is in itself a test of deftness and skill, enforcing extreme poetic concision, it should come as no surprise that Muldoon adds more even constraints to the traditional form. For a start his haiku rhyme in the first and third lines, and he also uses rhyme to knit the sequence together: the middle word of each haiku provides the rhyme word for the haiku five poems later. What is more, the middle line of the last haiku returns us to the beginning, completes the chain, by rhyming with the first and third of the fifth haiku. In ratcheting up these formal constraints is Muldoon sacrificing the freedom and spontaneity of the haiku form? Rather he seems to be experimenting with the ways in which severe constraint, cutting back, can lead to a new kind of freedom.

Haiku are traditionally concerned with images of the natural world, but the nature which gives Muldoon food for thought is almost entirely domestic and suburban. Throughout the sequence he barely steps out of his back-yard, unless it is to get into his car. The poems offer brief glimpses of family life, which revolves around the kitchen (food again) and the yard. The cast of the sequence include his wife ('Jean paints one toenail. / In the fork of a white ash, / quick, a cardinal'); his daughter ('I've upset the pail / in which my daughter had kept / her five – 'No *six*' – snails'); his cats and dogs. We pass along a chain of vivid moments, ironic glimpses of the ordinary, the minor events of everyday life. These are pleasing vignettes, but for readers used to the complex jamborees of 'Madoc' and 'Yarrow' the modesty of these poems may be disconcerting. Even as we admire Muldoon's quick eye and verbal economy there's an almost inevitable nagging thought that perhaps he's simply lost it – producing a poetic version of the mall sushi bar. Sensing that there must be a deeper message, we may be tempted to search for a twist. On the other hand what's winning about the poems is precisely their refusal to pretend to any greater significance.

Less a developmental sequence than variations on a theme, the haiku are nonetheless held together by a vestigial pattern or movement. The seasons pass into one another as Muldoon charts the year, recording at first his private concerns as a snow-bound winter turns into spring: 'The first day of spring. / What to make of that bald patch / right under the swing.' As spring becomes summer, and eventually we return to a new winter, Muldoon notes small but telling episodes of family life. Though nature scarcely threatens here, the poems still mark a preoccupation with food, with the need to keep something by: 'For most of a week / we've lived on a pot of broth / made from a pig's cheek.' This sense of reserves running low recurs in the final haiku ('The maple's great cask / that once held so much in store / now yields a hip-flask') and it's perhaps not too far-fetched to discern an underlying worry that, here in suburbia, the fodder of experience, the imaginative resources of the poet may be getting thin.

Seasonal growth, though hardly dramatic, appears both welcome and unwelcome: 'It seems from this sheer / clapboard, fungus-flanged, that walls / do indeed have ears.' And connected with this growth and change in the natural world is the question of ageing. The poet's birthday comes in the very middle of the sequence (right on target in haiku number 46), giving rise to disquieting thoughts of 'the thistles / which attend our middle age', or, of a hard pear, 'ripeness is not all'. Ageing, and a faint whiff of mortality, are again imaged in terms of cutting back, harvesting, bringing in the hay: 'No time since we checked / our scythe-blades, our reaping hooks / that are now rust-flecked.'

The scythe is rusted: nature here is something to observe and enjoy, to muse on and play with, not to work with and against. The country scene is a site of leisure (as 'Paunch' suggests), so there is no need to keep one's tools in good repair or to save the hay. Implicit in this view of nature is a contrast with the rural life of Muldoon's father – we recall the father's well-worn boots, one of the items in the mud room. When the poet sets light to the straw (rather than storing it for use) he is transported to the scene of Irish agrarian battles, sees the nineteenth-century insurgents his father was fascinated by in 'The Mixed Marriage':

> When I set a match
> to straw – Whiteboys, Bootashees,
> pikestaffs in the thatch

From the white-hot bales
Caravats and Shanavests
step with white-hot flails.

These sudden slippages from one scene to another occur repeatedly in *Hay*, recalling Muldoon's pleasure in the imagination's power to transport both poet and reader across time and space in *The Annals of Chile*. In the previous book these leaps and shifts seemed like displays of poetic prowess and control. The devices of the camera and the video recorder suggested that such cross-cutting, the poet's ability to subvert spatial and temporal relations, was a matter of technical mastery. But the fluid boundaries between times and places in *Hay* seem subtly different, more like involuntary and fortuitous dissolves than purposeful transformations. It's almost as though the poet is unable to keep his mind on pleasure, leisure and sex, much as he would like to. Muldoon can't stop the slippage or the "bleeding" of the image (a process for which he has coined the term 'imarrhage', with its connotations of violence and emergency). So far from using poetry to subvert or distort perspective, he seems to be at the mercy of his mind's eye.

It's worth pausing for a moment to recall Muldoon's statements on poetic 'intent' in his lecture 'Getting Round'. The lecture itself is an ingenious display of tightrope-walking between two seemingly entirely opposed positions. Muldoon argues on the one hand for an extravagant version of new critical control, insisting on total knowingness on the part of the poet: 'The point to which I've been getting round is that it's the poet's job to take into account, as best he or she is able, all possible readings of the poem.' On the other for an equally exorbitant version of Keatsian 'negative capability', or poetic unknowingness, embellished with the Japanese philosophy of Zen (itself an influence on the haiku). It's not, he argues, that the poet creates a connection between images, rather 'a connection sees me'. Muldoon resolves the discrepancy between these views with typical sleight of hand, arguing that it is the poem, not the poet, which 'creates the role of the first reader' – the poet himself is 'read by' the poem. While some version of this tension between destiny and accident has always been a feature of Muldoon's work (think, for example, of the 'singleminded swervings', of *Why Brownlee Left*) there is in this book a heightened awareness of the power of contingency, to the extent that the poet sometimes seems as much victim as master of his art. The disorientating, troublesome and often violent eruptions which repeatedly disturb the tranquillity or intimacy of the moment vividly illustrate this loss of control.

In the sestina 'Wire', for example, the poet 'roves out' into the

familiar North American suburban landscape, only to find himself
trapped inside a nightmarish 'rerun' of events in Northern Ireland:

> Then a distant raking through the gear-box
> of a truck suddenly gone hay-wire
> on this hillside of hillsides in Connecticut
> brought back some truck on a bomb-run,
> brought back so much with which I'd hoped to break —
> the hard line
>
> yet again refusing to toe the line,
> the bullet and the ballot-box,
> the joy-ride, the jail-break,
> Janet endlessly singing 'The Men Behind the Wire',
> the endless rerun
> of Smithfield, La Mon, Enniskillen, of bodies cut
>
> to ribbons as I heard the truck-engine cut
> and, you might have read as much between the lines,
> ducked down here myself behind the hide. As if I myself were on the run.
> The truck-driver handing a box-
> cutter, I'm sure, to the bald guy. A pair of real live wires.
> I've listened to them all day now, torn between making a break
>
> for it and their talk of the long run, the short term, of boxing clever,
> fish or cut bait, make or break,
> the end of the line, right down to the wire.

The poem ends with the poet a fearful fugitive, immobilised in
the landscape. If this is pastoral, then it is a pastoral which speaks
of war. The casual conversation of two sportsmen, out for the day,
gets loaded with other meanings as the eavesdropper is overwhelmed
by memories of a violent past, sucked into a terrifying fantasy scene.
(The circular, repetitive form of the poem, as elsewhere in Muldoon,
reinforces the sense of being haunted, of entrapment.) Here cliché
reveals its darker side – its very neutrality allows apparently innocent chatter about games and pastimes (boxing, fishing...) to be
transformed into something menacing and desperate. Is there a
suggestion, as the poet traverses his mid-life crisis ('make or break'),
that poetry itself is a game in deadly earnest? One way of reading
a poem such as 'Long Finish' is as Muldoon reassuring himself
that it's fine to live where nothing much happens, since even the
smallest changes of everyday life can be transmuted into something
of greater scope. There is certainly no need to fear that domestic
intimacy and suburban pastoral will become too idyllic – the terror
and violence of the wider world are never far away, and can erupt
unpredictably. 'Wire' presents a more sinister version of this scenario
– the poet cannot escape from the past at all, he is unable to move
on, to 'make a break' with his own history.

These instances of violence erupting in a rural setting are condensed in the image of mowing which recurs throughout the book. In 'The Plot' mowing is associated with beginnings, and endings through the metaphor of sex; in the 'Hopewell Haiku' mowing is a figure for ageing, hay for violent rebellion. Such images of life as a meadow to be mowed, mowing as love or war (being mown down), inevitably recall Andrew Marvell. Indeed Muldoon at one point refers to Marvell's eclogue, in which love and hay are intertwined: 'Saturday night. Soap. / Ametas and Thestylis / still making hay-ropes.' This may be *Hay*'s most obvious reference to Marvell – but the ghost of Marvell is everywhere in this book. Like Muldoon he's a poet for whom mowing represents many things, not least the ravages of civil war. In 'Upon Appleton House', for example, the mowers are represented as the force of civil war, the meadow as a scene of battle ('The Mower now commands the Field; / In whose new Traverse seemeth wrought / A Camp of Battail newly fought: / Where, as the Meads with Hay, the Plain / Lyes quilted ore with Bodies Slain'). But if mowing represents destruction for Marvell (as for Muldoon), it is also the precondition for renewal.

Marvell (known as 'the Patriot poet') is surely alluded to in the first lines of 'Aftermath':

> I
>
> 'Let us now drink,' I imagine patriot cry to patriot
> after they've shot
> a neighbour in his own aftermath, who hangs still between two sheaves
> like Christ between two tousle-headed thieves,
> his body wired up to the moon, as like as not.
>
> II
>
> To the memory of another left to rot
> near some remote beauty spot,
> the skin of his right arm rolled up like a shirtsleeve,
> let us now drink.
>
> III
>
> Only a few nights ago, it seems, they set fire to a big house and it got
> so preternaturally hot
> we knew there would be no reprieve
> till the swallows' nests under the eaves
> had been baked into these exquisitely glazed little pots
> from which, my love, let us now drink.

Here is another of Muldoon's experiments in poetic constraint. The three parts of the poem use three rhymes in all. (The significance of the number three throughout *Hay* is worth noting – from the three-line haiku to the three cakes of matzo bread to the three intertwining narratives of the final long poem. Is this Muldoon reflecting again on being in the middle, between beginning and end, or perhaps on being the male in the family, between wife and daughter?) The form is in fact a rondeau. We could read it as a belated reply to the pamphleteer in 'Lunch with Pancho Villa', who upbraids the poet for his self-indulgence ('People are getting themselves killed / Left, right and centre / While you do what? Write rondeaux?'). Here the rarefied pleasures of the rondeau are shown to be intimately connected with violence. The speaker of the poem becomes increasingly caught up in the violence he imagines. The first stanza pictures the aftermath of a "successful" rebel operation; the second the death of a comrade (the victim of a tit-for-tat killing?). The intimate address of the third part heralds a change of scene, as the poet and his partner are suddenly transported into the world of nineteenth-century secret societies, or perhaps to a moment in the Anglo-Irish war earlier this century. The burning of a 'Big House' (that marker of the Anglo-Irish Ascendancy) has been a recurrent feature of violent conflict in Ireland. The disturbing implication is that war needs to rage before you can drink your elegant drink; luxury, it seems, comes at the cost of a terrible mowing down. The poem implies not only that the violence of the past cannot be shaken off, but that no matter whether we live there or not, we are involved – there are no moral innocents or bystanders at the grisly carnival of history.

The final image of the couple toasting each other from their fine pots suggests, at one level, a reprehensible indifference to the suffering and destruction which made their pleasures possible. Yet it also seems that only in a consuming fire can the mud of the mud room, the muddle of ordinary life, be transformed into a new creation – something natural turned into a highly wrought artefact, through a force which is 'preternatural'. We return here to one of Muldoon's earliest intuitions, already evident in 'Dancers at the Moy', that violence and suffering are in some sense preconditions of creation. But if anything the disturbing relation between the horrors of history and present enjoyment has intensified. In 'Dancers at the Moy' the bones of the starved horses underpinned the creativity and energy of the dance. There is no such movement here – in an almost exaggerated display of lack of feeling the poem mirrors the hard, glazed and fired form of the pots. The poem offers a graphic enactment of the disturbing relation between art and violence – the image of the swallows' nests recalling an earlier image for the aesthetic, the swallow dipping into the mire in 'Incantata'. What's striking about 'Aftermath' is how small and fragile the achievement of art turns out to be – a less comforting notion of 'reprieve' would be hard to imagine.

If 'Aftermath' takes us back to the ruins of the Irish civil war, 'Third Epistle to Timothy' is haunted by the same historical moment. The poem is set in 1923, in the aftermath of civil war, when Muldoon's father was eleven years old, and working as 'a servant-boy at Hardy's of Carnteel'. It provides a point of concentration for the volume's concerns with pastoral, labour and violence – with mowing. The poem is, amongst other things, a subtle and moving lament for the hardships of his father's life; it's nearly midnight and he's on the point of falling asleep after another day's labour in the fields. The lines which follow imagine his father's dream, a waking dream which culminates in a vision. Indeed this looks like a return to a kind of primal scene, one which discloses (or at any rate pretends to) the imaginative provenance of the images of hay and the horse disease which has appeared in so many of Muldoon's poems over the years:

> That knocking's the knocking against their stalls of a team
> of six black Clydesdales mined in Coalisland
> he's only just helped to unhitch from the cumbersome
> star of a hay-rake. Decently and in order
> he brought each whitewashed nose
> to its nosebag of corn, to its galvanised bucket.
> One of the six black Clydesdale mares
> he helped all day to hitch and unhitch
> was showing, on the near hock, what might be a bud of farcy
> picked up, no doubt, while on loan to Wesley Cummins.

The disease has been picked up from the stable of a Protestant and a Unionist, a local farmer to whom Patrick Muldoon himself has been loaned, to help with saving the hay. In the context of the recent war even the most seemingly innocent of activities is politically loaded: the mowing machine is a gun carriage; Cummins himself a dragoon. Memories of recent violence are inescapable, including one of the volume's central images, burning hay :

> A year since they kidnapped Anketell Moutray from his home at
>   Favour Royal,
> dragging him, blindfolded, the length of his own gravel path,
> eighty years old, the Orange county grand master. Four A Specials shot
>   on a train
> in Clones. The Clogher valley
> a blaze of flax-mills and haysheds. Memories of the Land League.
>   Davitt and Biggar.

The poem movingly evokes the father's isolation as a child – a lone farm boy, he is mistreated by Cummins, who employs biblical rhetoric to give vent to his prejudice and hatred ('Decently and in order... let all Inniskillings be done'). He alludes to Job ('as the

sparks fly upward / man is born into trouble') but as the title suggests he is fondest of quoting mottos from the epistles of St Paul:

> 'Though you speak, young Muldoon...' Cummins calls up from
>   trimming the skirt
> of the haycock, 'Though you speak with the tongue
> of an angel, I see you for what you are... Malevolent.
> Not only a member of the church malignant but a *malevolent* spirit.

We could think of Cummins as a perverse embodiment of the poet
(after all he's always quoting Paul); like the poet he mixes up his
allusions and twists clichés to his own ends. He takes moralistic
biblical pronouncements about how to live the good life, and sub-
verts them to express his own baneful prejudices.

The question of how to live your life is central to the poem,
and not just because of Cummins's ill-willed pronouncements. It's
hard to imagine a rural existence more different from Muldoon's
leisured relationship to the countryside. The contrast in the book
between his father's life of labour, privation, subjection, perhaps
above all 'order', and Muldoon's muddle of self-indulgence and
self-gratification (indecency and disorder) could not be more stark.
The portrayal of his father's early life might suggest that it's a bad
conscience about his own life of ease and indulgence which causes
the poet to see Caravats and Shanavests in the straw he burns in
'Hopewell Haiku'. Yet at the same time the poem implies that what
father and son share is their capacity for dream. In addition to the
Marvellian echoes, there is, surely, a background presence here of
Frost's early poem 'Mowing'. On the face of it, Frost's poem sets
up a distinction between the truth of fact, (associated with work),
and the fictions and fantasies spun from indolence ('no dream of the
gift of idle hours'; 'the fact is the sweetest dream that labor knows.').
But just as Frost's poem ironically doubts its own premise, so
Muldoon questions the contrast between labour and fantasy.

In 'Third Epistle to Timothy' Muldoon dreams his father's
dream – it's a dream which derives from labour but is far from
sweet, nor does it stay in the realm of fact. Its truth is the truth of
fantasy; it's a dream of escape into an other world of tenderness
and possibility. The poem ends with the vision of a time before
creation, of a world of pure potentialities. The father's reverie
conjures up an extraordinary – and extraordinarily moving – sight
of an innumerable band of lost spirits, an image of haycock after
haycock each topped by a child:

> Hardy's last servant-girl, reaches out from her dais
> of salt hay, stretches out an unsunburned arm
> half in bestowal, half beseechingly, then turns away to appeal

> to all that spirit-troop
> of hay treaders as far as the eye can see, the coil on coil
> of hay from which, in the taper's mild uproar,
> they float out across the dark face of the earth, an earth without form,
>   and void.

There's something almost achingly distressing about these lines. The implication is surely not that Hardy's last servant-girl has moved on to another position, but that she is dead. A kind of guardian spirit, she represents the ultimate in loss and grace at the same time (half in bestowal, half-beseechingly). How delicately Muldoon offers this image, counterpointed as it is by the quiet disturbance, the 'mild uproar' of the candle flame, a flame which seems both to protect the boy and inspire his vision.

This return to a vacant, pre-Genesis world is vitally important. For what is being honoured here is the intensity, the power of the father's imagination, his capacity to give shape to otherwise empty possibilities. So while Seamus Heaney famously compares his writing to the digging of his farmer father, Muldoon portrays his father as a subversive, fantasising spirit, able to transcend, if only fleetingly, the shackles of drudgery, of decency and order, which Cummins tries to impose on him. He suggests, if you like, that his father was a poet too. In playing out his father's reverie poetically here, and – in the final poem of the volume – realising his dream of emigrating to Australia, Muldoon is offering a deeply felt and touching tribute. The father's boots which appear in 'The Mud Room' ('so worn / it was hard to judge where the boots came to an end / and the world began, given how one would blend / imperceptibly into the other'), even evoke, one might suggest, a kind of negative capability – an ability to merge with one's surroundings which is not opposed to, but rather arises out of, the world of strenuous and repetitive work.

'Third Epistle to Timothy' is written in regular ten line stanzas, the last rhyming with the first and thus bringing it full circle. Apart from this the poem doesn't rhyme except in one bizarre, almost terrifying sense – it rhymes with the other long poems in *Hay*, 'The Mud Room' and 'The Bangle (Slight Return)'. What is more these poems in turn 'rhyme' with 'Yarrow' and 'Incantata'. Each poem uses the same ninety rhyme words, and in the same order as they first occur in 'Yarrow', but in different verse forms, so that the repetition is undetectable unless you are looking for it. What is Muldoon up to here? There are many kinds of repetition in *Hay* – loops, refrains, mottos, recurrent clichés – but this is a repetitive device beyond anything which an attentive reader of the individual poem could be expected to grasp. In one sense, since the rhyme scheme originated in 'Yarrow', we could say that a kind of ghostly maternal template is now structuring Muldoon's work – the mother is an invisible frame or presence, even in poems which are ostensibly about the father. But beyond this, we have to reckon with an increasing obsession on Muldoon's part with arbitrary formal constraint as such. The rhyme scheme template – invisible to the 'naked eye' – is reminiscent of the formal experiments associated with the French group Oulipo (Ouvroir de Littérature Potentielle). Perhaps the best known member of the group was Georges Perec, who wrote his novel *La Disparition* without using the letter 'e' (an extraordinary feat considering that this is the commonest vowel in the French language). Muldoon too seems interested in the way that mechanical tasks may generate patterns, at the same time releasing him from the tyranny of established plot expectations, liberating him from dependence on reality, and the psychological control of meaning.

We have been here before, of course. Muldoon, who styles himself in *Hay* as 'a Prince of Serendip', has always been fascinated by the way extreme formal constraint may allow more accidents to happen, with how artifice converges with contingency and the possibility of chance discoveries. Unexpected substitutions of the artificial and the natural occur at many points in the volume, from the cosmetic made of birdshit in 'Nightingales', to Muldoon's astonishment at Jimi Hendrix's technologically unsupported wizardry: 'I'm taken aback (jolt upon jolt) / to think that Hendrix did it all "by hand".' Doing it 'by hand' suggests the stamp of individual intention (Muldoon contrasts this with the 'worst excesses' of Conlon Nancarrow's pre-calculated music.) But clearly, even the hand can slip, producing the unanticipated. In one poem, 'Errata', Muldoon sends up his own obsession with this process through a series of semantically charged 'corrections':

> For 'mother' read 'other'.
> For 'feather' read 'father'.
> For 'married' read 'marred'.
> For 'religion' read 'region'.

The spark of a new meaning is struck from the clash between what was intended and what (accidentally) occurred. But since it was the poet who invented the errata (though not the verbal similarities on which they are based), this is clearly a matter of control after all.

Muldoon's preoccupation with the relation between predetermined form and chance is at one level, as I've suggested, merely a new version of Robert Frost's famous definition of the figure a

poem makes as a tension between the predestined and the unforeseen. Yet this book takes the conflict between these ideas – the poet's
absolute subjection to chance and his absolute control over his
material – to the limit. The final poem in the book 'The Bangle
(Slight Return)' is an extraordinary, excessive assault on this issue.
Formally the shape of the poem is absolutely predetermined – each
of the thirty sonnets uses six of the ninety rhyme words from
'Yarrow' (rhyming ababcdcdefgefg), in the order in which they
first occur in the earlier poem – which gets you to sonnet 15, and
then the whole pattern is repeated in reverse. Yet despite (or because
of) this unyielding structure, the sequence takes us on a journey
into confusion and chaos. The poem follows three different narratives at the same time, narratives which slip into one another, and
get increasingly mixed up as the poem progresses. The switch from
one story to another often hinges on some quirk of language, or on
poetic "dissolves" of the kind which Muldoon refers to as 'bleeding
images' – an apposite term, given the welter of blood spattered
across the pages of these sonnets. Like 'The Mud Room', 'The
Bangle (Slight Return)' is concerned with what it means to 'draw a
line', to trace a limit or make distinctions without denying the
variousness of things. How, in the flux and muddle of our lives,
can we set a boundary to something, stop it becoming something
else – hold on to it? It isn't a coincidence, I think, that the last time
Muldoon made use of this register was in poems such as 'Something
Else' and 'The Soap-Pig' in the elegiac volume *Meeting the British*,
written after the death of his father. Slippage and metamorphosis, as
we shall shortly rediscover, are intimately connected in his poetry
with the slide into non-being, with death.

The question of non-being, with its after-echoes of the conclusion
of 'Third Epistle to Timothy', is almost unceremoniously thrust at
the reader by the three epigraphs with which Muldoon prefaces
'The Bangle (Slight Return)'. The epigraphs offer different visions
of 'an earth without form and void'; the first is a quotation from
the Romanian philosopher E.M. Cioran: 'If it is true that by death
we once more become what we were before being, would it not have
been better to abide by that pure possibility, not to stir from it?
What use was this detour, when we might have remained forever in
an unrealised plenitude?' Life is a matter of choice and exclusion, of
narrowing down the range of possibilities – but on the other hand,
what use is an unrealised plenitude? The second epigraph also focuses
on a space in between – a suspension between life and death – as it
speculates on what foetuses dream about. Here pure possibility
seems to reveal its vacancy. Foetuses cannot dream (at any rate

not in any recognisable way) because they have not yet lived a life
– they have no experience, no knowledge of conflict with the world,
which (as the father's dream in 'Third Epistle' reveals) is the stuff
which dreams are made on, the fodder which nourishes the imagination, and perhaps the poem. The final epigraph is from *The
Importance of Being Earnest*, where Algernon is faced with the choice
between 'this world, the next world, and Australia'. Muldoon's
poem takes up the hint that Australia represents a kind of no-man's-
land between life and the after-life, a place where 'pure possibility'
can reign, as he imagines (yet another) alternative life for his father,
this time at the Antipodes.

'The Bangle (Slight Return)' offers a kind of crazed version of
Why Brownlee Left's concern with fate and possibility, with what
had to be and what might have been. Throughout the earlier volume Muldoon puzzled over how a poem can go somewhere, take
us on a journey, and yet its outcome be unforeseen. Life is a narrowing down of possibilities, an unavoidable exercise of choice; we
have to take one road and abandon the other. But in poetry we can
go in several directions at once, take the road not taken too. Holding open imaginative possibilities, alternative routes, is a familiar
Muldoon technique, and 'The Bangle (Slight Return)' is in this
sense another journey poem. But here so many possibilities are kept
in the air at once that the poem can't go anywhere very much,
though it moves at a fantastic pace nonetheless.

Muldoon is thinking about the plethora of abstract potentialities,
and its relation both to art and to a life in which we have to
choose and act. The subject-matter may be serious (or 'earnest')
but this is one of Muldoon's wildest and funniest poems to date.
As we might have come to expect, from what we know of the
book so far, the narrator of the poem is in a restaurant, and in the
course of the poem much eating and drinking goes on. (The
restaurant is in Paris 'off the Champs-Elysées', so the narrator is
nearly a goner, has almost made it to the Elysian fields, or – at
the very least – is on the way out). Muldoon is reading Virgil
(who 'talks' to him and thus becomes his guide through the law-
less journey which follows), and writing a poem in his head. But
at the same time he is enjoying a most unusual meal, since he
refuses to make the kinds of choices on which a meal is usually
based. He drinks various kinds of wine, both white and red
(Veuve Cliquot, Châteauneuf du Pape, Muscadet, Côtes du Rhône
– his tastes are pretty "middle of the road", if not *nel mezzo del
camin*) in no particular order, much to the starchy disapproval of
the waiter, who

when he saw me tend
towards another bottle of the Côtes du Rhône
licked the end

of his pencil, drew a line
and began to catalogue,
with all the little tuts and twitters and whistle-whines
that are the mark of capability and godlike

reason, the damage done by my convoy,
my caravan,
of consommé, salad and ray's wing braked

on a bed of bockchoy.

Significantly, here it is the waiter who is drawing a line, and at a number of points in the poem, dressed in 'full-length white empyrean', he is given quasi-divine status. Like God, he has command of the total range of possibilities which are listed and distinguished on the menu. He can survey them all, without doing himself damage by gross indulgence, by trying to consume them all without making a choice. In the course of his binge, the narrator begins to flirt, or imagines he is flirting, with a woman at another table who reminds him of a reporter he once knew in Belfast. Here is another rather hopeless and pathetic middle-aged figure, fondly imagining he still has it in him, fantasising sexual possibilities. Things rapidly descend into chaos after the mid-point of the sequence (sonnet 15), surely another allusion to the poet's mid-life crisis. It becomes clear that nothing will come of this flirtation, that the narrator is losing his grip on reality. The woman's male companions make pointed remarks about his girth, and he ends up discovering that he does not even have the money to pay for his meal. This decline in his fortunes is punctuated by snatches from the children's ballad, 'The Love-Sick Frog' ('a frog he would a-wooing go') – an ominous accompaniment, since the amorous frog ends up getting eaten.

The gastronomic confusion of the poem is reflected at many other levels. The restaurant scene keeps slipping into other narratives – one the story of Aeneas's flight from Troy, as told by Virgil, and in particular his return to the burning city and attempt to rescue his wife Creusa. The other is an imagined version of Muldoon's father's emigration to Australia, which in fact would have resulted in Muldoon himself remaining a pure possibility. But this imaginary past itself splits in different variations. In one, the father arrives in Australia where, among other things, his pony's belly is torn open by a wild animal. In another he only gets as far as the 'packet boat' from Stranraer to Larne, which turns round in the middle of the Irish Sea. Possibly, he does not even get that far as, unable

to find the ferry timetable: 'the cow-pony's innards / packed themselves back into the manganese- / red suitcase that would never
now burst open on the border / of Queensland and wherever'.
With this witty and exuberant gesture Muldoon takes the figures
of the horse and the suitcase which recur throughout his work
(think of the briefcase and the valise in *Madoc – A Mystery*) and
makes them one. The suitcase, in its ability to contain variety,
offers an image for the poem. In a suitcase, or perhaps its full-
scale counterpart the wagon train, you can take your entire world
with you, just as the poem has a kind of self-containment which
allows it to pack everything it needs for its own journey. But in
this poem the suitcase opens and everything compressed inside
comes tumbling out, recalling the bale of hay in the title-poem
('I'm itching to cut the twine, to unpack // that hay accordion, that
hay-concertina'). Despite the power of the poem to compress and
contain, it is when it starts to expand and explode (or catch fire –
in 'Hay' the bales begin to glow, just as straw and hay burst into
flame throughout the book), that the poet can really begin to play.
    The question of poetic control and its limits, of how far one can
define and hold to a direction amidst the plenitude of possibilities,
is introduced right at the start of 'The Bangle (Slight Return)', as
Virgil addresses the poet:

> 'The beauty of it,' ventured Publius Vergilius Maro
> 'is that your father and the other skinnymalinks
> may yet end up a pair of jackaroos
> in the canefields of Brisbane...
>
> 'The beauty of it is that I delivered them from harm;
> it was I who had Aeneas steal
> back to look for Creusa, I who had her spirit rub
>
> like a flame through his flame burnished arms...

The aesthetic power of poetry, its beauty, is inseparable from its
being all made up, determined by the imagination of the poet.
And yet, despite Virgil's pronouncements, the poet-narrator finds
himself at the mercy of whim and accident, rather than in control
of the poem's direction. The shifts between the three narratives
depend on accidents of language and event – or so Muldoon
would have us think (he refers, for example, to the 'The Tyre
Courier' rather than 'The Tyrone Courier', suddenly making
Northern Ireland both Trojan and Tyrian). The casual actions of
the woman in the restaurant trigger unpredictable associations,
conjure up other scenes. The flashing of her bracelet calls up
images of Muldoon's father's hair glinting with Brylcreem; when

she lights a cigarette the poet sees the smoke of burning Troy: 'The streel of smoke. The tink and tonk / as the Greeks hastened from tent to tent / / in their nightclubbers' boots and short skirts.' It's not accidental that both these examples are about flames, for the poem is full of flashing lights, sparks, fires, glitter and glimmer, and all kinds of incendiary devices. Hay burns, as we know, throughout the rest of the book – and in part, these conflagrations are a figure for inspiration, the unpredictable explosion of the poem. But there is something else at work here too. Flame and fire are elusive and intangible, they slip through your fingers. Now past mid-life, the poet is aware that all kinds of past possibilities are unattainable, gone forever. At the end of the poem Creusa (famously figured by Virgil as a flame), who blurs with the woman in the restaurant, and with the former Belfast colleague, 'slipped forever from my arms'.

Total control, complete wish-fulfilment, is – it seems – an illusion in art as in life. Try as he might, the poet cannot keep the poem on course, ruefully reflecting that

> ...there's many a slip
> twixt what one supposedly determines
> and the al-al-al-al-aleatory...

The poem sustains a tension between the desire to choose and act, to give shape and direction to the journey, to hold onto something ('As the packet tried to hold to hold to hold / its course) and the inevitability of slippage. Holding on to one thing means setting others aside, and this involves drawing a line, using the power of language to define and distinguish. Muldoon worries about the difference between being aware of variety and being mired in it, as he was mired in the drek of the mud room.

As 'The Bangle (Slight Return)' progresses, not only do the three narratives become increasingly confused, but it also starts to get mixed up with other parts of *Hay*, turning into other poems, in particular 'Errata' and 'Symposium'.

> It was downhill all the way after that. The opprobrium
> of the waiter of waiters. To have your cake
> and eat bigarroons *and* Bonderay au Foin? His new imperium
> sweeping clean through the muskeg
>
> in which my da and your man had ridden their cock
> horses roughshod over my *crise*
> *d'un certain âge*, my da trying in vain to kick-
> start the cow-pony, my calling out 'Creusa, Creusa, Creusa'
>
> as the packet reached the mid-way- and turning-point.

Poetic meaning depends on the ability to keep to a structure, to maintain the pattern which both distinguishes and connects the lines. But as this poem progresses the poet seems to lose the ability to keep things separate, as he lapses into a drunken reverie:

> Even as I myself tried to keep myself on an even
> keel as if I had indeed been put
> drunk into the Newhaven-
> Dieppe packet-boat...

What makes the poetic plethora of alternatives and unrealised possibilities different from simply inebriation, what differentiates it from the pure potentiality which, as the Cioran epigram suggests, is non-being or death? This question is sharpened by the Marvellian echoes which return here: 'As one put drunk into the Packet-boat / Tom May was hurried hence and did not know't. / But was amazed on the Elysian side, / And with an Eye uncertain, gazing wide, / Could not determine in what place he was.' Muldoon presents himself as a drunken poetaster, who has died from over-indulging in food and drink. What differentiates the poet's capacity to entertain and play with endless possibilities from death in which, equally, nothing really happens any longer? What differentiates Louis MacNeice's celebration of the 'drunkenness of things being various' from plain drunkenness?

At the end of 'The Bangle (Slight Return)', amidst the almost terminal confusion, the poet discovers he is unable to pay for his meal – it turns out that (in American slang) a 'muldoon' is a stolen credit card. In a book so concerned with how to hold a line, with how to define and preserve an identity, as your life becomes entwined with others and death becomes a felt possibility, to discover your credentials are fake may seem like the final blow. A fundamental way in which we define our identity is in terms of the past, but in this poem the past is all made up. Life is a series of impressions that can be summoned, but it lacks the central core which would give it all meaning. But the poem, with its extraordinary energy, offers its own answer to the question of whether borrowings from, and entanglements with others really do threaten to erase uniqueness. For a Muldoon, we could say, *is* something stolen. Not only do other poets – Marvell, Virgil, Frost and many others – speak through his lines, but he trades too in the worn-out language of platitude and cliché. The resulting confusion is far from an indistinguishable and anonymous mixture. The poetic voice reveals a constancy which lies beyond the opposition of intention and chance, beyond anything the writer could deliberately aim at or hold onto. Even as the poet loses his grip, he is buoyed up by his own unmistakable idiom.

Postscript

Critical judgement is always at the mercy of time. Like any significant author, Muldoon demands patience of the reader, and this is not only because the complexity of his language and ideas has to be allowed time to unravel in the mind. This is poetry whose ingenuity is matched by a richness and density which no amount of re-reading can exhaust. I have no doubt that my account of *Hay* will soon be superseded by those of others able to look on the book from a greater distance. It's only over time that it will become clear, for example, whether *Hay* really is a turning point in Muldoon's work, and – perhaps more importantly – whether he happens to be moving in the right direction. This element of doubt is of course essential to any arresting and innovative work – there's always a question mark over a new book by any pioneering contemporary. With typical legerdemain, however, Muldoon responds to this difficulty of knowing by addressing it in his work. It's as though he's trying to anticipate our doubts by dramatising his dialogue with himself, his concern about whether this is the end or a fruitful new beginning.

We might regard this as further evidence of his refusal to stand behind what he says, to speak in an unqualified voice. While it could be construed as openness and honesty, Muldoon's apparent confession of poetic crisis can more plausibly be read as yet another game of doubles, an ironic holding of himself at arm's length. Yet again the poet teases us with our inability to tell which is the "real" Muldoon – the seeming clarity of much of the recent poetry may be still another veil. Similarly, in laughing at himself as an irresponsible Don Juan figure, taking liberties with women and words, refusing to select and allowing his appetite to range, Muldoon may be seeking to forestall the suggestion that he has sacrificed feeling and authenticity for the sake of technical flourish. He's always trying to stay one step ahead. He sends up the idea that he is merely making selfish use of things, manipulating the materials of his craft, keeping his distance rather than getting involved. Apparently, we can't even take his worries seriously. Like Byron, his mentor in such forms of ironic displacement, Muldoon adopts these modes of poetic self-defence as much as a matter of style as out of genuine anxiety – he performs his dilemmas, jokes about them, sets himself up as Byron does his narrators.

This teasing acknowledgement of the problem of technique and feeling doesn't dispel our doubts, of course. Indeed, in some sense it makes them more acute. Muldoon's poetry has no fear of artifice – the intricate, often obscure rhyme schemes, the intellectual conceits on which many of the poems are based, point to a distinctively baroque sensibility. Of course, the contrivances of the baroque were not in themselves inimical to feeling; on the contrary, they often served to compress and intensify it. Muldoon too is adept at intensifying emotion through the use of highly-wrought poetic devices, and indeed it could be argued that it is only the intricacy of his work which allows him to do justice to the depth and complexity of the feelings he explores. At the same time his dazzling ability to play with language heightens the poetry's characteristically elusive stance; Muldoon's continual sidestepping may often seem like disavowal of the emotions his work so powerfully conveys. Yet this seemingly endemic uncertainty is itself emotionally charged. It speaks to a world in which the question of feeling is inseparable from the question of identity and its fractures, in which nostalgia for a sense of place vies with a suspicion of tradition and its constraints. Muldoon's work registers the force of our longings for the securities of the past – but at the same time refuses to let us forget how scenes of apparent harmony or repose are invariably built on some previous history of violence. The pressure of conflict, its fateful repetitions and reprises, is central not only to Muldoon's sense of history, but to his poetics. As a way of seeking to restore sense to the world when our habitual reponses are disabled and disrupted, art has an anxious, indissoluble affinity with violence.

There's a version of Muldoon which is all about breaking things – iconoclasm, 'destructed' sonnets, 'exploded' sestinas. It's a take on his work which Muldoon has frequently encouraged, suggesting that the poet's task is above all to disrupt. He undoubtedly likes to play the *enfant terrible*, but it is not just bravado when he asserts that his poetry strives less for peace than disturbance. On the other hand he would not be the powerful writer he is, were his poetry concerned simply with the overturning of pattern and rule. The impulse to disturb and unsettle has always been counterbalanced in his work by a profound sense of order and design, of the spontaneous echoes and associations through which language speaks to us. He has even suggested that there may be an objective, involuntary element to the verbal repetitions, slippages and connections which characterise his work: 'I believe that these devices like repetition and rhyme are not artificial, that they're not imposed, somehow, on the language. They are inherent in the language.

Words want to find chimes with each other, things want to connect.'¹ This may sound odd coming from a poet renowned for the artfulness and contrivance of his structures, not least the arbitrary and predetermined structure of the rhyme-words which his recent long poems employ. Yet it is surely Muldoon's talent for listening to the patterns of the language which allows him to create his intricate, often plangent and moving poems.

Muldoon's work makes demands of us – and I hope I have not glossed over this fact in the preceding pages. Yet for all the complexities, his work has a verve and impetus which makes it, in another sense, compellingly readable ('like watching television', as one enthusiastic new reader put it recently), and I have tried to communicate this excitement too. Muldoon's unlikely combination of vulnerability, elusiveness and immediacy of impact is unique in contemporary poetry. His is a style superbly equipped to capture that insistent modern experience – the sense that it is precisely when we think we know our place that we are furthest from home.

Notes

Introduction *(pp.9-23)*

1. Helen Vendler, 'Anglo-Celtic Attitudes', New York Review of Books, 6 November 1997, 59.
2. John Carey, 'The Stain of Words', *Sunday Times*, 21 June 1987, 56.
3. Michael Hofmann, 'Muldoon – A Mystery', *London Review of Books*, 20 December 1990, 18.
4. Hofmann, 18.
5. Mark Ford, 'Little Do We Know', *London Review of Books*, 12 January 1995, 19.
6. Paul Muldoon, 'Getting Round: Notes Towards an *Ars Poetica*', *Essays in Criticism*, 48 (2), April 1998, 109.
7. Vendler, 58.
8. Seamus Heaney, *The Redress of Poetry* (London: Faber, 1995), 3-4.
9. Muldoon, 'Getting Round', 126.
10. John Haffenden, *Viewpoints: Poets in Conversation* (London: Faber and Faber, 1981), 133.

CHAPTER ONE: *New Weather* *(pp.24-41)*

1. See 'Notes for "Chez Moy: A Critical Autobiography"' (unpublished MS., 1994).
2. Patrick Kavanagh, *Collected Pruse* (London: Martin Brian and O'Keeffe, 1973), 282.
3. Muldoon, 'Notes for "Chez Moy: A Critical Autobiography"'.

CHAPTER TWO: *Mules* *(pp.42-60)*

1. Muldoon, 'Notes for "Chez Moy: A Critical Autobiography"'.

CHAPTER THREE: *Why Brownlee Left* *(pages 61-85)*

1. Haffenden, 133.
2. Matthew 6.26.
3. Robert Frost, 'The Figure a Poem Makes', *Norton Anthology of American Literature*, second edition, vol.2, ed. Nina Baym et al (New York: W.W. Norton, 1985), 1033-34.
4. Seamus Heaney, *The Government of the Tongue* (London: Faber and Faber, 1988), 94.
5. 'Paul Muldoon writes…', *Poetry Book Society Bulletin*, 106, Autumn 1980, 1.
6. Muldoon, 'Notes for "Chez Moy: A Critical Autobiography"'.
7. Paul Muldoon, 'Between Ireland and Montevideo', the first Waterstones Lecture, delivered on 29 May 1994 at the Hay-on-Wye Festival of Literature (unpublished MS.).
8. Edna Longley, *Poetry in the Wars* (Newcastle upon Tyne: Bloodaxe Books, 1986), 211.
9. Haffenden, 141.
10. *Poetry in the Wars*, 222.

CHAPTER FOUR: *Quoof* *(pp.86-110)*

1. Tim Kendall, *Paul Muldoon* (Bridgend: Seren, 1996), 94-5.
2. John Kerrigan, 'The New Narrative', *London Review of Books*, 16-29 February 1984, 22.

CHAPTER FIVE: *The Wishbone* and *Meeting the British* *(pp.111-134)*

1. 'An Interview with Paul Muldoon', interviewed by Clair Wills, Nick Jenkins and John Lanchester, *Oxford Poetry*, 3 (1), Winter 1986-7, 18.
2. Quoted in Clair Wills, 'The Lie of the Land', *The Chosen Ground: Essays on the Contemporary Poetry of Northern Ireland*, ed. Neil Corcoran (Bridgend: Seren, 1992), 134.
3. Personal interview, 2 June 1987.
4. Samuel Hynes, *The Auden Generation: Literature and Politics in England in the 1930s* (Faber and Faber, 1976), 349.

CHAPTER SIX: *Madoc – A Mystery* *(pp.135-156)*

1. Carey, 56.
2. Haffenden, 136.
3. Gwyn Williams, *Madoc: The Making of a Myth* (London: Eyre Methuen, 1979), 67.
4. Paul Muldoon, 'Introduction to a Dramatised Reading of "*Madoc – A Mystery*"', held in Manhattan Theatre Club (May 1992).

CHAPTER SEVEN: *The Prince of the Quotidian* and *The Annals of Chile* *(pp.157-185)*

1. Wallace Stevens, 'The Noble Rider and the Sound of Words', *The Necessary Angel: Essays on Reality and the Imagination* (London: Faber and Faber, 1942), 36.
2. Muldoon, 'Getting Round', 123.
3. Ford, 19.
4. 'An Interview with Paul Muldoon', interviewed by Lynn Keller, *Contemporary Literature*, 35 (1), Spring 1994, 9.
5. Stevens, 20, 36.
6. Cathal Bui Mac Giolla Ghunna, 'The Yellow Bittern', in *The New Oxford Book of Irish Verse*, ed. Thomas Kinsella (Oxford, 1986). The same 'bibulous bittern' appears in the closing lines of 'Yarrow'.
7. Muldoon, 'Between Ireland and Montevideo'.
8. Vendler, 59.

CHAPTER EIGHT: *Hay* *(pp.186-214)*

1. *Muldoon in America*, interviewed by Christopher Cook, BBC Radio 3, 1994.

Postscript *(pp.215-217)*

1. 'Interview with Paul Muldoon', interviewed by John Redmond, *Thumbscrew*, 4 (Spring 1996): 4.

Select Bibliography

Poetry Volumes and Selected Pamphlets:

New Weather (London: Faber and Faber, 1973).

Mules (London: Faber and Faber; Winston-Salem: Wake Forest University Press, 1977).

Why Brownlee Left (London: Faber and Faber; Winston-Salem: Wake Forest University Press, 1980).

Quoof (London: Faber and Faber; Winston-Salem: Wake Forest University Press, 1983).

The Wishbone (Oldcastle: Gallery Press, 1995).

Mules and Early Poems (Winston-Salem: Wake Forest University Press, 1985).

Selected Poems 1968-1983 (London: Faber and Faber, 1986).

Meeting the British (London: Faber and Faber; Winston-Salem: Wake Forest University Press, 1987).

Selected Poems 1968-1986 (New York: Ecco Press, 1987).

Madoc – A Mystery (London: Faber and Faber; New York: Farrar, Straus & Giroux, 1990).

The Prince of the Quotidian (Oldcastle: Gallery Press; Winston-Salem: Wake Forest University Press, 1994).

The Annals of Chile (London: Faber and Faber; New York: Farrar, Straus & Giroux, 1994).

New Selected Poems 1968-1993 (London: Faber and Faber, 1996).

Kerry Slides, with photographs by Bill Doyle (Oldcastle: Gallery Press, 1996).

Hopewell Haiku (Easthampton: Warwick Press, 1997).

Hay (London: Faber and Faber; New York: Farrar, Straus & Giroux, 1998).

Libretto:

Shining Brow (London: Faber and Faber, 1993).

Plays:

Monkeys (BBC, 1989).

Six Honest Serving Men (Oldcastle: Gallery Press, 1995).

Books for Children:

The O-O's party, New Year's Eve (Dublin: Gallery Press, 1980).

The Last Thesaurus (London: Faber and Faber, 1995).

Translation:

The Astrakhan Cloak: Poems in Irish by Nuala Ní Dhomhnaill with translations into English by Paul Muldoon (Oldcastle: Gallery Press, 1992).

Editor:

The Scrake of Dawn: Poems by Young People from Northern Ireland (Belfast: Blackstaff Press, 1979).
The Faber Book of Contemporary Irish Poetry (London: Faber and Faber, 1986).
The Essential Byron (New York: Ecco Press, 1989).
The Faber Book of Beasts (London: Faber and Faber, 1997).

Articles:

'Paul Muldoon writes…', *Poetry Book Society Bulletin*, 106, Autumn 1980, 1.
'Paul Muldoon writes…', *Poetry Book Society Bulletin*, 118, Autumn 1983, 1.
'A Tight Wee Place in Armagh', *Fortnight* (Belfast), July/August 1984, 19 & 23.
'Paul Muldoon writes…', *Poetry Book Society Bulletin*, 162, Autumn, 1994, 1-2.
'Getting Round: Notes towards an *Ars Poetica*', *Essays in Criticism*, 48 (2), April 1998, 107-28.
'The Point of Poetry', *Princeton University Library Chronicle*, LIX: 3 (Spring 1998), 503-16.

Selected Interviews:

'Paul Muldoon', interviewed by John Haffenden, *Viewpoints: Poets in Conversation* (London: Faber and Faber, 1981), 130-42.
'A Conversation with Paul Muldoon', interviewed by Michael Donaghy, *Chicago Review*, 35 (1), Autumn 1985, 76-85.
'Reclaiming Poetry', interviewed and profiled by Alan Jenkins, *Sunday Times*, 14 December 1986.
'An Interview with Paul Muldoon', interviewed by Clair Wills, Nick Jenkins and John Lanchester, *Oxford Poetry*, III (1), Winter 1986/7, 14-20.
'Q&A: Paul Muldoon', interviewed by Kevin Barry, *Irish Literary Supplement*, 6 (2), Fall 1987, 36-37.
'Way down upon the old Susquehanna', interviewed and profiled by Blake Morrison, *The Independent on Sunday*, 28 October 1990, 37.
'Lunch with Paul Muldoon…', interviewed by Kevin Smith, *Rhinoceros*, 4, 1991, 75-94.
Muldoon in America, interviewed by Christopher Cook, with readings by Paul Muldoon, BBC Radio 3, 1994.
'An Interview with Paul Muldoon', interviewed by Lynn Keller, *Contemporary Literature*, 35 (1), Spring 1994, 1-29.
'Interview with Paul Muldoon', interviewed by John Redmond, *Thumbscrew*, 4, Spring 1996, 2-18.

Selected Reviews and Critical Discussions of Paul Muldoon:

Jonathan Allison, 'Questioning Yeats: Paul Muldoon's "7 Middagh Street"', *Learning the Trade: Essays on W.B. Yeats and Contemporary Poetry*, ed. D. Fleming (Connecticut: Locust Hill, 1993), 3-20.
John Banville, 'Slouching Toward Bethlehem', *New York Review of Books*, 30 May 1991, 37-39.
Richard Brown, 'Bog Poems and Book Poems: Doubleness, Self-Translations and Pun in Seamus Heaney and Paul Muldoon', *The Chosen Ground: Essays on the Contemporary Poetry of Northern Ireland*, ed. Neil Corcoran (Bridgend: Seren, 1992), 153-67.

John Carey, 'The Stain of Words', *Sunday Times*, 21 June 1987, 56.

Neil Corcoran, 'The Shy Trickster', *Times Literary Supplement*, 28 October 1983, 1180.

Mark Ford, 'Little Do We Know', *London Review of Books*, 12 January 1995, 19.

John Goodby, 'Elephantiasis and Essentialism', *Irish Review*, 10, Spring 1991, 132-37.

Ian Gregson, *Contemporary Poetry and Postmodernism: Dialogue and Estrangement* (New York: St Martin's Press, 1996).

Hugh Haughton, 'Lord of the Red Herrings', *The Independent on Sunday*, 9 October 1994.

Seamus Heaney, *Place and Displacement: Recent Poetry of Northern Ireland* (Grasmere: Trustees of Dove Cottage, 1984).

––––– 'The Pre-natal Mountain: Vision and Irony in Recent Irish Poetry', *The Place of Writing* (Atlanta: Scholar's Press, 1989), 36-53.

––––– 'Filling the cup above the brim', *Sunday Independent* (Dublin), 25 September 1994.

Michael Hofmann, 'The Recent Generations at their Song', *Times Literary Supplement*, 30 May 1986, 585-86.

––––– 'Muldoon – A Mystery', *London Review of Books*, 20 December 1990, 18-19.

Mick Imlah, 'Abandoned Origins', *Times Literary Supplement*, 4 September 1987, 946.

John Kerrigan, 'The New Narrative', *London Review of Books*, 16-29 February 1984, 22-23.

Tim Kendall, *Paul Muldoon* (Bridgend: Seren, 1996).

Edna Longley, *Poetry in the Wars* (Newcastle upon Tyne: Bloodaxe Books, 1986).

––––– 'Way down upon the Susquehanna', *Irish Times*, 3 November 1990.

––––– *The Living Stream: Literature and Revisionism in Ireland* (Newcastle upon Tyne: Bloodaxe Books, 1994).

Lucy McDiarmid, 'From Signifump to Kierkegaard', *New York Times*, 28 July 1991.

Sean O'Brien, *The Deregulated Muse: Essays on Contemporary British and Irish Poetry* (Newcastle upon Tyne: Bloodaxe Books, 1998).

Bernard O'Donoghue, ' "The Half-Said Thing to them is Dearest": Paul Muldoon', *Poetry in Contemporary Irish Literature*, ed. Michael Kenneally (Gerrards Cross: Colin Smythe, 1995), 400-18.

Helen Vendler, 'Anglo-Celtic Attitudes', *The New York Review of Books*, 6 November, 1997, 57-60.

Clair Wills, *Improprieties: Politics and Sexuality in Northern Irish Poetry* (Oxford: Oxford University Press, 1993).